# Pretend Play
# in Childhood

# Pretend Play in Childhood

## Foundation of Adult Creativity

**Sandra W. Russ**

American Psychological Association • Washington, DC

Published by
American Psychological Association
750 First Street, NE
Washington, DC 20002
www.apa.org

To order
APA Order Department
P.O. Box 92984
Washington, DC 20090-2984
Tel: (800) 374-2721; Direct: (202) 336-5510
Fax: (202) 336-5502; TDD/TTY: (202) 336-6123
Online: www.apa.org/pubs/books
E-mail: order@apa.org

In the U.K., Europe, Africa, and the Middle East, copies may be ordered from
American Psychological Association
3 Henrietta Street
Covent Garden, London
WC2E 8LU England

Typeset in Goudy by Circle Graphics, Inc., Columbia, MD

Printer: United Book Press, Inc., Baltimore, MD
Cover Designer: Mercury Publishing Services, Inc., Rockville, MD
Cover Art: Susan Finsen, Jazz Hands 1, 2012, mixed media, 18" square

Library of Congress Cataloging-in-Publication Data

Russ, Sandra Walker.
  Pretend play in childhood : foundation of adult creativity / Sandra W. Russ.
    pages cm
  Includes bibliographical references and index.
  ISBN 978-1-4338-1561-4 — ISBN 1-4338-1561-3  1.  Play—Psychological aspects.
2.  Cognition in children. 3.  Creative ability. I. Title.
  BF717.R77 2014
  155.4'18—dc23
                                    2013016988

British Library Cataloguing-in-Publication Data
A CIP record is available from the British Library.

Printed in the United States of America
First Edition

http://dx.doi.org/10.1037/14282-000

This book is dedicated to Dorothy and Jerome Singer,
with deep appreciation for leading the way in the play arena
and for their profound judgment about the meaning of play
in child development.

# CONTENTS

# ACKNOWLEDGMENTS

I appreciate all of the excellent help I received from Maureen Adams at American Psychological Association Books in developing this book. Also, the editorial comments of Beth Hatch improved the manuscript, as did Erin O'Brien's copyediting. I also want to thank graduate students Jessica Dillon Hoffmann and Karla Fehr for their scholarly research on a number of projects in the area of play that added to the content of this book. And thanks to Jessica for transcribing the play sessions that are included. Finally, I thank my husband, Tom Brugger, for his loving support of my work.

# Pretend Play
## in Childhood

# INTRODUCTION

Pretend play is the creative elixir of childhood. The world of pretend play is one in which children can be free to express themselves, their ideas, their emotions, and their fantastic visions of themselves, of other people, and of the world. Pretend play is a natural event in childhood. Play occurs in all cultures and circumstances. Children enjoy it and have fun in the process of playing. Play serves many purposes in child development and has consequences for adult development. We learn about play from many sources. Theory and research, of course, provide the building blocks of what we know. But case studies of creative children and creative adults offer a different perspective and a reality-based understanding of the importance of play. Case studies can point the way for future research.

The main thesis of this book is that pretend play is a foundation of adult creativity. Pretend play introduces the child to the creative experience. Because so many of the cognitive and affective processes central to creativity

http://dx.doi.org/10.1037/14282-001
*Pretend Play in Childhood: Foundation of Adult Creativity*, by S. W. Russ

occur in play, pretend play can facilitate and nurture the development of these processes. Pretend play is not the only way in which to develop creative potential, but it is an important one for children.

Why is creativity important? We live in a time of rapid change. Adults in the workplace must think flexibly to adapt, learn new skills, and innovate. How can we prepare for this state of continual change as a society? At the same time that the need for creativity is increasing, pretend play and creative exploration is being deemphasized in schools. The topics of pretend play and creativity are especially important at this time because of the decrease in time for all types of play in childhood and the increased focus on academics in the learning process. Modern societies demand highly developed creativity in science, engineering, and the arts in an increasingly complex world. Creative thinking and expression are also important for the personal well-being of children and adults. It is important that we develop environments for children at home and at school that ensure optimal development of creative potential. Development of children's creative potential will benefit children and, as they become creative adults, will benefit society as well.

It is difficult to "catch" the creative events in pretend play, just as it is difficult to "catch" and understand transformations in the creative act. But we are making progress as a field of study. This book reviews what we have learned about the importance of pretend play from a variety of sources. On the basis of research findings, it discusses in depth the relationship between pretend play and creativity and the processes involved in each. Examples of creative play in children are presented. Examples of creativity from the lives of creative adults that illustrate and support some of the findings with children are discussed. Good pretend play abilities set the stage for adult creativity in the sciences and the arts.

The purpose of this book is to review all aspects of pretend play and creativity, from the point of view of both theory and research, and to illustrate how play lays the foundation for adult creativity. What is the role of pretend play in the development of creativity? What are the processes in pretend play? How do they relate to creative processes? How do the processes used in play reemerge in adult creativity? How do these processes show themselves in the creative work of the adult? For example, how is affect expression in pretend play similar to affect expression in the narrative of a story or poem? How is using blocks to represent different objects similar to generating hypotheses for scientific experiments? Is there evidence that play facilitates creativity?

The area of pretend play and creativity is interdisciplinary in nature. Scholars and researchers from a variety of disciplines have contributed to the literature. Research and scholarship is found in fields of creativity, child development, education, child therapy, and literature and biography. A variety of perspectives and methods of inquiry provides a more comprehensive understanding of play and creativity than does one viewpoint alone.

The first chapter in this volume, "Pretend Play and Creativity: An Overview," is an introductory one that defines pretend play and creativity and gives a general overview of processes involved in creativity and play. It presents a proposed model of pretend play and creativity. Chapter 2, "Evolutionary, Psychoanalytic, and Developmental Theories of Pretend Play and Creativity," presents theories of pretend play, from Vygotsky to Fein to Jerome and Dorothy Singer. It discusses the functions of pretend play and its role in evolution. What implications does research on animal play have for the role of play in child development and creativity? Chapter 3, "Cognitive Processes in Pretend Play and Creativity," reviews the research on cognitive processes in play and creativity. Chapter 4, "Affective Processes in Pretend Play and Creativity," reviews the research on affective processes in play and creativity. In both of these chapters, transcripts of children's pretend play that illustrate individual differences in cognitive and affective processes in play are presented. Details of the Affect in Play Scale (Russ, 1987, 2004) are also given.

Chapter 5, "Case Studies in Science and Technology," compares some of the research findings in the play and creativity area with case studies of adult scientists. What processes in play are similar to those of scientists and engineers? What do they look like in adult creative expression? Examples from scientists and inventors such as Steve Jobs and Barbara McClintock are presented. The same question is asked about artists in Chapter 6, "Case Studies in the Arts." How are the processes called on by the poet Stanley Kunitz or the painter Frida Kahlo similar to what occurs in childhood play? How are processes different in the arts than in the sciences?

Chapter 7, "Facilitating Pretend Play and Creativity in Training Programs," reviews the research literature that focuses on facilitating pretend play and facilitating creativity in children. Research from my own research program on play facilitation is described, with some examples of creative play. Transcripts of adult–child interaction in play intervention studies are presented. Suggestions for enhancing creativity in play at home and in school are offered.

Chapter 8, "Play, Culture, and the Modern World," first discusses play in different cultures and then reviews research findings that compare children's play in the United States and in Italy. Finally, changes in children's play skills in the United States over the past 23 years are discussed, with implications for child development. The impact of video games is also considered.

Finally, in "Afterword: Converging Evidence," I summarize the major points in the volume and provide suggestions for the future.

On a personal note, I have long been intrigued by the area of play and creativity. I played a lot as an only child. I loved to play and pretend. As an undergraduate at the University of Pittsburgh, I became fascinated by the area of creativity. How did someone come up with a new idea? How did emotion influence the creative process? My master's thesis project explored anxiety and creativity. Later, as I worked as a child therapist, I observed many children use play to work out problems. Their thinking seemed to become more flexible and creative as well. What was the link between play and creativity? How could I study the relationship between play and creativity? At Case Western Reserve University, I developed the Affect in Play Scale, a measure of affect in fantasy in pretend play. It filled a need in the play area for a measure of affect expressions in fantasy play. With my students, I have carried out a number of studies using this instrument. I have also taught a number of seminars on creativity. I have tried to generate interest in creativity and play in undergraduate and graduate students over the years and to send the message that there is creative potential in each individual. In this book, I hope to stir the passions of the scholars and researchers who will go forward to discover the next pieces in the puzzle of pretend play and creativity.

# 1

# PRETEND PLAY AND CREATIVITY: AN OVERVIEW

Creativity and pretend play are both multidimensional. Many cognitive and affective processes are involved, and there are differences across individuals for each process. There is overlap among processes that occur in pretend play and processes that occur in creativity. This introductory chapter first reviews definitions of creativity, with a focus on creative products and creative people. It emphasizes the cognitive and affective processes involved in creativity and considers how different creative processes are involved in different stages of creative production. Next, it reviews definitions of pretend play, with a focus on cognitive and affective processes in pretend play. Finally, it presents a model showing the overlap between pretend play and adult creativity. This chapter provides only an overview of processes that occur in both the pretend play of the child and the creative acts of the adult; later chapters present the theories and research in greater depth.

http://dx.doi.org/10.1037/14282-002
*Pretend Play in Childhood: Foundation of Adult Creativity*, by S. W. Russ

# DEFINITIONS OF CREATIVITY

When we think about *creativity*, we encounter different aspects of the construct. First there is the creative product—the actual artwork or scientific discovery that the field labels as being creative. There is also the person who is the maker of the creative product. What are the internal processes that enable an individual to think in a creative fashion? The distinction between product and process is an important one (Golann, 1963; Mackinnon, 1962).

## Creative Product

What features need to be present for something to be labeled as *creative*? There have been numerous attempts to identify criteria for determining whether a product is creative. There is a consensus among creativity scholars that two criteria are necessary. For a product to be judged as creative, it must be (a) unique, original, and novel and (b) useful, adaptive, and aesthetically pleasing, according to the standards of the specific discipline. The product must be original, of good quality, and appropriate to the task (Sternberg, Kaufman, & Pretz, 2002). Torrance (1988) concluded that newness is a major criterion for a creative product. A product is creative if old facts are integrated in new ways, new relationships emerge from old ideas, or there is a new configuration.

But novelty alone is insufficient. The product must also be useful or aesthetically pleasing. Vernon (1989) offered a comprehensive definition of creativity that included these major components: "Creativity means a person's capacity to produce new or original ideas, insights, restructuring, inventions, or artistic objects, which are accepted by experts as being of scientific, aesthetic, social, or technological value" (p. 94). Inevitably, experts in the relevant discipline must judge the product. Thus, there is always the involvement of cultural values and norms when judging a product as creative.

Given the high standards for a product to truly be creative, the question is often asked, Can children be truly creative? Children can generate new ideas and new configurations and make aesthetically pleasing artwork, but they rarely have the cognitive sophistication or the knowledge to really contribute to a field in a new way. However, if age norms are taken into consideration, then we can consider children as generating creative products (Russ, 1993). We can ask the question, Is this product new and of good quality for this age group? Using age norms is the common practice in assessing children for many abilities. A 9-year-old's solution to a problem can be judged on criteria of adaptiveness and originality for the age group. Thurstone (1952) stated that if a discovery is new to the thinker, even though it had already occurred to someone else, then it is a creative act. Children as well as individuals new to a field often have many creative acts that have been previously thought of or discovered by someone else.

*Everyday Creativity*

Ruth Richards (1990) introduced the concept of *everyday creativity*, which has widely influenced the field. Everyday creativity is the "originality of everyday life" (Richards, 2007, p. 26). It is the ability to adapt flexibly to changing environments. Richards (1990) described everyday creativity as real-life creativity at work or at leisure. A new and effective way of handling budget problems or of managing caretaking of an ill parent would qualify as examples of everyday creativity. Children's days are filled with everyday creativity. Making up new games or new ways to dress their dolls or new models of rocket ships are instances of everyday creativity.

Everyday creativity can also be judged on a continuum of less creative to more creative. In fact, Richards developed the Lifetime Creativity Scales (Richards, Kinney, Benet, & Merzel, 1988) to assess everyday creativity. However, often in everyday creativity there is not a specific lasting product that we think is necessary for creativity. Rather, creativity is "in the moment," often accompanied by a subjective experience of joy or deep satisfaction. This in-the-moment quality and positive subjective experience often occur in pretend play in children and in the creative experience of adults. One might consider pretend play to be an example of everyday creativity in children.

*Little-c and Big-C Creativity*

Another important distinction in the creativity literature is that of little-c and big-C creativity. *Little-c creativity* involves the novel and task-appropriate creative events that occur on a daily basis (Plucker & Beghetto, 2004). *Big-C creativity* refers to the groundbreaking major creative discoveries that transform a field. Einstein's theory of relativity would be an example of big-C creativity, whereas the invention of intermittent windshield wipers would be on the continuum of little-c creativity. Plucker and Beghetto (2004) pointed out that the social context partially determines what is little-c or big-C creativity. It is probable that individuals who demonstrate a large number of little-c events would be more likely to make a groundbreaking discovery in an area. Simonton (1988) showed that eminent creators have a number of failed ideas—they experiment with ideas a lot and also are highly productive. One might speculate that children who have a large number of little-c events, or many examples of everyday creativity, are more likely to become eminent creators in adulthood. Play is one place where examples of little-c creativity and everyday creativity occur.

*Four-C Model*

Beghetto and Kaufman (2007) introduced the concept of *mini-c*. Mini-c events are those productions or expressions that are new to the person but not necessarily novel. The standards for evaluation are lower than for little-c creativity.

Kaufman and Beghetto (2009) proposed a *four-C model* of creativity that reflects the developmental trajectory of creativity. First, mini-c levels of creativity occur in the child. Exploration and pretend play could be ways in which the child begins to experience and experiment with mini-c creativity. Next, individuals may progress to little-c creative events. Everyday creativity begins to occur as individuals master challenges and opportunities in daily living.

A new category of creativity introduced by Kaufman and Beghetto (2009) is that of *pro-c*. Pro-c is a category for individuals who are professional creators. Pro-c includes creative acts that follow years of immersion in a field that then make a contribution to the domain. The individual has professional level status. Finally, the big-C category is reserved for those major contributions that alter the direction of a domain. The idea of a progression of levels of creative events is interesting and places creativity within a developmental framework. It offers guidance about how to help children and adolescents develop their creative potential. It also emphasizes the early childhood experience with mini-c and little-c that prepares the way for adult creativity.

*Levels of Contribution*

Sternberg, Kaufman, and Pretz (2001) proposed the *propulsion theory of creative contributions*. They described eight levels of creative contributions to a field. The first four (*replication, redefinition, forward incrementation*, and *advance forward incrementation*) stay within the framework of the existing paradigm. For example, forward incrementation pushes the field forward a little in the same direction. The next four categories (*redirection, reconstruction/redirection, reinitiation*, and *integration*) break the paradigm. For example, reinitiation involves moving to new starting point. Kaufman (2009) offered the example of Marcel Duchamp's urinal, called "Fountain," in a 1917 art exhibit. The category of integration merges different domains.

## Creative Person

The creative person generates the creative product. Historically, only eminent individuals were considered to be creative. Guilford (1950, 1968) introduced the concept of a *continuum of creativity*. Guilford (1968) thought that all individuals possessed creative abilities to some degree: "Creative acts can therefore be expected, no matter how frequent or how infrequent, of almost all individuals" (p. 82). This was an important concept because it implied that creativity could be studied in all individuals, children and adults. Runco (2004) expanded on this concept and proposed that all individuals have creative potential. A number of factors determine whether that potential is developed and expressed. As a society, we should focus on helping individuals develop their potential.

What are the characteristics involved in creative production? Personality traits of creative individuals have a long history of investigation in the creativity literature. Major research programs in the area of creativity led to a personality profile of the creative individual (Barron, 1969; Gough, 1979; Mackinnon, 1965; McCrae & Costa, 1987; Roe, 1972). Barron and Harrington (1981) reviewed the literature and concluded that the following personality traits are conducive to creativity:

- tolerance of ambiguity,
- openness to experience,
- unconventional values,
- independence of judgment,
- curiosity,
- preference for challenge and complexity,
- self-confidence,
- propensity for risk taking, and
- intrinsic motivation.

They also listed high valuation of aesthetic qualities in experience, broad interests, high energy, autonomy, ability to accommodate conflicting traits in one's self-concept, and a firm sense of the self as "creative." The research base for the personality studies is mainly with adults, but the research with children is consistent with the adult literature.

Most recently, the Openness to Experience trait has emerged as important in creativity. Openness to Experience, one of the Big Five dimensions, includes intellectual curiosity, aesthetic sensitivity, liberal values, and emotional differentiation (McCrae, 1987). The relationship between Openness to Experience and creativity has been well-researched in adults. McCrae (1987) found that divergent thinking was related to Openness to Experience and suggested that Openness to Experience may serve as the catalyst for creative expression and exploration. In validating the Creative Achievement Questionnaire, S. H. Carson, Peterson, and Higgins (2005) found that it related strongly to both divergent thinking and Openness to Experience. L. A. King, McKee-Walker, and Broyles (1996) also found relationships between verbal creative ability and Openness to Experience, and Zhiyan and Singer (1997) found relationships between daydreaming and Openness to Experience. More recent, Furnham, Crump, Batey, and

Chamorro-Premuzic (2009) found that Openness to Experience was the best personality predictor of divergent thinking.

Personality consists of the interaction of a number of cognitive, affective, and interpersonal processes. The study of specific cognitive and affective processes has been especially fruitful for the study of creativity and the understanding of the creative process itself. Cognitive and affective processes within the person have been associated with creative acts and the generation of creative products.

## COGNITIVE AND AFFECTIVE PROCESSES IN CREATIVITY

What are the processes that occur within individuals that enable them to produce a creative product? Much of the research in the creativity area has focused on this question. There are many processes that can be involved in the creative act. Cognitive processes and affective processes are involved in creativity. Personality characteristics are also associated with creative production. Interpersonal processes play a role in some forms of creativity. In 1993, I developed an integrated model of creativity after reviewing the creativity literature. This model identifies cognitive and affective processes and global personality traits that have been associated with creativity in the research literature. Although the research findings in these areas, especially the affective processes area, have continued to evolve, the types of processes identified in the 1993 model are still appropriate. Figure 1.1 lists the cognitive and affective processes important in creative production. What is presented in this chapter is a basic overview of the processes. Research findings about the creative processes and pretend play are presented in later chapters.

### Cognitive Processes

Much of the research in the area of creativity has focused on cognitive processes. Guilford (1950, 1967, 1968) made major theoretical contributions to the area of creativity by identifying cognitive processes not previously focused on in tests of intelligence. Guilford identified cognitive processes that were unique to creative thinking: divergent production abilities and transformation abilities.

*Divergent thinking* is the ability to generate a variety of solutions to a problem or associations to a word. Divergent thinking is thinking that goes off in different directions, rather than funneling in to one best solution to a problem, as in convergent thinking. A typical item on a divergent thinking test might be "How many uses for a brick can you think of?" As Guilford (1968) stated, "Divergent thinking is a matter of scanning one's stored information

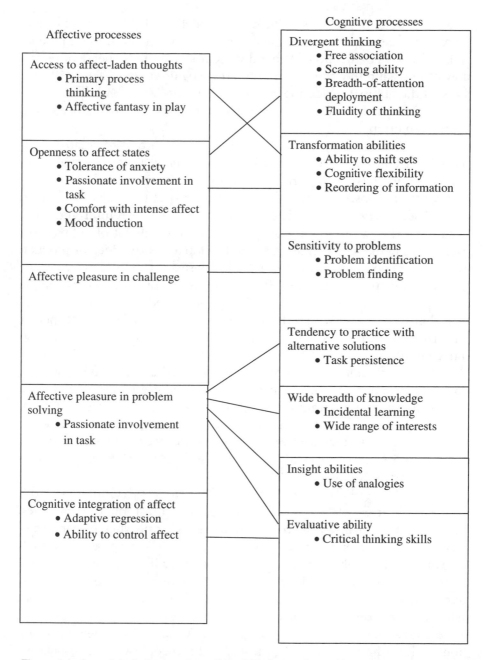

*Figure 1.1.* A model of affect and creativity. Affective and cognitive processes important in creative production. Hypothesized reciprocal connections among these processes. From *Affect and Creativity: The Role of Affect and Play in the Creative Process* (p. 9), by S. W. Russ, 1993, Hillsdale, NJ: Lawrence Erlbaum Associates, Inc. Copyright 1993 by Lawrence Erlbaum Associates, Inc. Reprinted with permission.

to find answers to satisfy a specific search model" (p. 105). A broad base of search and free-ranging scanning ability increases divergent thinking production. Wallach (1970) thought that divergent thinking is dependent on the flow of ideas and the "fluidity in generating cognitive units" (p. 1240). He stressed the ability to "ride the associative currents" (p. 1240). This ability to make remote associations increases the probability of thinking of a novel, creative solution.

A second category of cognitive processes important to creative ability is what Guilford (1968) termed *transformation abilities*. These abilities enable individuals to transform or revise what they know into new patterns and configurations. Cognitive flexibility is necessary to break out of an old set and see a new solution. The individual reorders or reinterprets what is currently known in a new way. The ability to break out of old patterns increases the likelihood that one will develop a creative idea or product. An old but good test of this ability to break sets is the Luchins water jug problem (Luchins & Luchins, 1959). A set is created in solving a simple math problem. Then, when a problem is presented with a simpler solution than the one for which the set was created, many individuals persist with the old, established set. Luchins referred to this perseveration as *cognitive rigidity*.

Much of Guilford's (1968) research focused on identifying specific cognitive processes that made up these two broad categories of abilities—divergent thinking and transformation abilities—and devising tests of them. He conceptualized these cognitive processes as being separate from personality traits. However, recent research has demonstrated that personality and affective processes influence divergent thinking and transformation abilities (Baas, De Dreu, & Nijstad, 2008).

Mednick's (1962) *associative theory* is consistent with Guilford's (1968) conceptualization of divergent thinking and transformation abilities. Mednick conceptualized creative thinking as occurring when disparate elements come together in new combinations for a useful purpose. Individuals who are able to combine remote elements are more likely to generate novel associations and ideas. Mednick proposed that individuals with flat associative hierarchies were more likely to generate remote associations. A *flat associative hierarchy* is one in which many ideas are connected but with weak associations between the ideas. A *steep associative hierarchy* has fewer associations with stronger bonds among the ideas. Thus, people with flat associative hierarchies would have more interconnected minds with wider ranges of solutions to problems or stimuli (Russ & Dillon, 2011a). They would have more ideas and more remote associations. A flat associative hierarchy would increase the likelihood that individuals would come up with novel ideas or creative products.

Divergent thinking and transformation abilities are cognitive processes that are uniquely important for creative production. An individual who is high on the continuum of divergent thinking and who is able to break out of old thinking habits would have the advantage in producing something new when compared with individuals with less ability in these two areas. However, there are a number of other cognitive abilities that are important to creativity as well as for problem solving in general.

The ability to try alternative problem-solving approaches is another important cognitive ability. Although this flexible approach to problem solving may be a subtype of transformation ability (i.e., the ability to shift sets and perceive alternative solutions), task persistence and engaging in trial-and-error behavior are often mentioned as being important in creative problem solving (Weisberg, 1988).

Sensitivity to problems and problem finding is another ability that has been found to relate to creativity (Getzels & Csikszentmihalyi, 1976; Guilford, 1950; Runco, 1994a). One must be able to identify the problem to be solved that others may have missed. Reiter-Palmon (2011) concluded that problem finding involves problem identification and the structuring and definition of the problem. In ill-defined problems, both divergent thinking and convergent thinking processes are involved. The activation of different ways of perceiving a problem is a divergent process. The integration of various problem representations involves evaluation.

A wide breadth of knowledge is an often-cited characteristic of creative individuals (Barron & Harrington, 1981). Although memory capacity is involved, a wide range of facts, information, and analogies from broad life experience provides much to draw from when attempting to develop a novel solution or configuration.

Insight ability during problem solving has been much studied in relation to creativity. Sternberg (1988) and Sternberg and Davidson (1982) postulated that three type of insights are involved in creativity. *Selective encoding* involves separating relevant from irrelevant information. *Selective combination* entails synthesizing isolated pieces of information into unified wholes; information is organized in new ways. *Selective comparison* involves relating new information to old information. It seems that both divergent thinking and transformation partially underlie these insight abilities.

There is some debate as to whether insight occurs in a flash or in slow incremental steps. Weisberg (1986, 1988) stressed the incremental nature of problem solving. Novel products evolve in small steps that use memory searches. There are few real leaps of insight. However, Metcalfe (1986) presented evidence that some insight tasks are different from memory retrieval tasks. She used a "feeling of knowing" paradigm to determine whether similar processes were involved in an insight problem and a memory-based trivia problem. In two studies, she found that people could predict memory performance fairly well but could not predict performance for insight problems. She concluded that insight problems involve a sudden illumination that cannot be predicted in advance.

Analogies and the application of ideas from one domain to another are often part of the insights that occur in creative problem solving. Langley and Jones (1988) developed a computational model of scientific insight. They stressed the importance of the use of analogies in creative problem solving. Insight involves the recognition, evaluation, and elaboration of analogies. Memory processes are important in recognizing and applying appropriate analogies to new situations.

Although not unique to creative thinking, evaluative ability is essential to the creative act (Guilford, 1950; Runco, 1991). The creator must think critically and evaluate the product. The creative product must be good, aesthetically pleasing, or meaningful.

It may seem reasonable to expect a strong relationship between intelligence and creativity. However, because most of our intelligence tests measure convergent thinking and do not tap divergent thinking or the ability to think flexibly and break out of a set, most of the research has found small positive relationships between intelligence and creativity measures. Intelligence tests do measure critical-thinking ability and memory for general information as well as abstract thinking ability. These cognitive processes are important in creative problem solving. But the processes that are relatively unique to creativity—fluid divergent thinking and flexibility of thought—are not represented on most intelligence tests. K. H. Kim (2005) performed a meta-analysis and concluded that the relationship between creativity and IQ is negligible, supporting the hypothesis that creativity and intelligence are separate constructs. However, the average correlation was .20, suggesting some association. In a review by Batey and Furnham (2006), correlations between intelligence and divergent thinking ranged from .20 to .40.

How one defines and measures intelligence is important. If components of creative thinking are included in intelligence measures, then the relationship is stronger. *Fluid intelligence*—the ability to solve novel problems—was related to a creativity measure for high IQ individuals. Batey and Furnham (2006) concluded that fluid intelligence may be important for early stages of creativity or mini-c creativity.

For children, divergent thinking has usually had small positive relationships with intelligence (Russ, 2004). Findings with children are consistent with findings with adults. However, with very young children (3–5 years), when cognitive processes are still differentiating, intelligence and divergent thinking may be intertwined and the association could be stronger.

## Affective Processes

The recognition of affective process in creative production is a relatively recent phenomenon. Whereas research on cognitive processes began in the 1950s, research on affective processes began in the 1980s. There was early theorizing and some research from the psychoanalytic tradition that pointed the way for research on affect and creativity. In 1993, I attempted to synthesize the theoretical and research literature to identify affective processes unique to or important in creative production (Russ, 1993; see also Figure 1.1). Since the 1990s, research on affect and creativity has mushroomed.

*Affect* is defined as a broad set of events that includes emotions and drives and involves feeling states that are pervasive (Izard, 1977; Moore & Isen, 1990). *Emotion* is a subset of affect that is defined as a state of aroused feeling or agitation. Affect is the broader category. *Affective processes* refer to the different dimensions of affect, or types of affective events, that occur within the individual. Most theorists think that cognition is involved in affective processes. One rationale for the relationship between affect and creativity is that the involvement of emotion broadens the search process for information or memories (Isen, Daubman, & Nowicki, 1987). A broader search process would enable more divergent thinking or more flexible thinking, which would increase the likelihood of a creative solution. Another way affective involvement could aid creativity, especially artistic creativity, is through access to emotion-laden memories so important to the writer or visual artist.

On the basis of theory and the research literature, five affective processes have emerged as important to creative production (Russ, 1993, 2004).

- *Openness to experiencing affect states.* There are individual differences in the ability to experience positive and negative emotions and mood states. These specific feeling states function differently in the creative process and are reviewed in Chapter 4. Much research has been carried out using a mood induction paradigm in which mood is manipulated with film, memories, or music. Positive mood states in particular have been found to increase creativity. Results are mixed with negative mood states (Baas et al., 2008).
- *Access to affect-laden thoughts, images, and fantasy.* This is the ability to think about ideas, images, and fantasy that includes affect. Thoughts involving affect themes such as aggression, sex, affection, or fear illustrate this blending of affect and cognition. The psychoanalytic concept of primary-process thinking is an example of this type of cognitive–affective process that involves flexibility of thought as well as affect content (Holt, 1977).

- *Affective pleasure in challenge*. This process involves the excitement and tension that comes with identifying a problem and wanting to immerse oneself in the task. Both positive and negative affect could be involved. Runco (1999b) discussed how tension is involved in creativity. The anticipation of resolution of tension could be a motivating factor in creative problem solving.
- *Affective pleasure in creative problem solving*. The joy of the creative act is a well-known phenomenon (Csikszentmihalyi, 1990). The tendency to take deep pleasure in solving a problem or completing an artistic production or in self-expression is an important component of creativity.
- *Cognitive integration and modulation of affect*. This is the ability to control, think about, and regulate the affective events one experiences and not be swept away. Although this process is probably more cognitive than affective, it warrants inclusion because it involves both cognition and affect and is important in the creative process.

There are other broad motivational systems that are important in creativity. The area of motivation subsumes needs, drives, and affective processes. *Intrinsic motivation* is the motivation that comes from within the individual to do a task, whereas doing a task for recognition or reward comes from *extrinsic motivation*. Amabile (1983) has an extensive research program that supports the importance of doing something for the love of it in creative work. Curiosity is a motivational state found to be important in creativity (Berlyne, 1966). Both curiosity and intrinsic motivation are often categorized as personality traits. Conflict resolution and self-expression also motivate the individual to resolve an internal conflict or to express intense emotions. There are many anecdotal accounts of individuals using the arts as a form of therapy to deal with emotional problems or daily stresses. The psychoanalytic concept of *sublimation* occurs when a personal conflict is channeled into a specific creative endeavor and is transformed into a universal symbol or resolution. These different affective processes and motivational systems work in different ways in different areas of creativity for different individuals and for different types of creativity tasks.

## STAGES OF CREATIVITY

When thinking about creative processes, it is useful to think about stages of creativity that occur when producing a creative product. The first well-known attempt to conceptualize stages was that of Wallas in 1926.

Although Wallas's stages are rather global, his four-stage model has held up fairly well (Runco, 2007). His model consisted of the following stages:

1. *Preparation stage:* information gathering, identifying the problem, and mastering the knowledge. In this stage the basic techniques and methods and content of a particular domain are mastered. The violinist learns the technique and the chemist masters the content and scientific method of the domain.
2. *Incubation stage:* Ideas incubate without the individual directly, logically working on the problem. It is in this stage that processes unique to creativity are so important. Problems are not consciously worked on. Much restructuring and free-associating occurs outside of awareness.
3. *Illumination stage:* The solution to the problem occurs. This stage is often referred to as the "aha" experience of the creative scientist. However, many theorists have pointed out that reaching a solution is a gradual process in most instances (Gruber & Davis, 1988; Weisberg, 1988).
4. *Verification stage:* The solution must now be evaluated. The hypothesis must be tested; the invention must be put into practice and refined; the musical composition must be played.

Gruber (1989) pointed out that Wallas's (1926) stage model is incomplete. It does not include the early stage of problem finding, which is now thought to be so important (Getzels & Csikszentmihalyi, 1976; Runco, 2007). In addition, Vinacke (1952) stressed that the stages of the creative process are not so ordered. People go back and forth among the stages when producing something creative. Sometimes they let their thoughts roam, sometimes they think critically and test ideas. It is the ability to shift between stages and types of thinking and affective experiences that may be so important to creativity. Psychoanalytic theorists refer to this ability as *regression in the service of the ego* (Kris, 1952).

I proposed that the stages most unique to creative problem solving are Stages 2 and 3, incubation and illumination (Russ, 1993). Cognitive and affective processes important to creativity occur during these stages. One can speculate as to which cognitive and affective processes are important in different stages of creativity (Russ, 1993). (See Table 1.1; personality traits are also included in this table.)

Creative cognitive processes of divergent thinking and transformation abilities would be important during the incubation stage, when thoughts can freely roam. Access to affect themes and emotions would also aid the search process during this phase. Affect symbols and affect-laden memories could be manipulated and recombined and fused. Openness to Experience should

## TABLE 1.1
### Stages of the Creative Process and Cognitive–Affective Processes

| Wallas's stages | Cognitive abilities | Affective processes | Personality traits |
|---|---|---|---|
| Preparation | Sensitivity to problems<br>Wide breadth of knowledge<br>• Master knowledge base | Affective pleasure in challenge | Curiosity<br>Tolerance of ambiguity<br>Risk taking<br>Intrinsic motivation<br>Preference for challenge and complexity |
| Incubation | Divergent thinking<br>Transformation abilities<br>Tendency to practice with alternative solutions | Access to affect-laden thoughts<br>• Primary process<br>Openness to affect states | Openness to experience<br>Tolerance of ambiguity<br>Self-confidence<br>Preference for challenge |
| Illumination | Evaluative ability<br><br>Insight abilities | Access to affect-laden thoughts<br>Openness to affect states<br>Affective pleasure in problem solving | Self-confidence |
| Verification | Evaluative ability | Affective pleasure in problem solving<br>Cognitive integration of affect | Intrinsic motivation |

Note. From *Affect and Creativity: The Role of Affect and Play in the Creative Process* (p. 16), by S. W. Russ, 1993, Hillsdale, NJ: Lawrence Erlbaum Associates, Inc. Copyright 1993 by Lawrence Erlbaum Associates, Inc. Reprinted with permission.

also be an advantage during this phase because there would be a richer store of experiences and memories available to call on for the task. In the illumination stage, insight and evaluative, critical-thinking abilities would be important, as would affective pleasure in problem solving. The role of affect in recognizing the best solution would also be important. The aesthetic appreciation of the best artistic or scientific solution is important in creative production.

Different processes would be important in the preparation and verification stages, which require more logical cognitive processes, memory, and critical-thinking abilities. Affective pleasure in challenge would be important in this first preparation stage, as would personality characteristics of intrinsic motivation and curiosity. In the verification stage, having the intrinsic motivation to see the project through and the self-confidence to "put the idea or project out there" for possible criticism would be essential. Although most of these hypotheses about what processes are important in what stages have not been tested, the point of this speculation is that having a variety of cognitive and affective abilities is advantageous for different parts of a creative task. When incubation is useful in generating associations and ideas, then individuals who are better at using the processes that facilitate idea generation will have the advantage. In developing creativity in children, these particular cognitive and affective processes should be targeted.

## INTERACTION OF COGNITIVE, AFFECTIVE, AND PERSONALITY PROCESSES

There is a complicated interaction among different processes of cognition and affect and personality traits. Personality traits are reflections of cognitive and affective processes. Throughout development, interactions among these traits and processes occur. There are numerous possible configurations of these processes and traits in individuals. Many possible profiles exist and have implications for creativity. Runco (2004) presented the concept of *creative potential*—that each individual has the potential for creativity. If we think of creativity as emerging from cognitive and affective processes within the individual, within the context of various personality traits, some of which increase the likelihood of a creative act, then there are many different routes to creativity. Many different types of creative profiles exist (Russ, 1993). For children, there are many possible ways to enhance cognitive and affective development that would facilitate creative thinking. When we think of creative potential in children, there are many avenues through which that potential can be developed.

Different profiles of creative processes are likely in different domains of creativity. High access to affective memories could be important for fiction writers whereas high ability to use analogies may be important to the chemist. Feist (1999) concluded that some personality traits are domain general and some are domain specific. And for many areas, talent for the domain would be important in addition to creative processes. So where does pretend play come into the creativity picture? In pretend play, many of the cognitive and affective processes important in and unique to creativity occur and are developed. We can observe these processes when we watch children play.

## DEFINITIONS OF PRETEND PLAY

What is *pretend play?* There are many definitions, but one of the most concise is that of Fein (1987). She defined pretend play as a symbolic behavior in which "one thing is playfully treated 'as if' it were something else" (p. 282).

The block can represent a telephone. Fein also thought that pretense involves feelings and emotional intensity, so that affect is intertwined with pretend in play. Both cognition and affect are expressed. She viewed play as a natural form of creativity. In most children, pretend play starts at about 2½ years of age and continues, in more complex forms, until 9 or 10.

Pretend play involves make-believe and fantasy. Klinger (1971) thought that play and fantasy had a common origin. J. L. Singer (1981) conceptualized that internal fantasy was expressed in play; play was the externalization of fantasy. Interestingly, Piaget (1945/1967) thought of fantasy as *interiorized play*. Sherrod and Singer (1979) identified processes involved in both pretend play and fantasy: the ability to form images, skill in storing and retrieving formed images, possessing a store of images, skill in recombining and integrating these images as a source of internal stimulation and divorcing them from reality, and reinforcement for skillful recombining of images. They thought it was the last two processes that are unique to fantasy and play activities. However, it is possible that engaging in play could facilitate the other processes. Children who engage in play could become more adept at recombining images and could have more access to stored images that are affect-laden. D. G. Singer and Singer (1990) conceptualized pretend play as a vehicle for practicing with ideas and images. Pretend play is also a vehicle for practicing with manipulating affect-laden content (Fein, 1987). The idea that in play children practice, rehearse, and work in depth with ideas, images, fantasy, and affect is central to understanding the important role pretend play has in laying the foundation for creativity. Vygotsky (1930/1967b) thought that creative imagination originated in children's play.

Krasnor and Pepler (1980) developed a model of play that involves four components: nonliterality, positive affect, intrinsic motivation, and flexibility. They believed that pure play involves all four components. Again, both cognitive and affect processes are involved. All of these four processes overlap with processes identified as important in creativity. Krasnor and Pepler thought that play reflected the developmental level of the child and could be used as a diagnostic tool. They also thought that play could be a causal agent in developmental change.

The study of pretend play can tell us about the development of cognitive and affective processes and how they interact (Russ, 1987; D. G. Singer & Singer, 1990; D. L. Singer, 1973). Slade and Wolf (1994) stressed the importance of studying the role of play in both the development of cognitive structure and in the mastering of emotions. Historically, these two domains have been studied separately, usually from different theoretical and research traditions. Morrison (1988) noted that Piaget did not consider affect to be important in cognitive development, whereas Freud did. Just as in the area of creativity, where much of the research emphasis was on cognitive processes, so it has been with play. Most of the measures of pretend play have measured cognitive processes. Rubin, Fein, and Vandenberg (1983) spoke of the "cognification" of play, because of the lack of measures of affective processes. Today, there are more measures available of affect in play and more interest in studying affect in play. With increasing interest in the whole area of emotional intelligence and emotion regulation, development of affective processes in children is increasingly investigated.

## COGNITIVE AND AFFECTIVE PROCESSES IN PRETEND PLAY

We can observe and measure many processes in the verbal expressions and behaviors in pretend play. Cognitive and affective processes occur as well as interpersonal processes and problem-solving approaches (Russ, 2004). In all of these processes, the child has moved into the "as if" space that Fein (1987) described. What processes can we observe and measure when we watch children play?

Cognitive processes that have emerged from the research and clinical literature are as follows:

- *Organization*. Story narratives often occur in play. Even though nonlinear and jumping around in time and space, children's stories do have organized sequences of events that differ in coherence, elaboration, and complexity. There are sequences that include indications of cause and effect.
- *Fantasy and make-believe*. Stories and events are made-up and diverge from real life. Events are pretend events. Fantasy elements are part of the story.
- *Symbolism*. This is the ability to transform ordinary objects (e.g., Lego blocks, blocks, clay) into representations of other objects (e.g., a block becomes a milk bottle, a Lego block becomes a bear).
- *Divergent thinking*. Children generate a variety of ideas, story themes, transformations of objects and symbols in pretend play.
- *Recombining of objects, images, and story events*.

Affective processes that have emerged from the research and clinical literature are as follows:

- *Expression of emotion*. Children express a variety of affect states and emotions in pretend play. Story narratives and pretend play events include positive and negative emotions. An example of happy emotion would be a doll having fun going down a slide. An example of an angry emotion is one puppet hitting another.

- *Expression of affect-laden themes or symbols.* Many images and content themes in play are affect-laden. A gun is associated with aggression, even though no anger is actually expressed. A monster might be associated with fear, if the context suggested it.
- *Experiencing pleasure and joy in play itself is an affective process.* The ability to deeply engage in the task and experience positive affect is frequently observed in children when they play.
- *Emotion regulation and modulation of affect.* The ability to contain and modulate both positive and negative affect is an important part of play.
- *Cognitive integration of affect.* The ability to integrate affect into a cognitive context is a major occurrence in play. Affect is expressed within a narrative context. For example, aggression is expressed within a story about a hockey match.

Interpersonal processes that have emerged from the research and clinical literature are as follows:

- *Perspective taking.* Role taking with multiple figures involves taking the view of the other character.
- *Empathy.* The expression of concern and caring about others can be observed in play. Role taking involves taking the perspective of the other, which is involved in empathy.
- *Interpersonal schema and self–other representation.* How others are viewed emerges in pretend play. Whether others are nurturing or malevolent, trustworthy or indifferent, can often be observed in play. The developmental level of self–other differentiation and capacity to trust emerges in play scenarios.
- *Communication.* The ability to communicate with others about feelings, thoughts, and actions is expressed between figure representations.
- *Problem solving and conflict resolution.* How figures resolve interpersonal conflicts and internal conflicts can be observed in play.

## OVERLAP BETWEEN PRETEND PLAY AND CREATIVE PROCESSES: A MODEL OF PRETEND PLAY AND CREATIVITY

The processes in play that most overlap with the processes important in creative production are the cognitive and affective processes. My proposed model, shown in Table 1.2, depicts the overlapping cognitive and affective processes that occur in both play and creativity. Only a brief sketch of this model is presented here. The theoretical and research base for the model is

TABLE 1.2
Model of Creativity and Pretend Play

| Creative processes in pretend play | Examples in play |
| --- | --- |
| Divergent Thinking | Block transformations |
| | Different story ideas and elements |
| Broad Associations | Wide fantasy and remote images |
| Cognitive Flexibility/Recombining Ideas | Use toys in different ways |
| | Manipulating story elements |
| | Loosening of time and space |
| Insight and problem solving | Building novel objects |
| | Playing with mechanical objects |
| Perspective-taking | Role playing |
| | Pretending to be different characters |
| Narrative Development | Story plots and sequences |
| Affect themes and symbols | Monsters; cops and robbers |
| | Yummy food |
| Emotional expression | Dolls fighting; Dolls hugging |
| Joy in pretending | Pleasure and absorption in the play |
| Integration of affect/affect themes | Placing emotion in an appropriate narrative |

presented in Chapters 2, 3, and 4. Although interpersonal processes are central to child development and can be observed in play, except for perspective taking, there is little research on interpersonal functioning and creativity in children. We can speculate about how interpersonal functioning effects creativity, but it is not included in the model.

Before discussing specifics of the model, a quotation from Erik Erikson ("Obituary: Erik Erikson," 1994) beautifully summarizes the relationship between play and creativity:

> You see a child play, . . . and it is so close to seeing an artist paint, for in play a child says things without uttering a word. You can see how he solves his problems. You can also see what's wrong. Young children, especially, have enormous creativity, and whatever's in them rises to the surface in free play. (para. 29)

In this quotation, Erikson states that play is a creative production for the child. Play is creativity. The child is making something out of nothing, as is the artist. He also said that much is nonverbal, but words are an integral part of play for many children, especially as they get older. Also, the statement that things rise to the surface implies that deep-seated ideas and feelings are expressed, many of which may be unconscious or out of awareness. Play is a place in which problems are solved. Adults use creative work to express and work through personal problems as well (Niederland, 1973). Pretend play is an early form of this creative activity. Child therapists have utilized play as a form of personal problem solving since the 1930s (A. Freud, 1965). One can see what problems the child is struggling with. One can also see how the child's play compares with that of other children of the same age. In that way, play can be an assessment tool for child development.

Research supports the relationship between pretend play and creativity in children (Russ, 2004; Russ & Fiorelli, 2010). Much of this research is reviewed in later chapters. The strongest relationships that emerged from a meta-analysis of play and child development were the associations between pretend play and divergent thinking, and pretend play and perspective taking (Fisher, 1992). Research continues to support the robust relationship between pretend play and divergent thinking. There is growing evidence that pretend play can facilitate creativity (Dansky, 1999). Recently, Lillard et al. (2013) challenged the conclusion that pretend play relates to and facilitates creativity. However, it is my opinion that many well-done studies do support the relationships between processes that occur in pretend play and processes that occur in creative production.

## Overlapping Cognitive Processes in Play and Creativity

Research has suggested that overlap exists for three of the cognitive processes important in creativity: divergent thinking, transformation, and insight (see Table 1.2). Divergent thinking is a key cognitive process unique to creativity (Guilford, 1968). In pretend play, children practice divergent thinking (D. G. Singer & Singer, 1990). Divergent thinking occurs in play in many ways. Not only does it occur in both play and creative production, but research also suggests that play facilitates the development of divergent thinking ability (Dansky, 1999). Transformation ability, shifting sets, and recombining ideas and images, are important in creativity and occur in play. In play, the use of symbolism and fantasy involves a constant recombining of images and a manipulation of ideas. Cognitive flexibility is an inherent part of fantasy and make-believe. The "as if" nature of pretend requires a certain amount of cognitive flexibility. Insight is important in creative thinking, and research has suggested that play facilitates insight on problem-solving tasks (Vandenberg, 1980). Vandenberg (1980) stated that in both play and creativity, one is creating novelty from the commonplace and has a disregard for the familiar.

## Overlapping Affective Processes in Play and Creativity

Pretend play is infused with affect, and access to emotion and affect-laden cognition is an advantage for creative production. This is especially true in the arts but also in the sciences. If emotion broadens the associative process and aids with divergent thinking, then scientific creativity would be aided as well. Affect processes important in creativity occur in play (see Table 1.2).

Play is an arena in which children express both positive and negative emotion and become comfortable with that emotion. This is especially true for negative emotions (e.g., anger, sadness, fear, disgust) around which the child often feels conflicted or ashamed. Play is a safe place where the child can control the pace of the expression and slowly modulate or, as Waelder (1933) said, "digest" the event or emotion.

The same is true for affect-laden ideas, images, or fantasy. The affective content may be symbolized. *Affect-laden cognition* refers to thoughts and images that contain emotional content. Examples in children's play would be monsters, vampires, witches, birthday cake, and war games. The psychoanalytic concept of primary-process thinking is an example of this kind of emotion-laden thinking (Holt, 1977). Fein's (1987) concept of affect symbols is another. Fein viewed play as symbolic behavior organized around emotional and motivational issues. Symbolic units represent affective relationships such as fear of, love for, or anger at. An affective symbol system represents real or imagined experience, and symbols can be manipulated in pretend play. This manipulation and recombining of affect symbols is important in the arts and also could influence divergent thinking and transformation abilities. However, Fein thought that divergent thinking activities such as daydreaming, pretend play, and drawing could activate the affective symbol system. Bidirectionality is probably true for many cognitive and affective processes important in creativity.

Joy and pleasure in creative problem solving can be seen in children in many areas but certainly in pretend play. The pleasure in make-believe and total engagement in a task crucial for creativity occurs in uninhibited play. Csikszentmihalyi's (1990) concept of *flow* in creative tasks can also be observed in play when a child is totally engaged and loses track of time. We can only speculate as to the importance of this experience in childhood. It is certainly likely that this joyful experience, when felt in childhood in whatever form, is something the adult strives to recapture. Play introduces the child to the feeling that accompanies creative expression. It could also be the beginning of an aesthetic sense in the child. This desire to experience this deep pleasure could be a motivating force for adult creativity. Pleasure in challenge could also be involved in an intricate pretend experience. The intricate imaginary worlds or *paracosms* described by Root-Bernstein and Root-Bernstein (2006) would be an example of a challenging play task that could involve tension as well as pleasure.

Cognitive integration and modulation of affect refer to how the child deals with emotion. How well is affect integrated into the fantasy in the play? Is there a narrative around intense anger? Is the emotion sufficiently modulated so that the child stays in the play story? Sarnoff (1976) stated that the effective use of fantasy reflects a cross-situational, cognitively based structure that results in the ability to modulate the expression and experience of otherwise disruptive emotions. Sarnoff's conceptualization is consistent with Erikson's (1963) concept of mastery in play. Children use play to gain mastery over traumatic events and everyday conflicts. Psychoanalytic theorists also viewed play as a vehicle through which children could express negative emotions and slowly process them. Getting into the habit of using play, and later fantasy and thought, to think about problems and negative emotions could also set the stage for adult creativity.

## CONCLUSION

Research supports the relationship between pretend play and creativity. There is an overlap among cognitive and affective processes important to and unique in creativity and cognitive and affective processes that occur in pretend play. If we think of pretend play as a form of a creative act—as a form of creativity—then the relationship is obvious. Pretend play could also be a vehicle for mini-c creativity to occur as well. In pretend play, children can explore and experiment with mini-c forms of expression. Which specific processes are important in different creative domains needs to be identified through research. Which of these processes can be developed through play also requires further investigation.

The cognitive and affective processes described here are relatively discrete categories. Although they may become quite complex over time, we can conceptualize them as discrete categories that can be measured. Some of the other characteristics of the creative process such as self-expression, self-actualization, sublimation, or conflict resolution are more complex entities that are more difficult to operationalize and measure. But they are important concepts in adult creativity. Can we see the seeds of these complex variables in a child's pretend play? Child therapists would say yes, because they use play to help the child resolve conflicts (Chethik, 1989). Expression of emotion in a pretend way could be the beginning of sublimation. There is little research evidence that ties these concepts to pretend play. But they should be considered and further investigated. In the next chapter, I turn to an overview of different theories of play and functions of play in child development.

# 2

# EVOLUTIONARY, PSYCHOANALYTIC, AND DEVELOPMENTAL THEORIES OF PRETEND PLAY AND CREATIVITY

Theory can help us understand the role of pretend play in creativity. In particular, the function of play in evolution has implications for the function of play in child development. This chapter first reviews play from the perspective of evolutionary theory and animal play. Next, it reviews psychoanalytic and developmental approaches to the understanding of play and creativity.

## EVOLUTIONARY THEORY, PLAY, AND CREATIVITY

### Play in Animals

The study of play in animals can teach us about the role of play in evolution. Did play ability contribute to the survival of the individual? Did play ability aid the survival of the species? Is the play we see today a leftover remnant of a previous form that no longer has a function, or has play taken

http://dx.doi.org/10.1037/14282-003
*Pretend Play in Childhood: Foundation of Adult Creativity*, by S. W. Russ

on new functions? Burghardt (2005) addressed these questions and presented an excellent review of the animal play literature. He reviewed play research in primates, mammals, reptiles, birds, fish, and invertebrates such as spiders and bees. Burghardt's thesis was that human play is continuous with animal play in many ways. He stated, "All play . . . should be viewed as a product of evolutionary history" (p. 110). We can follow the continuity of play as it evolves in these different species. However, the picture of the evolution of play is complicated and complex.

Burghardt (2005) offered five criteria that must be present for an event to be classified as play in animals:

1. The behavior has limited immediate function. Some elements of the behavior do not contribute to current survival.
2. The behavior is done for its own sake. The behavior is intrinsically motivated.
3. The behavior is different from the complete performance when it is serious. For example, play fighting does not have all the behaviors of real fighting.
4. There is repeated performance in a similar form during a predictable period in the animal's life.
5. The behavior occurs in a relaxed field. The behavior occurs when the animal is not hungry or stressed and is healthy.

There are a number of different classification systems for animal play. According to Power (2000), less complex forms of animal play are locomotor play and object play. Different levels of complexity can still meet Burghardt's (2005) criteria. *Locomotor play* is sustained movement without any immediate benefit. *Object play* is exploratory play during which objects are manipulated.

Pretend play does occur in animals. Burghardt (2005) summarized the area of animal pretend play:

> Whenever animals treat an inanimate object as if it were a biologically meaningful one and independent information is available to show that the animal is able to make the distinction between it and the biologically appropriate one, then pretend play could be validly indicated, even if the cognitive underpinnings do not rely on imitation or are otherwise humanlike. (p. 101)

Note that the concept of "as if" is used in this definition as it is in the definitions of children's pretend play reviewed in Chapter 1. There is a consensus that pretend play does occur in apes and other primates, but many animal researchers have identified pretend play in cats, foxes, and dogs as well. For example, a cat playing with a ball of yarn as if it were prey involves pretense. An interesting question is how the internal mental representation of the ball for the cat differs from the mental representation of the child when playing with a baby doll as if it were real.

## Evolutionary Advantage of Play

What is the advantage of play behavior, especially pretend play behavior, to the individual and to the species? Groos (1901), one of the early play theorists, concluded that playful versions of necessary activities occur early in life. In general, animal play is viewed as practice and rehearsal for behaviors necessary for adult survival. Through play, the individual gains mastery over these behaviors.

Mitchell (2007) reviewed the advantages of practice through play for animals in preparation for adult behaviors. Most animals enact their own activities. Pretense that is based on others' activities occurs almost exclusively among the great apes and dolphins. Mitchell gave examples of this type of pretense: simulating another's behavior, acting as if someone or something has an imaginary property, substituting one object for another, and acting as if something absent were present (pp. 65–66). One example he gave of dolphin symbolic pretense was a young dolphin that observed, through an underwater window, a person blowing cigarette smoke. The dolphin then obtained a mouthful of milk from the mother, went back to the window, and squirted the milk in simulation of the smoke.

Practice with activities necessary for daily life in adulthood also can apply to practice with processing emotions. Positive emotions often accompany play in animals. Apes laugh when tickled or played with (Provine, 2001) and rats "laugh" when tickled and seek out opportunities to be tickled (Burgdorf & Panksepp, 2001). Burghardt (2005) pointed out that although much play in animals appears to have positive emotions associated with it, it has negative emotions present as well, such as fear and anger. Mitchell (2007) pointed out that Lorenz (1950/1971) thought that animals displayed pretend feelings. Burghardt concluded, "Play may serve as a means of arousing emotions in settings where their serious deployment is muted through comfortable and socially constrained contexts" (p. 140). He pointed out the similarity between this conceptualization and Sutton-Smith's (2003) idea that play in children triggers virtual emotions in safe contexts. The concept that animals and children use play to experience, rehearse, process, and, from a psychoanalytic perspective, work though emotions is important when we think about the value of play. In the creativity and child development literature, the emotional aspect of play is often overlooked. The simplistic view that play is fun and only fun does a disservice to the role of play and contributes to the growing cultural shift that devalues play and reduces time for play.

To determine whether play is adaptive, it is important to carry out both correlational studies and experimental studies. *Correlational* studies look at the relationship between the amount and type of play and an adaptive behavior. *Experimental* studies examine cause and effect. Burghardt (2005) raised a key question: "How do we demonstrate that play is adaptive [in animals]?" (p. 114). This question is also central in the area of child development. Are the processes that we see in play reflections of cognitive and affective development, or does play behavior also help these processes develop?

Smith (2007), from reviews of animal and child play research, concluded that play may be a facilitative experience but does not hold a major adaptive role in child development. Boyd (2009), however, from his reviews, concluded that play offers a major advantage for development. Boyd stated, "Play evolved through the advantages of flexibility; the amount of play in a species correlates with its flexibility of action" (p. 14). He proposed that practice in nonurgent situations can refine skills and neural pathways. Play is especially important in the development of art and creativity. Boyd proposed that all art evolved from animal play. Play helps develop a flexibility of mind that is facilitative of creativity.

**Implications for Play in Children**

Burghardt (2005) drew a number of conclusions about animal play that, in my opinion, are quite relevant to the conceptualization of play in children. First, play is heterogeneous. Factors that control one system of play are not the same as those controlling another. This argues against a unitary play drive or one play system. Even play fighting in animals can reflect different motivational systems: either aggressive or sexual. Especially in highly playful species, play involves multiple behavior systems. Also, as the organism develops, systems become differentiated. Behavioral reorganization occurs and behavioral systems become differentiated. So, for example, in children, cognitive and affective systems in play may become differentiated over time.

A second important conclusion is that play can have different functions at different ages. There may be critical periods for play to be adaptive in specific ways. There are critical periods for play to affect experience that in turn influences neural development. Play can help with the immediate life stage but not necessarily with a future stage. It is hard to evaluate the long-term benefits of play because play is only one of several ways to enhance development. This principle is true for children as well. For example, when we consider creativity, there are many processes involved in the creative act. Though play can help develop those processes, there are many other ways to facilitate their development as well.

Third, play occurs in a "relaxed field." A risk-free environment is necessary for play to occur in animals. Children also benefit from a safe, supportive environment in developing play behavior. Children who have experienced traumatic events and who have been diagnosed with post-traumatic stress disorder have shown constriction in their play behaviors (Gil, 1991; Terr, 1990).

If play is preparation for necessary activities in adulthood for animals, what are the necessary activities for humans that pretend play especially can prepare them for? Necessary activities for humans fall into two broad categories:

1. *Practice with problem solving*. Certainly, practice with problem solving is relevant. Pretend play can be rehearsal for a variety of problems that children face on a daily basis. Practice with divergent thinking should help generate ideas in many different situations. Practice with manipulating ideas and images should develop flexibility in thinking that is useful.
2. *Processing of emotion*. The use of pretend play to express, process, and integrate emotions should help the child feel comfortable with a range of emotions, learn to modulate and integrate emotions, and think about and manipulate affect-laden cognition. Learning to manage negative emotions, such as fear and anger, and memories of stressful events are important tasks of childhood.

Many of the functions of play observed and investigated in children have their evolutionary roots in animal behavior. And many of these functions are important in creative production.

## PSYCHOANALYTIC THEORY, PLAY, AND CREATIVITY

One important aspect of pretend play is that it involves emotion—the expression of emotion and the expression of affect-laden cognition. A number of theorists in developmental fields have investigated play, affect, and imagination. Early theorists who viewed pretend play as a way for children to process and manage emotions were the psychodynamic and psychoanalytic theorists Anna Freud (1966) and Melanie Klein (1955). They were not focused on creativity. Rather, they wanted to help children better deal with emotional problems. They brought pretend play into the therapy room. Play was a place where children expressed emotions and fantasy themes, both positive and negative, and rehearsed ways of dealing with memories and everyday problems. Children do this on their own in normal child development. Child therapists could then use play in therapy to bring problems to the surface and help the child resolve the issues.

Anna Freud (1966) viewed children's pretend play as a direct expression of fantasy and instincts in a more accessible and less disguised form than in adults. She was cautious in her interpretations about what child's play might mean. Melanie Klein (1955), however, thought that play for the child was the same as free association for the adult. Unconscious processes were expressed in play. The conceptualization of fantasy and affect expression in play evolved from Sigmund Freud's (1915/1958) theory of affect and primary process. What follows is a brief description, with more detail given in Chapter 4.

Psychoanalytic scholars viewed pretend play as a safe place where primitive, forbidden, affect-laden thoughts, feelings, and actions could be expressed. This conceptualization was based on Freud's theory of the unconscious and primary process. In 1915, Sigmund Freud first conceptualized *primary-process thought* as an early, primitive system of thought that was drive-laden and not subject to rules of logic or oriented to reality. A good example of primary-process thinking is the kind of thinking that occurs in dreams. Dreams are illogical, are not oriented to rules of time and space, and frequently include affect-laden content and images.

Affect is a major component of primary-process thinking. Access to primary process has been hypothesized to relate to creative thinking because associations are fluid, and primitive images and ideas can be accessed and used. In this mode of thinking, ideas are easily interchangeable, and attention is widely and flexibly distributed (Arlow & Brenner, 1964). Therefore, access to primary-process thinking should broaden the search process and enable a variety of associations. This broadened search process would facilitate creative thinking.

Research with adults and children has supported the relationship between access to primary-process thinking and creative cognition (Russ, 1993; Suler, 1980). Pretend play in children is a place where primary process is expressed. Waelder (1933) described play as a leave of absence from reality. Play is a place to let go and allow illogical primary-process thinking to occur. He described the play process as one in which the child repeats an unpleasant experience over and over until it becomes manageable. As he put it, the child "digests" the event. Theoretically then, children who are more able to access affect-laden primary-process ideas and images in play should be better divergent thinkers and more flexible in their problem-solving approach. They should also have more access to emotions and affect-laden memories. These abilities should increase the odds that they will be creative as adults.

# DEVELOPMENTAL THEORY, PLAY, AND CREATIVITY

Much of what has been written about the development of creativity in children has focused on the role of play in creativity. This is because play and creativity are so intertwined (Fein, 1987; Sawyer, 1997; Vygotsky, 1930/1967b). Research findings support the relationship between pretend play ability and creativity in children. There are many studies from many different researchers who have found significant, positive relationships between play and different components of creativity (divergent thinking, insight, flexibility) independent of intelligence; these are reviewed in later chapters. Because so many of the cognitive and affective processes important in creativity also occur in pretend play, we now turn to play and the development of play in children. Parts of this chapter are based on an earlier review (Russ & Fiorelli, 2010).

**Emergence of Pretend Play**

Hirsh-Pasek and Golinkoff (2003) concluded, in a review of the literature, that the type of play varies as a function of age. Play is first evident at 3 to 9 months, when children try to fit novel objects into their existing world through exploration. Significant development in play occurs around two years, when children are able to use objects in the appropriate way. Before 2 years of age, children play with objects similarly no matter what their actual functions are. Around 2 years of age, children recognize that a telephone is used to talk to someone, and a plate is used to hold food. Also around the age of two, children begin to discover pretend play. They are able to pretend to hear a voice from the telephone, for instance. In the 3rd and 4th years, pretend play is especially evident. Children are able to think symbolically, not be confined to a single use of an object, and consider worlds outside their own. They are now able to recognize that although a plate is typically used to hold food, it can also be used as a steering wheel for an imaginary car. Play follows developmental stages in which a child moves from reacting to characteristics of objects to exploring objects to symbolically using objects (Belsky & Most, 1981).

As children develop, their play becomes more complex. Dansky (1999) pointed out that in high-level play, children display all seven dimensions of original thinking described by Milgram: associative fluency, imagery, curiosity, fantasy, problem finding, metaphoric production, and selective attention deployment. He concluded that individual differences in play have implications for individual differences in creativity. Dansky also theorized that adopting the "as if" frame in play may open the door to a mode of problem solving where one can play with ideas and possibilities, which is so important in creativity.

Just as it is important in creativity to play with ideas and images, it is also important to play with affective processes. Affect expression in play occurs from a young age. It is notable that when we compare affect expression in the play narratives of children from 6 to 10 years of age, we do not find developmental differences in the amount of affect expression over these years.

In reviewing different theoretical approaches to pretend play, it is important to keep in mind the overarching evolutionary framework of play as preparation for adult life. Pretend play provides practice with problem solving and with processing of emotions. Many play theorists have focused on cognitive problem-solving benefits of play.

## Play and Creative Problem Solving

Sawyer (1997) conceptualized pretend play in young children as being improvisational. Improvisation is important in adult creativity. Sawyer pointed out that pretend play is unscripted yet has loose outlines to be followed. The concept of generating something that is unscripted and spontaneous is important because play is one of the first experiences the child has with a creative experience.

Vygotsky (1930/1967b) theorized that imagination developed out of children's play (Smolucha, 1992). He stated, "The child's play activity is not simply a recollection of past experience but a creative reworking that combines impressions and constructs from them new realities addressing the needs of the child" (p. 7). Through play, children develop *combinatory imagination*, the ability to combine elements of experience into new situations and behaviors. Combinatory imagination is important in both artistic and scientific creativity. Pretend play can also be conceptualized as practice with divergent thinking and can directly aid idea generation in creativity (Dansky, 1999; D. G. Singer & Singer, 1990). Vygotsky also thought that pretend play fostered "inner speech" that helps with language and cognitive development (L'Abate, 2009).

One of the most influential theorists in the area of cognitive development was Jean Piaget. Piaget was a stage theorist who proposed that there is a qualitative change in children's thinking as they go through different stages (Piaget, 1932). Important to the area of creativity is the preoperational stage, from 2 to 7 years, during which children begin to use mental imagery and symbolic representation. One object can represent another. This age is also the dominant period for pretend play. Piaget spoke of symbolic play that uses the imagination as "ludic" play (D. G. Singer & Revenson, 1996). He thought that one of the purposes of symbolic play was to help the child differentiate reality from fantasy. Another major purpose was for rehearsal of life experiences.

Piaget proposed a theory of adaptation (1945/1967). Runco (2007) pointed out that Piaget's theory of adaptation is relevant to the development of creativity. The theory of adaptation involves both the process of assimilation and accommodation as important developmental functions. D. G. Singer and Revenson (1996) described *adaptation* as "the continuous process of using the environment to learn and learning to adjust to changes in the environment" (p. 15). *Assimilation* is taking in information and fitting that information into existing notions and frameworks about the world. *Accommodation* is revising one's worldview to fit the new information. Accommodation and assimilation can occur in pretend play. Piaget (1962) viewed the creative imagination as "assimilation activity in a state of spontaneity" (p. 289). But Runco stressed that for adaptation to begin to occur, there must be a sense of disequilibrium to go into action. Runco (1999b) has written extensively on the importance of disequilibrium to the creative process. There must be some tension or perceived problem to begin the creative process. For children, there must be a challenge or problem for the child to manage.

Developmental theorists Vygotsky (1967a) and Piaget (1951) both believed that interaction through peers fosters problem solving and play development. Vygotsky (1967a) identified a zone of proximal development, which includes tasks that are too difficult for the child individually but that are possible with guidance from adults or more skilled peers. Hirsh-Pasek and Golinkoff (2003) cited a study by McCune, Dipane, Fireoved, and Fleck (1994) that demonstrated that the level of a child's play increases with adult involvement but not adult control. With guidance and demonstration from the researcher, children engaged in more complex and creative make-believe play and abstract thinking. Through these interactions, children are encouraged to participate in solving more advanced problems and increasing the complexity of play. Children are then able to adapt these newly learned skills and incorporate them into future interactions (Tudge & Rogoff, 1989).

Piaget also emphasized the importance of peers in the development of problem-solving skills but suggested that peers need not be more advanced. Through interactions with others at a similar developmental stage, children learn different perspectives, discuss possible resolutions, and decide on the best solution. Children develop problem-solving skills, as well as advance their play skills, through this resolution process.

Piaget's concept of compensatory play is similar to Waelder's conceptualization of children digesting primitive ideas or unpleasant experiences in play (see the earlier psychoanalytic section). In *compensatory play*, a child expresses affect about the unpleasant experience symbolically in play. The expression then "enabled a child to dissociate the unpleasant act from its context and then assimilate it into his behavior" (D. G. Singer, & Revenson, 1996, p. 48).

Harris (1989) proposed that imaginative understanding is developed in play and enables children to understand others' mental states and affective experiences. His research supports that proposition.

These developmental theorists have suggested and research has supported that it is within play that children are able to create and solve problems for themselves, learn how to interact with others, discover a sense of power, learn how to cope with life events, and develop language (Hirsh-Pasek & Golinkoff, 2003). Although research is reviewed in detail in Chapters 3 and 4, a few studies are presented here. Research has demonstrated that play and play interventions lead to an improvement in problem-solving ability (Drewes, 2006; Fisher, 1992). In one study, Sylva, Bruner, and Genova (1976) demonstrated that self-guided play serves to teach problem solving. In another study, 4-year-olds were either given an opportunity to play or a training experience, followed by a task requiring problem solving. On the first task, participants given the play opportunity performed equally as well as those participants trained in the specific task. The second task was related but more complex than the first. On this task, children who had the play opportunity were faster and required fewer hints than those who were trained on a similar, yet less difficult, task (Smith & Dutton, 1979).

Research has demonstrated that divergent thinking, which is associated with creativity and more advanced problem solving, improves through divergent play (Pepler & Ross, 1981). Children who first engaged in divergent play were much more successful at the subsequent divergent task of building a city from a pile of blocks. Through such play, children are able to create and solve new problems, an essential process in the development of problem-solving skills. The children who engaged in prior convergent activities were discouraged by the problem-solving task. They were less likely to think in novel ways; they often got stuck on one incorrect solution and were much more likely to give up before the task's completion. This suggests that without proper play, creative processes may be hindered. If a child is never given opportunities to creatively find solutions to problems or engage in activities that have more than one answer, they are likely preventing full development of such processes.

Wyver and Spence (1999) examined the relationship between play and problem solving further and identified an element of reciprocity. They found that the development of divergent problem solving facilitates the development of play skills and vice versa.

Elkind (2007) suggested that the problem-solving process only occurs if children are developmentally ready. The most effective way to develop this skill is through child-initiated and child-guided play, not at the instruction or control of the more advanced adult. As Hirsh-Pasek and Golinkoff (2003) suggested, a child begins to consider symbolic play only after fully exploring the objects in his or her world, not at the instruction of the parent. Similarly, it seems problem solving can only begin once children develop an understanding of their surroundings. In other words, an elementary understanding is necessary to develop such skills. As children increasingly engage in pretend play during the preschool years, research supports that they are also developing problem-solving skills. Furthermore, children are developing the skills to interact, play, and solve problems cooperatively with their peers (Ashley & Tomasello, 1998; Brownell & Carriger, 1990, 1991).

## Fein's Theory of Play, Affect, and Creativity

Fein (1987) was a major developmental theorist who stressed the importance of affect in play in the link to creativity. Fein proposed an affect symbol system that gets activated in pretend play and is important in creativity. An affective symbol stores information about emotional events and is manipulated and worked with in pretend play. Fein viewed play as a natural form of creativity. Her focus on affect in play is a major contribution to the affect and creativity area. She studied 15 master players (children who were excellent at pretend play) and concluded that good pretend play consists of five characteristics:

1. *Referential freedom*. The "as if" concept is important in that one object is treated as if it were another, and one person functions in multiple roles. Time and place change. Object substitutions and transformations occur. Fein theorized that transformations occur when a representational template is mapped onto persons and objects in the environment. These representations can be manipulated and are detached from practical outcomes. The ability to engage in referential freedom begins at 2 years of age.

2. *Denotative license*. The child takes a divergent stance with respect to actual experience. There are pretend events, not just object substitution in an accurate account of events.

3. *Affective relations*. Symbolic units represent affective relationships such as fear of, love for, anger at. Fein proposed an affective symbol system that represents real or imagined experiences at a general level. These affective units are affect-binding, representational templates. The templates store salient information about affect-laden events. The units are then "manipulated, interpreted, coordinated, and elaborated in a way that makes affective sense to the players" (p. 292). These affective units are a key part of pretend play. Fein viewed pretend play as symbolic behavior organized through emotional and motivational

issues. Fein implied that this affective symbol system is especially important for creative thinking. She stated that divergent thinking abilities such as daydreams, pretend play, or drawing could activate the affective symbol system.

4. *Sequential uncertainty*. The sequence of events in pretend play has a nonlinear quality.
5. *Self-mirroring*. Children are aware of the pretend quality of the play. The self is observed from a distance through play.

The concept of the affective symbol system is a major contribution to the affect and creativity area. It provides a way to think about playing with affect representations as well as playing with ideas. Both occur in pretend play and are important for the creative development of children. Children who have a rich affect symbol system and who can express it and manipulate affective representations should be more creative in many domains.

I have pointed out (Russ, 1993, 2004) that Fein's conceptualization of an affective symbol system is consistent with the concept of primary process. Both concepts refer to affect-laden cognition, often but not always unconscious, that facilitates the creative process. Both concepts emphasize the manipulation of affect-laden cognition that should foster flexibility in thinking and broad associations crucial in creativity.

## Russ's Integrated Model of Play and Creativity

I have stressed the importance of pretend play in helping children to access emotional memories and fantasies (Russ, 1993). My integrated model of pretend play and creativity (discussed throughout this volume) identifies key cognitive and affective processes in play that are also important processes in creativity. In particular, the importance of affective processes in play and creativity are highlighted. I developed a measure of play ability that assessed both cognitive and affective processes in play. Affect themes in the fantasy play narrative were focused on in this measure of play—the Affect in Play Scale (Russ, 1993, 2004; see also Appendix A, this volume). These affect themes consisted of affect-laden images, including primary-process content and emotional interactions between puppets. By developing a measure of affect expression in the play narrative with a standardized task and scoring system, the relationship between affect in play and creativity could be investigated. In my research, affect expression in play has been related to divergent thinking in a number of studies (i.e., Russ & Grossman-McKee, 1990), to teacher ratings of fantasy ability (Kaugars & Russ, 2009), to creativity in story telling (Hoffmann & Russ, 2012), and to emotion in memory narratives (Russ & Schafer, 2006).

## Cognitive–Affective Interaction

D. G. Singer and Singer (1990) proposed a cognitive–affective framework for pretend play, a "central conception from which we can explore the nature of imaginative play and its role in childhood" (p. 290). They reviewed Tomkins's (1962, 1963) model of affect and suggested that play is reinforcing when it permits expression of positive affect and the appropriate control of negative affect. This formulation is consistent with research by Golomb and Galasso (1995). In a study with preschoolers, they found that when affective valence of an imagined situation was negative, children modified the theme to diminish their fear, such as by imagining a friendly monster. In a positive affect situation, they embellished the theme to enhance the pleasure. Golomb and Galasso concluded that children monitor and regulate affect in play so as not to exceed a certain threshold, while still having enough emotional involvement to enjoy the play. Shmukler (1982–1983) viewed imaginative play as lying at the cognitive–affective interface and reflecting a general capacity for divergent thinking.

The concept that a balanced cognitive–affective interaction is important for children to be able to regulate emotion and still be in control of cognition and action is consistent with the idea of *adaptive regression* (Holt, 1977), or regression in the service of the ego (Kris, 1952). Some psychoanalytic theorists have stressed that it was controlled access to primitive, affect-laden ideation that was important in creative work. The individual—child or adult—needed to be able to go back and forth between free associations, be they affect laden and illogical, and critical evaluative thought. This flexibility in thinking is also consistent with Wallas's (1926) stages of creativity, reviewed in Chapter 1. In his stage model, the creative individual goes back and forth between the incubation stage, where free-roaming searches and associations occur, and the verification stage, where ideas are critically evaluated, refined, and tested. This flexibility requires individuals to have some control of the process and their emotions. Play theorists have proposed that pretend play is one place where this type of emotion regulation is learned (Berk, Mann, & Ogan, 2006).

Morrison (1988) placed cognitive–affective development in an interpersonal framework. He thought that the cognitive integration of affect occurs within safe interactions with the parents. Representations of self and others are fused with affect. In play, the child reconstructs past experiences and explores definitions of self. Old metaphors are constantly reworked. In this way, the child develops reflective thought. Conflicts from early interpersonal experiences can be a major form of creative thinking in that the metaphors of early experience are reworked in creative acts.

Although cognition and affect is discussed in different sections throughout this book, the interaction between these processes is constant. In that sense, it is an artificial distinction. Nevertheless, it is useful in organizing discussions about play and play research to treat cognitive and affective processes in separate sections. But it is important to keep in mind that interaction is occurring between the processes.

## Playfulness

Much has been written about the construct of playfulness as being important in the development of creativity. Often, when thinking about children's play, the playful aspect of the child comes to the fore. *Playfulness* has been defined as the capacity to "frame or reframe a situation in such a way as to provide oneself (or possibly others) with amusement, humor, and/or entertainment" (Barnett, 2007, p. 977). It has also been described as "an internal predisposition to bring a playful quality to interactions within the environment and across a variety of contexts and episodes" (Trevlas, Grammatikopoulos, Tsigilis, & Zachopoulou, 2003, p. 33). Lieberman (1977) described five components of playfulness in children: physical spontaneity, cognitive spontaneity, social spontaneity, manifest joy, and sense of humor. *Physical spontaneity* is level of movement and coordination during play. *Cognitive spontaneity* is taking on different roles and variety of object use. *Social spontaneity* is the flexibility of interactions with others. *Manifest joy* is the expression of enthusiasm and enjoyment while playing. *Sense of humor* is the tendency to clown around and joke. Playfulness in children has been found to relate to divergent thinking.

Interestingly, there is little research that has investigated the relationship between playfulness and capacity for pretend play. Burghardt (2005) commented on the need for research on this question. The constructs of pretend play and playfulness may be related but may be different constructs. In a longitudinal study with a small sample of 21 children, pretend play was related to teachers' rating of playfulness 4 years later (Christian, 2011). A significant positive correlation was found between the composite play score and teacher reported playfulness ($r = .37$, $p = .05$), with a medium effect size. Examining the specific play scores, significant positive correlations were found between organization ($r = .46$, $p < .05$), imagination ($r = .38$, $p < .05$), frequency of positive affect ($r = .46$, $p = .01$), total affect score ($r = .36$, $p = .05$), and teacher reported playfulness. Interestingly, a trend level negative association occurred between frequency of negative affect ($r = -.34$, $p = .06$) in play and teacher reported playfulness. Children with organized play narratives that expressed more imaginative elements and positive affect in play were considered more playful 4 and 5 years later when rated by their classroom teacher.

In this study, there was a relationship between quality of pretend play and playfulness, but a large portion of the variance was not shared. Thus, there could be many children who have a high quality of pretend play but who do not demonstrate the playfulness attitude in other circumstances. Or there may be playful children who do not show much pretense in pretend play. This is an important question for future investigation.

## CONCLUSION

Researchers in the area of animal play and evolution have proposed that play in young animals prepares them for adult activities. Some theorists believe that animal play and elements of pretend are associated with flexibility in cognition and behavior. A number of theorists and researchers in child development also think that play, especially pretend play, has a major role in the development of creativity. From Vygotsky's (1930/1967b) concept of imagination developing from children's play, to Sawyer's (1997) concept of play as improvisation, to Piaget's (1932) concept of adaptation, to Anna Freud's (1966) ideas about pretend play and fantasy, play has been thought to be central to creative problem solving. Affect in play was especially important in Fein's (1987) affective symbol system. Dorothy and Jerome Singer have emphasized the interaction between cognition and affect in play (D. G. Singer & Singer, 1990). My integrated model attempts to pull together what is known about cognition and affect in play and creativity (Russ, 1993). Many of the theorists in the play and child development area have based their concepts on observations of children. What does the research say about the importance of pretend play in creativity? The next two chapters focus on the research findings about the relationship between cognitive processes in pretend play and creativity (Chapter 3) and between affective processes in play and creativity (Chapter 4).

# 3

# COGNITIVE PROCESSES IN PRETEND PLAY AND CREATIVITY

The purpose of this chapter is to review the research on pretend play and creativity, with a focus on cognitive processes. Ideally, researchers would be able to identify specific cognitive processes in play (e.g., divergent thinking, symbolism, fantasy elements) and then determine their correlates in creative production. However, the field is not yet focused on specific components of play. Most studies are rather global in nature. Therefore, this chapter includes studies that are most relevant to the area of cognitive creative processes. Some research studies do measure specific cognitive processes in play and their correlates. The Affect in Play Scale (Russ, 1987, 1993, 2004), which measures specific cognitive and affective processes in play, is described in detail in this chapter. Research with that scale is also reviewed here (and in Chapter 4).

This chapter first gives a brief overview of the concepts behind research in the area of cognitive processes in play and creativity. Next, it describes the Affect in Play Scale. Then it reviews the research literature in the area of

http://dx.doi.org/10.1037/14282-004
*Pretend Play in Childhood: Foundation of Adult Creativity*, by S. W. Russ

play and creative cognitive processes: play and divergent thinking; play and insight; play, everyday creativity, and coping; play and perspective taking; play and creative narratives; and wordplay and creativity. Methodological issues are discussed throughout. Finally, a summary and suggestions for future research are presented.

## RESEARCH ON PRETEND PLAY AND COGNITIVE PROCESSES: AN INTRODUCTION

There is strong empirical support for the relationship between pretend play and creativity in children. A number of different researchers with different child populations have found significant associations between pretend play and creativity, using various measures of play and of creativity. Some studies attempted to isolate the specific components of play that were important in the creativity task; others used more global measures of play. Most of the research has focused on cognitive processes, both in play and in creativity.

In 1983, Nathan Kogan stated, "The research directed toward the issue of the play–creativity linkage may well represent the most promising set of findings in the children's creativity literature over the past decade" (p. 642). Although the theoretical link between play and creativity had existed for some time, the research investigating the link began in the early 1970s. Since Kogan's prescient analysis, empirical evidence has continued to build and support the relationship between play and creativity.

In a meta-analysis conducted by Fisher (1992), 46 studies were included in the play and child development area up to 1987. He investigated the impact of play on cognitive, affective–social, and linguistic processes. Both correlational and experimental studies were included. In general, he found a modest effect size (ES) of .347. The largest ESs were for divergent thinking and perspective-taking criteria (.387 and .392, respectively). Both of these abilities are important cognitive processes in creative thinking. Divergent thinking involves generating a variety of ideas about and associations to a problem, which increases the odds of finding a novel solution. Perspective taking, taking the view of the other, is important in many domains of creativity, especially literature. Perspective taking is also crucial for interpersonal functioning. Fisher concluded that play does result in improvement in children's development. The strongest effect size was for cognitive abilities important in creative thinking. Divergent thinking, cognitive flexibility, and insight emerge in pretend play and in creative production.

Two major categories of cognitive processes important in creativity are divergent thinking and transformation abilities (reviewed in Chapter 1).

Guilford (1968) identified both of these processes as being important in and unique to creative problem solving. *Divergent thinking* is thinking that goes off in different directions. For example, a typical item on a divergent thinking test is "How many uses for a brick can you think of?" Guilford thought that the key concept underlying divergent production abilities was variety. Wallach (1970) thought of divergent thinking as being dependent on the flow of ideas and the "fluidity in generating cognitive units" (p. 1240). Divergent thinking involves free association, broad scanning ability, and fluidity of thinking. It has been found to be relatively independent of intelligence (Runco, 1991). *Transformation abilities* enable the individual to reorganize information and break out of an old set. They enable the individual to transform or revise what he or she knows into new patterns or configurations. Flexibility in thinking is involved. Insight is a third cognitive ability that is important in creativity (Sternberg, 1988). Research has supported relationships between pretend play ability and these cognitive processes.

There has been some criticism of the idea that divergent thinking is important in creative production. Silvia, Winterstein, and Willse (2008) concluded that divergent thinking is relevant for beginners in an area but not important at the expert level of creativity. Kaufman, Plucker, and Baer (2008) concluded that divergent thinking tests do not predict creative ability in many studies.

Some of the strongest evidence for the relationship between divergent thinking and creativity is the strong predictive validity of the Torrance Test of Creative Thinking (K. H. Kim, 2008). This test battery assesses various aspects of divergent thinking and originality. The Torrance test was administered to children in the 1950s. Cramond, Mathews-Morgan, Bandalos, and Zuo (2005) carried out a 40-year follow-up and found that the Torrance test did predict creative achievement 40 years later. In a reanalysis by Plucker (1999), both Torrance test scores and IQ were predictive of creative achievement. Torrance scores were stronger predictors of creative achievement than were IQ scores. Recently, Runco, Millar, Acar, and Cramond (2011) carried out a 50-year follow-up. They found that Torrance scores were predictive of personal creative achievement, and Torrance scores and IQ combined were predictive of public achievement. These follow-up studies provide stronger empirical support that divergent thinking ability in childhood is predictive of creative functioning in adulthood. Tests of divergent thinking continue to be widely used as a measure of creativity in children and adults. However, it is important to be aware of the mixed findings of predictive validity in the research literature.

To study cognitive and affective processes and their correlates in play, we need to be able to measure play. What follows is a description of the Affect in Play Scale. A detailed manual for the scale can be found in Appendix A.

## THE AFFECT IN PLAY SCALE

The Affect in Play Scale (APS; Russ, 1987, 1993, 2004) was developed to meet the need for measures that assessed both cognitive and affective processes in pretend play. The scale consists of a standardized play task and a criterion-based rating scale. The APS is appropriate for children from 6 to 10 years old. The play task consists of two human puppets, one boy and one girl, and three small colored blocks that are laid out on a table. The puppets have neutral facial expressions. The task is individually administered. All children are given the same instructions and prompts. In essence, the child is asked to play with the puppets any way they like for 5 minutes. The play is videotaped and scored according to a detailed rating system.

The instructions are free-play instructions that leave much room for the child to structure the play and present themes and affects that are habitual to him or her. The instructions are as follows (see Appendix A):

> I'm here to learn about how children play. I have here two puppets and would like you to play with them any way you like for 5 minutes. For example, you can have the puppets do something together. I also have some blocks that you can use. Be sure to have the puppets talk out loud. The video camera will be on so I can remember what you say and do. I'll tell you when to stop.

Complete instructions and scoring manual can be found in Russ (2004) and in Appendix A of the present volume.

The APS measures cognitive processes on a 5-point Likert scale for imagination and organization ability. Criteria for rating imagination include amount of fantasy and pretend elements, transformations of blocks, and novel content. Organization criteria include quality and complexity of the plot and coherent story sequences. The APS also measures the amount and types of affective expression in the fantasy play. It measures affect themes in the play narrative. Both emotion-laden content and expression of emotion in the play are coded. In the development of the scale, Holt's (1977) scoring system for primary process on the Rorschach and J. L. Singer's (1973) play scales were used as models. In addition, the work of Izard (1977) and Tomkins (1962, 1963) was consulted to ensure that the affect categories were comprehensive and covered all major types of emotion expressed by children in the 4-to-10 age group.

The major scores from the APS are as follows:

- *Organization* (1–5 global rating). This score measures the organization of the play and considers the quality of the plot and complexity of the story. For example, a score of 1 would be given for a series of unrelated events, and a score of 5 would be given for a story with an integrated plot with elements of cause and effect.

- *Imagination* (1–5 global rating). This score measures the novelty and uniqueness of the play, the ability to pretend, and the ability to transform the blocks. A score of 1 would be given to play that has no block transformations and no fantasy elements. A score of 5 would be given to play that includes many block transformations, novel elements, and many story elements. In some studies, organization and imagination scores are combined to yield a quality of fantasy score.

- *Total frequency of units of affective expression.* A unit is defined as one scorable expression by an individual puppet. In a two-puppet dialogue, expressions of each puppet are scored separately. A unit can be the expression of an affect state, an affect theme, or a combination of the two. An example of an affect state is "This is fun." An example of an affect theme is "Here is a bomb that is going to explode." The expression can be verbal ("I hate you") or nonverbal (one puppet punching the other). The frequency of affect score is the total number of units of affect expressed in the 5-minute period.

- *Variety of affect categories.* There are 11 possible affect categories: happiness/pleasure, anxiety/fear, sadness/hurt, frustration/disappointment, nurturance/affection, aggression, oral, oral aggression, anal, sexual, competition. The variety of affect score is the number of different categories of affect expressed in the 5-minute period. These 11 affect categories can be divided into subsets of positive (happiness, nurturance, oral, sexual, competition) and negative (anxiety, sadness, frustration, aggression, oral aggression, anal) affect. Also, primary-process affect themes can be scored (aggression, oral, oral aggression, anal, sexual, competition). Primary-process content includes affect-laden oral, aggressive, and libidinal content around which children experience early intense feeling states. It is a subtype of affect in cognition that is based on psychoanalytic theory (Russ, 1987, 1996).

- *Mean intensity of affective expression* (1–5 rating). This rating measures the intensity of the feeling state or content theme. Each unit of affect is rated for intensity on a 1-to-5 scale. This particular score has not been used much in recent years because the scoring is labor-intensive, and it is highly correlated with the other affect scores.

- *Comfort*. Comfort in play is rated on a 1-to-5 scale. Comfort includes the involvement of the child in the play and his or her enjoyment of the play. It captures both the joy the child experiences and the involvement in the play itself. Although this score on the surface taps emotional involvement, it repeatedly loads on the cognitive factor with imagination and organization.

Finally, if desired, an affect integration score is obtained by multiplying one of the cognitive scores by the frequency of affect score. The affect integration score is useful because it attempts to measure the construct of cognitive modulation of emotion. It taps how well the affect is integrated and controlled by cognitive processes.

The APS was adapted for use with younger preschool children. The Affect in Play Scale–Preschool version (APS–P; Kaugars & Russ, 2009) is appropriate for children from 4 to 5 years old. The props consist of a number of stuffed and plastic animals, a car, and a ball. The instructions are much more structured than in the original version and help engage the young child into the play process. Scoring criteria are similar to the APS but also score for amount of pretend, functional, and no-play episodes.

### Reliability

Interrater reliability has been consistently good. Because a detailed scoring manual was developed and a careful training process is in place, interrater reliabilities in a large number of studies with different raters have usually been in the .80s and .90s, with a few in the .70s. For example, in our recent study using intraclass correlation coefficients that measure absolute agreement, $r = .94$ for organization, .96 for imagination, .95 for comfort, .96 for affect, .97 for variety of affect, .95 for positive affect, and .98 for negative affect (Hoffmann & Russ, 2012). Similar interrater reliabilities were found with the preschool version of the scale as well (Kaugars & Russ, 2009). Internal consistency of the frequency of affect score has also been good. We compared the 2nd and 4th minutes of the play with the 3rd and 5th minutes. Using the Spearman-Brown split-half reliability formula, there was good internal consistency of $r = .85$ (Seja & Russ, 1999).

### Validity

Construct validity for the APS was developed by investigating the relationships between the scores on the APS and theoretically relevant criteria (Anastasi, 1988). Weiner (1977) stressed that by finding hypothesized relationships between a measure and theoretically relevant criteria, conceptual validity is developed. Validity is developed for both the measure (as a good measure of the variable) and also for the theory that predicts a relationship between the variable and the criteria. So, for example, if the imagination score on the APS relates to a divergent thinking test, as hypothesized, then validity for the score is supported but so is the theory that imagination in play relates to divergent thinking in another area. For the APS, a number of studies have been carried out with the theoretically relevant criteria of creativity, coping, emotional understanding, experience of affect, and others (for a review, see Russ, 2004). Many of the studies relevant to the creativity are discussed in this chapter and in Chapter 4.

## PLAY AND DIVERGENT THINKING

What does divergent thinking in play look like? As D. G. Singer and Singer (1990) said, pretend play is practice with divergent thinking. Different stories are made up, Lego blocks represent many different things, and characters assume different roles. One facet of imagination in play is divergent thinking ability.

Before reviewing the research, it might be useful to give an example of what divergent thinking looks like in play. In the following example of divergent thinking in play, a 7-year-old girl was administered the APS. I first presented this narrative with a different focus (Russ, 2004). In this transcript, one can see the many different transformations the girl makes with the blocks and the many different scenes and story sequences that she develops. The dialogue is between the puppets.

> Hey, want to play with the beads that I'm using to make my necklace? OK. Like my necklace? Yeah. Now I am going to make mine. [*Blocks are beads for the necklace.*] Like my necklace? Yeah. I do. Let's go to the playground. There's a tunnel and a funny slide, It goes sort of straight. [*Blocks are the tunnel and slide.*] OK. Let's go. Whee! Whee! OK, now let's go home. Now what can we do? I don't know . . . how about we draw? [*Pretending to draw.*] Like my person? Of course I do. Do you like mine? My flowers? Of course I do. Come on. Now what should we do? Let's write a story. I made a skyscraper. Nah, we could make a person. How should we do that? OK. That will be . . . no, no, how about just a skyscraper? [*Blocks are the skyscraper.*] Now what else could we do? I know what we could make this into. What? OK. A telescope. How do you like it? [*Blocks are the telescope.*] I think it's great! Now it's my turn . . . hmm. What could that be? A butterfly! [*Blocks are the butterfly.*] That's right. Now a funny telescope. [*Laughs.*] No, no, no. A playground where you go in, up, and climb down that way. Climb up there, go through here, slide down

the slide, and go up there. [*Blocks are the playground.*] Yeah! OK, now let's go to the playground again. This time we'll go on the swing. We'll have to take turns—or go on the double swing. [*Blocks are the swing.*] Two people have to go on there.

In this play session, this child used the blocks to represent a number of different things: a telescope, a slide, and a butterfly. She generated many ideas. She also had a number of different events in her story. In general, children who show this much divergent thinking in play should generate more ideas on divergent thinking tests, such as the Alternate Uses Test (Wallach & Kogan, 1965). There are many individual differences in divergent thinking ability in play.

## Research Studies

Dansky's (1980) theoretical rationale for the relationship between play and divergent thinking was that the process of free combination of objects and ideas that occurs in play is similar to the elements involved in creative thinking. He speculated that the free symbolic transformations inherent in pretend play create a temporary cognitive set that loosens old associations. Kogan (1983) also proposed that children's play involves a search for alternate modes of relating to an object, a process similar to searching for alternate uses for objects in divergent thinking tasks. The idea of a temporary loosening of a cognitive set suggests that engaging in play would result in improved divergent thinking immediately after a play session. In addition, the concept of practice with divergent thinking in play should lead to a general improvement in divergent thinking. The child would be more able to engage in a divergent thinking approach when the task called for it or when just generating ideas for fun.

A large number of studies have found relationships between play and divergent thinking. Some, but not all, of these studies are reviewed here. An early study by D. L. Singer and Rummo (1973) found a relationship between play and divergent thinking in kindergarten boys. Pepler and Ross (1981) also found a relationship between play and divergent thinking. Feitelson and Ross (1973) found that thematic play facilitated creative thinking. Pepler (1979) found that the expression of symbolic and representational play predicted performance on a divergent thinking task. Johnson (1976) found that social make-believe play was related to divergent thinking. Dunn and Herwig (1992) found no relationship between dramatic play and divergent thinking, but did find a negative relationship between nonsocial play and divergent thinking. Wyver and Spence (1999) found that divergent thinking on a semantic task was related to thematic and cooperative play in preschoolers.

Theoretically, pretend play should be predictive of divergent thinking over time. Guilford (1950) expected creative processes to be stable, and the few studies in the area do support this hypothesis. In a longitudinal study, preschool imaginative predisposition and expressive imagination in play related to later imagination and creativity (Shmukler, 1982–1983). Hutt and Bhavnani (1972) found that creative inventiveness in preschool play related to later divergent thinking. P. Clark, Griffing, and Johnson (1989) found a relationship between play and divergent thinking in preschool males that was predictive of divergent thinking over a 3-year period. These studies support the stability of the association between play and divergent thinking.

## Research With the Affect in Play Scale

In investigating the relationship between play and divergent thinking, it is important to begin to identify the specific processes that account for the relationship. We conducted a series of studies investigating the relationship between cognitive processes and affective processes in play and divergent thinking (Hoffmann & Russ, 2012; Kaugars & Russ, 2009; Russ & Cooperberg, 2002; Russ & Grossman-McKee, 1990; Russ & Peterson, 1990; Russ, Robins, & Christiano, 1999). This section focuses on cognitive processes in play in these studies.

We found both imagination ($r = .35$, $p < .001$) and quality of the organization of fantasy ($r = .30$, $p < .001$) to be significantly related to the Alternate Uses Test in first- and second-grade children (Russ & Grossman-McKee, 1990). These correlations were independent of verbal intelligence. The finding that the relationship was independent of intelligence is important and consistent with findings in the creativity literature. Measures of creativity usually have a modest relationship with intelligence tests. In the 1990 study, we found that verbal IQ did not relate to the play measure. We replicated these findings in a study with sample of 121 children (Russ & Peterson, 1990). In the replication sample, both imagination ($r = .42$, $p < .001$) and quality of fantasy ($r = .43$, $p < .001$) were significantly related to divergent thinking. These relationships also remained significant when IQ was partialed out. In both studies, affect in fantasy scores also related to divergent thinking.

In a recent study with 61 girls from kindergarten through fourth grade, we found that pretend play was related to divergent thinking (Hoffmann & Russ, 2012). As in previous studies, a pattern emerged in which the cognitive processes of pretend play (organization and imagination), as measured by the APS, were related to divergent thinking. Organization in play positively correlated with divergent thinking fluency, $r(46) = .32$, $p < .05$, and flexibility, $r(46) = .28$, $p < .05$, on the Alternate Uses Test. Imagination in play also positively correlated with fluency, $r(46) = .38$, $p < .05$, and flexibility,

$r(46) = .36$, $p < .01$. Children who were rated as having more organization and imagination in their play also generated more responses on the divergent thinking task. Organization and imagination in play accounted for 10% and 14% of the variance in fluency of divergent thinking, respectively. The magnitudes of these correlations are of a medium effect size (J. Cohen, 1992). The variety of affect expressed in pretend play was also found to relate to divergent thinking. Variety of affect, as measured by the APS, positively correlated with divergent thinking fluency, $r(46) = .25$, $p < .05$. Children who expressed a wider range of emotions during pretend play also generated more answers during divergent thinking. These results remained significant after controlling for verbal ability.

In a longitudinal study that followed the children in our 1990 study (Russ & Peterson, 1990), cognitive processes in play predicted divergent thinking over a 4-year period. We (Russ et al., 1999) followed up with 31 children and tested them in the fifth and sixth grades. The major finding was that quality of fantasy and imagination in first- and second-grade play significantly predicted divergent thinking on an Alternate Uses Test over a 4-year period ($r = .34$, $p < .05$; $r = .42$, $p < .01$, respectively; see Table 3.1). The association between play and divergent thinking remained stable. This relationship was independent of intelligence.

The relationship between early and later divergent thinking was also relatively stable during this 4-year period, with a correlation of .42. In an unpublished study (Russ & Cooperberg, 2002), we recruited 49 of the original 121 children when they were in high school. Early play, as measured by the APS, predicted divergent thinking in the 11th and 12th grades. The correlations were of similar magnitude to the previous follow-up sample in

TABLE 3.1
Longitudinal Pearson Correlations of Play Scale Variables
at First and Second Grade With Divergent Thinking and Coping Measures
at Fifth and Sixth Grade

| Affect in Play Scale | Divergent thinking | | Coping | |
| --- | --- | --- | --- | --- |
| | Fluency | Spontaneous flexibility | Frequency | Quality |
| Frequency of affect | .13 | .11 | .02 | −.03 |
| Variety of affect | .25 | .20 | .26 | .23 |
| Comfort | .24 | .17 | .20 | .22 |
| Mean quality | .34* | .25 | .34* | .33* |
| Organization | .27 | .16 | .34* | .28 |
| Imagination | .42** | .35* | .42** | .45** |

*Note.* $N = 30$. From "Pretend Play: Longitudinal Prediction of Creativity and Affect in Fantasy in Children," by S. W. Russ, A. L. Robins, and B. A. Christiano, 1999, *Creativity Research Journal, 12,* p. 135. Copyright 1999 by Lawrence Erlbaum Associates, Inc. Reprinted with permission.
*$p < .05$. **$p < .01$.

the fourth and fifth grades. Both imagination ($r = .30$, $p < .05$) and quality of fantasy ($r = .30$, $p < .05$) related to fluency on the Alternate Uses Test over a 9-year period. Nine percent of the variance in divergent thinking was accounted for by organization and imagination in early play. An important point in the two follow-up studies is that the Alternate Uses Test was given in a group format. Individual administration of this test might have resulted in stronger correlations.

The APS has also been used with preschool children (APS–P; Kaugars & Russ, 2009). We (Kaugars & Russ, 2009) found that the number of pretend episodes in the play related to divergent thinking on the Multidimensional Stimulus Fluency Measure (Goodwin & Moran, 1990).

## Methodological Issues

Recently, in an extensive review of the literature, Lillard et al. (2013) concluded that the evidence for the association between play and measures of creativity, including divergent thinking, was not strong. They concluded that the correlational studies were inconsistent and were not supportive of a true association. One of their major criticisms of the research was that the play and creativity measures were administered by the same individual, and bias might have occurred. In other words, the researcher might have inadvertently functioned in a way that better players were given higher scores on the creativity tests. Smith and Whitney (1987) also raised this issue. However, my review of the literature reached a different conclusion. I pointed out that a number of correlational studies (Lieberman, 1977; Russ & Grossman-McKee, 1990; D. L. Singer & Rummo, 1973) did use different examiners for the two tasks and still found significant relationships between play and divergent thinking (Russ, 1993). Since then, our study (Russ et al., 1999) used different examiners in significantly predicting divergent thinking from early play scores 4 years earlier. One could also make the argument that the divergent thinking task is administered in a standardized format. In my APS program, all play and creativity measures are scored in a blind fashion.

## Play as a Facilitator of Divergent Thinking

Given that the association of pretend play with divergent thinking has been supported in a number of studies, the next question is whether a pretend play experience can facilitate divergent thinking. Does the relationship only reflect similar cognitive processes that both pretend play and divergent thinking share, or is there also a causal relationship between play and divergent thinking?

There is some evidence that play facilitates divergent thinking. In several well-done experimental studies, pretend play did facilitate divergent thinking in preschool children (Dansky, 1980; Dansky & Silverman, 1973). In the Dansky and Silverman (1973) study, children who played with objects during a play period gave significantly more uses for those objects than did a control group. Dansky (1980) refined the earlier study and found that play had a generalized effect on objects that were different from those in the play period. He also found that the free-play condition facilitated divergent thinking only for children who engaged in make-believe play. Make-believe and the involvement of fantasy was the mediator of the relationship between play and divergent thinking.

A methodological criticism of the Dansky (1980) study was made by Smith and Whitney (1987), who raised the issue of experimenter bias. The same experimenter who administered the play intervention also administered the divergent thinking task. Thus, unconscious experimenter bias could be a factor. Smith and Whitney, in a carefully executed study, failed to confirm the hypothesis that play enhanced divergent thinking in preschool children. In their study, they had a different experimenter administer the divergent thinking task after the play task. However, it is possible that introducing a new examiner between the play task and the divergent thinking task could have interfered with the experimental set being induced by the play (Russ, 2004). If Dansky's rationale for the effect was correct, that pretend play loosens the cognitive set and old associations facilitate divergent thinking, then interfering with that process would interfere with the effect of play on divergent thinking.

However, in a 2001 study, we did not find an effect of play on divergent thinking (Russ & Kaugars, 2000–2001). This study was different from Dansky's (1980) study in that children did not play with objects. Rather, they played with puppets and blocks on the APS, making up stories. Also, the children were in first and second grades, rather than preschool. Eighty children were randomly assigned to one of four groups: a happy puppet playgroup, an angry puppet playgroup, a free-play group; and a control puzzle group. They were given different instructions about having the puppets play out a happy story or an angry story, or they were given the standard, neutral APS instructions in the free-play group (having the puppets do something together). The Alternate Uses Test was given immediately following the play, by the same examiner.

There was no effect for any of the play conditions on divergent thinking. The experimental affect manipulation did work for the angry group (on a mood check) but not for the happy group. Thus, the hypothesis remains untested for the positive affect group. Nevertheless, the free-play group did not differ from the control. It is possible that for pretend play that does not focus on play with objects, but instead is make-believe story play, effects on divergent thinking will be apparent over time but not immediately after the play. Christie (1994) cautioned against brief one-trial studies in the play intervention area. There is some evidence that when pretend play occurs in multiple sessions over time, increases in divergent thinking occur (Russ, Fehr, & Hoffmann, 2013). But there is no consensus yet in the field. These studies and methodological issues are reviewed in Chapter 7.

## PLAY AND INSIGHT ABILITY

Early research on play and creativity investigated play and insight ability. In a series of studies Sylva, Bruner, and Genova (1976) concluded that play in children 3 to 5 years of age facilitated insight in a problem-solving task. In one study involving three groups of children, one group played with the objects that were later used in the problem-solving task, a second group observed the experimenter solve the problem, and a third group was exposed to the materials. Significantly more children in the play and observation groups solved the problem than in the control group. The play group was more goal oriented in their efforts on the task and more likely to piece together the solution than the other groups.

Vandenberg (1978) refined the experimental methodology of the Sylva et al. (1976) studies and used a wider age group of 4 to 10 years. In this study, the experimental group played with the materials to be used in the problem-solving task, and the control group was asked questions about the material. The play group did significantly better on one of the two insight tasks following the intervention. Six- and 7-year olds benefited most from the play experience. Vandenberg concluded that the relationship between play and insightful tool use was mediated by age and the nature of the task.

Smith and Dutton (1979) also investigated play and insight ability. They compared four groups on two insight tasks in 4-year-old children. There was a play group, a training group, and two control groups. The play and training group did significantly better than the control groups on one task, and the play group did better than all other groups on the other insight task, which required motivational effort. There were more motivated problem solvers in the play group than the other groups. Again, motivation seemed to be influenced by the play activity.

Vandenberg reviewed the play and insight literature in 1980. He concluded that the studies consistently found that play facilitated insightful tool use and enhanced motivational task activity. Task type and age were mediating variables. Vandenberg pointed to the similarity between play and creativity. In both play and creativity, one is creating novelty from the commonplace and disregarding the familiar. There are other abilities related to creativity that relate to cognitive processes in pretend play. Coping ability and emotional understanding are abilities that relate to play and to creativity and involve common cognitive processes.

## PLAY, EVERYDAY CREATIVITY, AND COPING

Coping in an adaptive way with changing daily events and stressors is part of the definition of everyday creativity. Richards (1990) defined *everyday creativity* as the ability to adapt flexibly to a changing environment. Often, solutions are novel responses to challenging situations. Folkman and Lazarus (1980) devised a widely accepted definition of *coping* as the "cognitive and behavioral efforts made by individuals to master, tolerate, or reduce" (p. 223) stressful demands when "a routine or automatic response is not available" (Monat & Lazarus, 1977, p. 8). In other words, coping can be thought of as an active process of generating solutions to real-life problems or as a real-world application of a divergent thinking ability.

Thinking of a variety of solutions is one component in coping with stress. Theoretically, divergent thinking should relate to the ability to think of different solutions to problems. Creative problem solvers should be better copers because they bring their problem-solving skills to everyday problems. Good divergent thinkers should be able to think of alternative solutions to real-life problems. Some empirical evidence supports this relationship. D. Carson, Bittner, Cameron, Brown, and Meyer (1994) found a positive relationship between figural divergent thinking and teachers' ratings of coping. Consistent with this finding, I found a significant relationship between divergent thinking on the Alternate Uses Test and teachers' ratings of coping in fifth grade boys (Russ, 1988). We (Russ et al., 1999) found a significant relationship between divergent thinking and self-reported coping in fifth- and sixth-grade children.

What about the relationship between pretend play and coping ability? Why should play relate to coping? The link between play and coping could be the divergent thinking construct. Also, in play, children try out different solutions to everyday problems. Rehearsal of possible behaviors occurs in pretend play. There is some evidence that play relates to coping ability. We (Christiano & Russ, 1996) found that better players on the APS were better copers in an invasive dental procedure. They implemented a greater number and variety of cognitive coping strategies during the procedure. Good players also reported less distress during the procedure than children who had less affect and fantasy in their play.

Consistent with these findings, we (Perry & Russ, 1998) found that fantasy in play was related to frequency and variety of self-reported coping strategies in a group of homeless children. We (Goldstein & Russ, 2001) found that fantasy and imagination in play were positively related to the number and variety of cognitive coping attempts in thinking about what to do in a situation that required impulse control of aggression. In our longitudinal study (Russ et al., 1999), quality of fantasy and organization in play on the APS predicted self-reported coping over a period of 4 years (see Table 3.1). The coping measure used in that study was a self-report measure (School Coping Scale) that asked children how they would deal with typical problems that arise in the school situation—for example, what they would do if they forgot their lunch or if they were late for school. Responses were rated on number of realistic solutions and quality of the solutions. In this study, children who expressed more organized fantasy and better imagination could think of more and better alternatives on the coping measure.

In a recent study, we (Fiorelli & Russ, 2012) found a similar pattern of correlations over an 18-month period. Imagination in play in first through fourth graders predicted number of coping responses 18 months later. In the concurrent sample, organization and imagination in play positively related to coping responses ($r = .38$, $p < .05$; $r = .34$, $p = < .05$, respectively). Children who demonstrated greater organization and imagination in their play generated a greater number of coping responses. An important point is that, in almost all of these studies, cognitive components of the play, the imagination and organization of the fantasy, were related to coping, whereas the affect in play did not. The one exception was our study (Christiano & Russ, 1996) in which both affect and fantasy in play related to coping in the dental situation. Perhaps affective processes were important in coping in this anxiety-provoking situation. The other measures of coping in these studies may have been more cognitive in nature. The divergent thinking link between play and coping may be more cognitive in nature as well. Even though all of the play and coping studies came from my research program, different examiners, child populations, and coping measures were used in the studies, giving more confidence in the results. However, replication with other play measures is needed.

Pellegrini (1992) identified *flexibility* as a link between play and creativity. In a study of third- and fifth-grade boys, flexibility in rough-and-tumble play was predictive of a variety of prosocial problem-solving responses. Pellegrini proposed that, in play, children recombine behaviors and develop flexible strategies. A varied problem-solving repertoire aids in social competence.

## PLAY AND PERSPECTIVE TAKING

Understanding the point of view of the other person is important in child development. It is also important in certain domains of creativity, such as literature or marketing, where understanding the other is important.

Harris (1989) proposed that imaginative understanding may enable children to understand others' mental states and affective experiences. Research has supported the proposition that individual differences in fantasy in preschoolers significantly related to affective and cognitive perspective-taking tasks (Astington & Jenkins, 1995; Youngblade & Dunn, 1995). The meta-analysis by Fisher (1992) found one of the largest effect sizes was that between play and perspective taking. We (Seja & Russ, 1999) found that the cognitive, but not affective, components of play related to facets of emotional understanding. Children in the first and second grades were administered the APS and the Kusche Affective Interview–Revised (Kusche, Greenberg, & Beilke, 1988). The fantasy components of the play related to the ability to understand emotions of others and to remember and organize memories related to emotional events. These relationships were independent of verbal ability. A composite fantasy score accounted for 5% of the variance in emotional understanding when verbal ability was accounted for.

Consistent with these findings, we (Niec & Russ, 2002) found that quality of fantasy on the APS significantly related to self-reported empathy in children. Children who had better-organized fantasy and were more imaginative reported more empathy on the Bryant Index of Empathy for Children (Bryant, 1982). Again, affect expression in play did not relate to the empathy measure.

The results of these studies suggest that it is the cognitive processes in play that relate to understanding the view of the other. The imagination and flexibility required to put oneself in the shoes of the other person is a cognitive skill. The capacity to feel for the other is a different emotional process not tapped by the APS.

## PLAY AND CREATIVE NARRATIVES

Creating narratives, such as in storytelling, is another type of creativity that includes cognitive processes. Baas, De Dreu, and Nijstad (2008) conceptualized different creative tasks as fitting into one of three domains: (a) open-ended tasks, such as divergent thinking; (b) tasks that have a single correct solution, such as insight tasks; and (c) creative performance tasks in which creativity is subjectively judged by others, such as art or storytelling. Hennessey and Amabile (1988) asserted that storytelling tasks are excellent additions to creativity assessments because they do not rely heavily on age-relevant skills.

It is not known what role divergent thinking has in storytelling ability. A child's story can excel in a variety of creative areas, including fantasy, novelty, imagination, or likeability. A factor analysis using elementary school teacher ratings on nine dimensions of storytelling found four ratings to load highly and positively on a creativity factor: creativity of the story, imagination of the storyteller, novelty of the idea, and likeability of the story (Hennessey & Amabile, 1988). Using a consensus scoring system, in which scoring criteria are purposely left vague, Hennessey and Amabile (1988) found large individual differences between low and high creative stories, with strong interrater reliability between teacher-raters.

We (Hoffmann & Russ, 2012) investigated the relationship between play and storytelling in 61 girls and found that play did relate to creativity in storytelling, independent of verbal ability. For the storytelling measure, using the consensus system, imagination in pretend play positively related to creativity in storytelling, $r(44) = .26$, $p < .05$. Children rated as more imaginative in pretend play were also rated as telling more creative stories. Positive affect in pretend play also significantly related to story likeability, $r(44) = .30$, $p < .05$; creativity, $r(44) = .31$, $p < .05$; and imagination, $r(44) = .29$, $p < .05$. Children who expressed more positive affect during pretend play also tended to tell stories rated as more creative. Also of note, divergent thinking was significantly related to creativity in storytelling. Those children who had higher divergent thinking scores also tended to have higher amounts of affect, larger varieties of affect, and greater amounts of fantasy in the stories they told. These children were also more likely to be rated as having stories that were more likeable, novel, creative, and imaginative. Originality during divergent thinking was also positively related to storytelling affect expression and fantasy, as well as ratings of creativity and novelty. These results suggest a common creative ability across creative tasks, which has implications for development of creative writing abilities.

In a recent dissertation by Fehr (2012) using the APS–P with preschool children, pretend play was related to divergent thinking and to creativity in storytelling. Divergent thinking and storytelling were also related. Thus, similar associations occurred between play, divergent thinking, and storytelling in preschool and school-aged children.

## WORLDPLAY AND CREATIVITY

Root-Bernstein and Root-Bernstein (2006) studied paracosms and worldplay in creative adults. *Paracosms* are imaginary worlds, and *worldplay* is play with these worlds, usually continuing for a long period. Root-Bernstein and Root-Bernstein studied MacArthur "genius" fellows and a comparison group of college students who recollected their worldplay in childhood. Of the MacArthur fellows, 26% reported having imaginary worlds in childhood, compared with 12% of the college students. In addition, another 20%

reported some form of paracosm in childhood. These recollections of creative adults support the importance of fantasy play and imaginary worlds in childhood for these individuals.

## CONCLUSION

There is strong empirical evidence that pretend play relates to divergent thinking and to insight abilities. These relationships are independent of verbal intelligence. There is evidence that pretend play can facilitate insight in problem solving. There is also some evidence that pretend play facilitates divergent thinking. However, not all studies have replicated that finding, perhaps because of the fragility of the cognitive set induced by pretend play in one-trial studies. Longitudinal studies of play and divergent thinking support the stability of the association but do not indicate causation.

Pretend play also relates to measures of coping. Thinking of solutions to daily problems is one type of everyday creativity. Play also relates to perspective taking, which is so important in creative domains that require taking multiple perspectives of life and situations. There is some evidence that play relates to creativity in narratives. It is not clear what specific cognitive components of pretend play relate to and facilitate creative performance on tasks. These specific components or processes should be identified and investigated in future studies. One can speculate that in pretend play, children

- practice with the free flow of associations that is part of divergent thinking,
- practice with different solutions to problems and different types of object substitutions,
- practice with symbol substitution and recombining ideas and images,
- practice taking the view of the other in make-believe play,
- generate different story scenarios with different endings, and
- learn to manipulate and develop imaginary worlds.

Future research needs to determine what components of play relate to creativity tasks, whether there are critical periods when the benefits of play are more evident, what kind of play experiences most facilitate creative thinking, and whether specific training programs in schools and in the home are beneficial.

# 4

# AFFECTIVE PROCESSES IN PRETEND PLAY AND CREATIVITY

The purpose of this chapter is to review the research on pretend play and creativity, with a focus on affective processes. Affect and emotional expression are an integral part of pretend play. Children express all aspects of emotion in fantasy play. Processing emotions is one of the necessary activities of adulthood, and pretend play helps children prepare for that function. Because affect is also important in creative production, it is theoretically plausible that affect in play would also relate to creative thinking in children. Learning to process emotions could help creativity as well as problem solving in daily life.

One of the challenges in the field has been to find ways to measure affect in play. Much of the early research on play and creativity focused on cognitive processes. One of the reasons for this cognitive focus was the lack of reliable, standardized, and valid measures of affective processes in play. Rubin, Fein, and Vandenberg (1983) referred to this phenomenon as the "cognification" of play. I developed the Affect in Play Scale (APS; Russ, 1987, 2004) to meet

http://dx.doi.org/10.1037/14282-005
*Pretend Play in Childhood: Foundation of Adult Creativity*, by S. W. Russ

the need for a measure that focused on affect and to investigate the relationship between affect in play and creativity in children. This chapter reviews what we have learned about the role of affect in play and creativity from research with the APS as well as from other researchers. This chapter also reviews theories of affect, play, and creativity.

First, I review the concepts that underlie the relationship between affect in play and creativity. Because psychoanalytic theory and primary-process theory is, from my point of view, central to understanding this area, I review theory and empirical evidence in depth. Recent theories of affect and creativity are also reviewed. Next, transcripts of play samples are presented that illustrate what affective expression in play looks like. This is followed by a review of research studies on affect in play and divergent thinking and creative narratives. The chapter concludes with a summary of research findings and suggestions for future research.

## PRETEND PLAY AND AFFECTIVE CREATIVE PROCESSES: THEORETICAL BASIS

It is important to define the terms *affect* and *emotion*. Affect has been described as a broader concept, with emotion as a subset of affect (Tellegen, 1989). On the basis of the *American Heritage Dictionary* definition, Tellegen (1989) described affect as a feeling or emotion as distinct from cognition. Emotion is defined as a state of aroused feeling or agitation. Izard (1977) also viewed affect as a broad set of events that includes emotions and drives. Moore and Isen (1990) conceptualized affect as involving feeling states that are pervasive and nonspecific. They described emotions as interrupting events that are more specific in terms of stimuli and behavioral responses than are broader feeling states. Moods are often defined as being of longer duration than emotions without a clear trigger or object. Affect is the more inclusive concept. *Affective processes* refer to the different dimensions of affect, or types of affect events, that occur within the individual. Most theorists think that cognition is frequently involved in the affective processes, although they differ as to whether affect is always involved, the degree of involvement, and the type of involvement.

Historically, cognitive style theorists and psychoanalytic theorists were the first to think about the influence of affect on cognition and creativity. The *cognitive style* construct reflected an interface between cognition and personality (Kogan, 1976). Cognitive style included variables such as field dependence–independence (autonomy from stimulus field), reflection–impulsivity (reflection in problem solving), and style of categorization (breadth vs. narrowness). Individual differences in cognitive processes were associated with personality components. Research from the Menninger Foundation group of Gardner and Moriarty (1968) and of G. Klein (1970) paved the way for understanding the importance of the interaction between cognition and personality.

In the 1980s and 1990s, researchers began to conceptualize cognitive–affective interaction. Creativity researchers began to realize the importance of affect in the creative process. Amabile (1983) investigated intrinsic motivation and creativity. Csikszentmihalyi (1990) proposed the importance of *flow* to creativity. Both of these theorists stressed the importance of passion and love of the work in the creative process. Isen began her classic research on mood induction and creativity (Isen, Daubman, & Nowicki, 1987), which found that positive affect facilitated various types of creativity. Emotion in bipolar disorders and creativity began to be explored (Jamison, 1989; Richards & Kinney, 1990). Other theorists synthesized what was known about affect and creativity (Shaw & Runco, 1994; Russ, 1993). The focus of creativity research began to shift to the role of affect in the creative process.

## AFFECTIVE PROCESSES AND CREATIVITY

In the synthesis of the affect and creativity area proposed in my model and on the basis of theory and the research literature, five affective processes emerged that are important in creativity (Russ, 1993, 2004). These five processes were briefly described in Chapter 1. We revisit them here (see Figure 1.1). The five affective processes, briefly defined, are as follows:

- *Openness to experiencing affect states.* This is the ability to feel affect and specific emotions as they occur. Tellegen (1989) and others (L. Clark & Watson, 1991) have found that different types of affect states can be classified as positive affect or negative affect. Individuals differ as to how much they can experience positive and negative affect states. These specific feeling states seem to function differently in the creative process. In play, where even negative affect is pretend, it is possible that the actual valence of the emotion could be more positive than negative.
- *Access to affect-laden thoughts, images, and fantasy.* This is the ability to think about ideas, images, and fantasies that include affect. Thoughts involving affect themes such as aggression, sex, affection, or anxiety illustrate this blending of affect and cognition. The psychoanalytic concept of primary-process thinking, to be discussed in a later section, is an example of this type of affective process.

- *Affective pleasure in challenge.* This process involves the excitement and tension that comes with identifying a problem or mystery and wanting to immerse oneself in the task. A combination of positive and negative affect could be involved.
- *Affective pleasure in problem solving.* This is the tendency to take deep pleasure in solving a problem or completing an artistic production. Joy in creative production and deep immersion in the task may be involved.
- *Cognitive integration and modulation of affect.* This is the ability to control, think about, and regulate the affective events one experiences and not be swept away. Although this process is probably more cognitive than affective, it warrants inclusion because it involves both cognition and affect, and it is important in the creative process.

Whether these categories are truly separate dimensions of affect needs to be systematically investigated. However, they have separate theories, literatures, and research programs, so treating them as separate dimensions at this point makes some theoretical sense.

## Affect and Associations

Different theories of affect and creativity focus on different types of affective processes and different types of creativity. There is no one comprehensive theory that accounts for all variables and all research. Most theories propose that the involvement of emotion broadens the range of associations in some way that, in turn, increases the likelihood of novelty, divergent thinking, flexible thinking, or an original recombination of ideas.

One of the major roles of affect in creativity is to broaden the associative process. Individuals who are more open to experiencing emotions and/or to thinking about affect-laden images have more remote associations and a broader associative process. They can access more remote concepts and images, which is so important in generating original ideas, solutions to problems, and original narratives. Different theories of affect and creativity have different understandings about the mechanisms involved that broaden associations. The theories described next apply to pretend play and creativity as well, because pretend play involves these affective processes.

## Psychoanalytic Theory: Primary-Process Thinking and Repression

Historically, the first theory of affect and creativity was psychoanalytic. The key concept in the area of psychoanalytic theory and creativity is primary-process thinking. Primary-process thinking is included in the second category of affect important in creativity: affect-laden thoughts, images, and fantasy.

In 1915, Sigmund Freud first conceptualized primary-process thought as an early, primitive system of thought that was drive-laden and not subject to rules of logic or oriented to reality. A good example of primary-process thinking is the kind of thinking that occurs in dreams. Dreams are illogical, are not oriented to rules of time and space, and frequently include affect-laden content and images. Dudek (1980) thought of primary process as the surfacing of unconscious instinctual energy in the form of images and ideas. Holt (1977) categorized the drive-laden content in primary-process thought as oral, aggressive, and libidinal.

Primary process has usually been regarded as a blend of cognitive and affective processes (Martindale, 1981; Zimiles, 1981). Holt (1977), in developing a measure of primary process for the Rorschach, defined both content properties, which included affect-laden oral, aggressive, and libidinal content and formal properties which included more cognitive qualities of illogical thinking, loose associations, and fused images and ideas.

Affect is a major component of primary-process thinking. The concepts of drive-laden and instinctual energy bring one into the realm of affect. Rapaport (1951) used the term *affect-charge* in discussing primary-process thought. S. Freud (1895/1966) in the "Project for a Scientific Psychology" stated that primary-process thought is frequently accompanied by affect. I proposed that primary process is a subtype of affective content in cognition (Russ, 1987). Developmentally, primary-process content is material about which the child experienced early, intense feelings (e.g., oral, aggressive, libidinal). The child has to learn to regulate and integrate these intense emotions. Individual differences exist in how much access children and adults have to primary-process content, how much they express it in fantasy and play, and how they integrate it into imagination. Pine and Holt (1960) suggested that primary-process integration becomes a kind of cognitive style that reflects how one deals with affective material. Why are individual differences in primary-process expression important? Because access to primary-process thought has been hypothesized to relate to creative thinking. In primary-process thinking, associations are fluid and primitive images and ideas can be accessed and used.

According to classic psychoanalytic theory, primary-process thinking is characterized by *mobility of cathexis*—that is, the energy behind ideas and images is easily displaced (Arlow & Brenner, 1964). In this mode of thinking, ideas are easily interchangeable and attention is widely and flexibly distributed. Therefore, access to primary-process thinking should facilitate a fluidity of thought and flexibility of search among all ideas and associations. Flexibility and fluidity of thought are characteristic of two of the most important cognitive processes involved in creative thinking: divergent thinking and transformation abilities. Martindale (1989) stated, "Because primary-process cognition is associative, it makes the discovery of new combinations of mental elements more likely" (p. 216).

Affect in primary process aids in creativity as well. Psychoanalytic theory was the first to recognize the importance of emotion in the creative process. S. Freud's (1926/1959) formulation that repression of "dangerous" drive-laden content leads to a more general intellectual restriction predicts that individuals with less access to affect-laden thoughts, images, and memories would have fewer associations in general. The psychoanalytic concept of repression involves warding off the feeling of instinctive impulses or the ideational representations of the instincts (A. Freud, 1966). Both the feeling and the thought associated with the feeling are repressed. The purpose of the repression is to reduce the anxiety and the conflict by reducing the awareness of the dangerous content. If there is too little repression, then the individual can be overwhelmed with inappropriate images and affect and may act out behaviorally, as in the manic phase of bipolar disorders. If there is too much repression, then a major constriction of thinking can occur. Individuals who have good access to affective ideas and images—such as those in primary-process thinking in a controlled fashion (i.e., not be overwhelmed)—theoretically should have many associations.

### Regression in the Service of the Ego

An important point in psychoanalytic theory is that controlled access to primary-process thinking is facilitative of creative thought. The concept of *regression in the service of the ego* postulates that creative individuals could regress in a controlled fashion and tap into primary-process thinking (Kris, 1952). The creative individual could go back and forth between early, primitive primary-process thought and more mature, rational, secondary-process thinking. The creative individual could be distinguished from the individual with a thought disorder in that the creative individual was in charge of this regressive process and could critically and logically evaluate the loose, primitive associations and images.

A number of theorists have proposed that the concept of regression may not be necessary in understanding the relationship between primary process and creativity. Holt (1967) proposed that primary process was a group of structures with its own course of development. Arieti (1976) and Suler (1980) also suggested that the concept of regression to an earlier mode of thinking may not be necessary. Rather, primary-process thought may be a separate entity that develops simultaneously with secondary-process thought. A separate ability to cognitively integrate and modulate primary-process thinking is important in the critical evaluation stage of creative thought.

*Recent Conceptualizations*

Contemporary theories in cognitive psychology provide a framework for understanding primary process without the concept of instinctual energy or regression. I placed the primary process and creativity link within the current theoretical models of affect and cognition (Russ, 1996). In 1987, a classic study by Isen and colleagues began a series of studies that found that positive emotional states facilitated creative thinking. They concluded that the involvement of emotion broadens the search process for associations. Therefore, emotion facilitates divergent thinking and types of creativity that depend on generating associations. The involvement of emotion theoretically broadens the search process for associations by triggering associated memories, images, and thoughts.

Isen et al. (1987) were the first to apply Bower's (1981) associative network theory to creative thinking. Bower's theory proposed that each emotion is a memory unit—each emotion has a special node or unit in memory. The activation of the emotion unit aids the retrieval of events associated with it. It primes emotional thematic imagery for use in free association, fantasies, and perceptual categorization. Rholes, Riskind, and Lane (1987) expanded Bower's theory and discussed mood-related cognitions. Affect states activate a set of relevant mood-related cognitions, and a cognitive priming process occurs. I conceptualized primary process as mood-relevant cognition that triggers related associations in memory (Russ, 1993).

Another theoretical model is that of Getz and Lubart (1999), who proposed an emotional resonance model of creativity. In their model, emotions become attached to concepts or images labeled *endocepts*. Associations are emotion-based and may resonate with each other when triggered. Endocepts that are attached to related concepts resonate with one another and link concepts in memory. In this way, emotions contribute to the access and association of cognitively remote concepts in memory.

I proposed that individuals—adults and children—who are open to affect states and affect-laden cognition, including primary-process cognition, benefit in creative activities in three ways (Russ, 1993). First, as previously discussed, they can access affective cues that trigger and activate other ideation and memories in the search process. This broader associative network increases the likelihood of a novel idea or solution to a problem. This affective advantage would benefit creativity in both science and the arts. Increased divergent thinking and flexible thinking is involved in creative production in domains of science and art.

Second, more emotionally salient content is coded and stored when an individual is in an emotional state. For individuals who are more open to affect, more emotional content and memories would "get in," thus providing a richer network of affect-relevant associations. This storing of affective content is especially important in the arts, where one is often dealing with emotion and the transformation of emotion into universal symbols. There is evidence that more creative individuals are more open to experience (McCrae & Costa, 1987). Affective processes could then guide the search process for associations. There would be a rich store of emotional memories and associations on which to draw.

Third, affect could guide the selection process of the ideas and memories that are accessed. Some are more salient for the task than others. This conceptualization is consistent with Damasio's (1994) somatic-marker hypothesis. Damasio proposed that cognitive images become marked with physiological responses that reflect emotions. He applied his model to decision making, but we can extrapolate to divergent thinking. As associations occur, they are highlighted (or made salient) by positive and negative emotional responses. These emotional and physiological responses are rapid and out of awareness, or unconscious (Damasio, 1994; V. Simón, 1998). Damasio quoted the creative mathematician Henri Poincaré, who described a nonrandom process of associations in this thinking. Poincaré, according to Ghiselin (1952) stated that creation involves making "useful" combinations of ideas. One sifts through a minority of useful possibilities, as though a preselection process had already occurred. Only useful associations are considered.

When Poincaré (1913/1952) described this association process in his essay "Mathematical Creation," he described the shifting images and ideas involved in the incubation stage of problem solving. He stated that the picture is not thought out and determined beforehand. "Ideas rose in crowds. I felt them collide until pairs interlocked so to speak—making a stable combination" (p. 36). Here Poincaré described the fluidity of thought and associations that can occur during the discovery process. This description also reflects the loosening of control that is so often described by creative individuals during the process of discovery. However, the importance of recognizing the solution when it occurs is essential. The "stable combination" is recognized through an evaluation process. A preselective, unconscious selection process is also occurring, guided by affect.

Often, primary process is equated with the unconscious. Vernon (1989) spoke of the role of unconscious processes. Creative thinking is differentiated from logical problem solving in that it involves "a greater degree of free-flowing imagination and recourse to subconscious activities such as incubation and inspiration" (p. 37). He concluded that these subconscious activities occur in both artistic and scientific work, although more frequently in artistic expression. Martindale (1989) made the point that primary process is not necessarily unconscious and that much of it is conscious thought. Individuals who can tap into this primary process in the waking state and who can also evaluate and synthesize when appropriate should have the advantage in generating creative products. An example of conscious use of primary process is the free flow of associations in a Robin Williams monologue (Russ, 1993). In describing his process of improvisation, Williams said,

> And sometimes there are times when you're just on it—when you say the muse is with you and it's just flowing and that's when you know that the well is open again and you just put in the pipe and you stand back and say "yes."

He said, "You're in control, but you're not—the characters are coming through you" (Culbane, 1988, pp. 5, 14). Williams's description of being in control but not in control at the same time is common in descriptions of the creative process by writers and artists.

In summary, the psychoanalytic model of primary process and regression in the service of the ego stresses the importance of two types of affective processes in creativity: (a) access to affect-laden thoughts and images and (b) cognitive integration of affective material. Theoretically, these processes are important in the facilitation of creativity.

**Empirical Evidence for Primary Process and Creativity**

Primary process has been found to relate to creative cognitive processes in the research literature. Most of the research has used Holt's (1977) primary-process scoring system for the Rorschach as a measure of primary process. Holt's scoring system measures whether an individual can allow primary-process content to surface and be expressed and how well that content is controlled and integrated into cognition. In general, as psychoanalytic theory predicted, the ability to give good form responses to the Rorschach that contained primary-process content was significantly related to measures of divergent thinking and flexibility in problem solving in adults. For example, the adaptive regression score (integration of primary-process content) has been significantly positively related to several measures of creativity (I. Cohen, 1961), to divergent thinking (Pine & Holt, 1960), and to problem-solving efficiency (Blatt, Allison, & Feirstein, 1969). We (Murray & Russ, 1981) found a relationship between adaptive regression score and remote associations on Mednick's Remote Associates Test (Mednick, 1962).

Using a different approach that compared creative individuals with less creative individuals, Gamble and Kellner (1968) found that creative individuals had greater access to primary process. Dudek (1968) reported more primitive primary-process content in artists than nonartists and more primitive primary process in good artists than poor artists. She also found that top-ranked creative architects produced more libidinal (sexual) primary-process content than did lower-ranked architects (Dudek, 1984).

Gender differences have consistently been reported in studies with adults. Holt (1977) stated that, in general, primary-process integration on the Rorschach has been related to creativity in males but not in females: "Negative findings from well-executed studies came entirely from samples of females" (p. 413). The relationship between adaptive regression (AR) and divergent thinking (Pine & Holt, 1960) and between AR and associational fluency (Murray & Russ, 1981) occurred in adult men but not in adult women. In our study, the correlation between AR and Mednick's Remote Associates Test was $r = .36$, $p < .05$, for men and $r = -.27$ for women (Murray & Russ, 1981). There was a negative relationship for the female participants. Suler's (1980) thorough review of the literature also concluded that gender is an important moderator variable between primary-process thinking and creativity.

In children, age, gender, and specific measures and scores emerge as important factors (Russ, 1993). Dudek (1975) found no relationship between primary-process thinking on the Rorschach and divergent thinking on the Torrance Tests of Creative Thinking (Torrance, 1966) in fourth-grade children. However, in this study primary-process expression on a drawing task was related to divergent thinking. Dudek concluded that the relation between primary process and creativity is ambiguous in childhood and that children have not yet learned to use primary-process thinking effectively. In a 1989 study with fifth and sixth graders, Dudek and Verreault (1989) found that creative children gave significantly more primary-process responses than noncreative children, as measured by Holt's (1977) system applied to the Torrance tests. Gender differences were not examined or reported in these studies.

Rogolsky (1968), when using a new adaptive regression measure for the Rorschach, found a relationship between primary-process integration and artistic creativity for third-grade boys but not girls. In a series of studies from 1982 through 1990, I found gender differences in the relationship between primary process and creativity in children, similar to the adult literature (Russ, 1982, 1988; Russ & Grossman-McKee, 1990). For these studies, each child was individually administered the Rorschach and creativity measures, and Holt's (1977) system was used to measure primary process. Although Holt's system was designed for adults, when used with children, it measures primary-process content (i.e., fighting bears or food percepts) and adaptiveness of that content (mainly good form). Scoring of formal characteristics of thought such as condensations or illogical associations is a very small percentage of responses in children's protocols (Dudek, 1975; Russ, 1982). Typical aggressive content in children's protocols was fighting animals, exploding volcanoes, blood, and scary insects. Typical oral-libidinal responses were people eating, food, and mouths. In my studies, the mean percentage of primary-process content in the entire Rorschach protocol was about 50% for these child populations (Russ, 1982, 1988; Russ & Grossman-McKee, 1990).

In the first study, I found a relation between AR scores and reading achievement in second-grade children ($r. = 54, p < .001$; Russ, 1980). This relationship remained significant when IQ was partialed out ($r = .45$) and when productivity and perceptual accuracy (good form quality) were partialed out. In a follow-up study of these children when they were in the third grade, the size of the relation between third-grade AR scores and reading achievement remained consistent ($r = .52, p < .001$; Russ, 1981). Although reading achievement is not a creativity criterion, the rationale behind using reading as a criterion was that children who have access to primary-process thinking and integrated it well would be flexible problem solvers and be open to ideas. Thus, they would be better learners than children with less access to primary-process content, and this would be reflected in the reading score. There were noteworthy gender differences in this study. Although the correlations were not significantly different for boys and girls, there was a difference in the magnitude of the correlations for the genders ($r = .66$ for boys and $r = .24$ for girls).

The next series of studies investigated the relationship between primary process and creativity in children. The first study investigated the relation between primary-process thinking and transformation abilities in third-grade children (Russ, 1982). An adaptation of the Luchins water-jug problem (Luchins & Luchins, 1959) was used as the measure of transformation ability. This test assesses the ability to break out of a set and think of an alternative solution to a problem. The child must be able to discover a new, more adaptive approach and be able to shift sets. Gender differences again occurred. In this study, the AR score was related to the ability to shift problem-solving strategies ($r = .39, p < .01$) for boys. This relationship was independent of intelligence. There was no relationship for girls. This sample of children was followed to the fifth grade. Again, primary process on the Rorschach was related to divergent thinking (Alternate Uses Test; Wallach & Kogan, 1965) for boys but not for girls (Russ, 1988). Finally, in a study with second-grade children, percentage of primary process on the Rorschach related to divergent thinking in boys ($r = .72$) but not in girls (Russ 1988).

In all my studies with primary process in children, there were gender differences in the relationship between primary process and creativity (Russ, 1982, 1988; Russ & Grossman-McKee, 1990). At times the differences between the correlations for boys and girls were significant, and at other times the differences approached significance (Russ, 1982, 1988; Russ & Grossman-McKee, 1990). The pattern was consistent. For boys, primary process related to divergent thinking and to flexibility in problem solving and shifting sets (Russ, 1982). The integration of primary process (AR score) was usually the best predictor, but percentage of primary-process content was also a significant predictor in several studies (Russ, 1982, 1988; Russ & Grossman-McKee, 1990). For girls, there was generally no significant relationship. In one study, percentage of primary process related to flexibility in problem solving in one of the two samples (Russ, 1982).

An important finding in these studies was that boys usually expressed more primary-process content than did girls (Russ, 1982, 1988). In both samples with the third-grade population, boys had a significantly greater percentage of primary-process content than did girls (Russ, 1982). Specific analysis of the content categories revealed that boys had significantly more aggressive content than did girls. We also found that fourth- and fifth-grade boys expressed significantly more primary-process content than girls (Kleinman & Russ, 1988). These results are consistent with those of other studies in the child literature. Boys are consistently more aggressive than girls in their play and behavior (Maccoby & Jacklin, 1974). Girls recall fewer details of aggressive modeling (Bandura, 1965) and require longer tachistoscopic exposures than do boys for aggressive scenes (Kagan & Moss, 1962). I theorized that there may be more cultural taboos against expression of primary-process content for girls than for boys (Russ, 1980). Therefore, girls may not have the opportunity to practice manipulating primary-process thoughts and images, an advantage in creative thinking.

In summary, affect-laden primary-process thinking is related to cognitive processes important to creativity for males. For females, in most studies there was no relationship between primary process and creativity. A few studies found that pure access to primary process was related to creativity in females. One possible explanation for these sex differences is that females do not have as much access to primary-process thought because of cultural taboos and socialization processes. Because of the lack of access, girls do not learn to use primary process in creative tasks. They do not practice with or manipulate this affective content in imagination and then do not learn to apply it in creative endeavors. Another explanation could be that the Rorschach is a more valid measure of primary process for males than for females. There are many questions remaining to be answered in this research area.

## Mood Induction Framework

A more recent approach to understanding affect and creativity has been within a cognitive–affective framework. Research has specifically investigated how affect influences cognitive processes important in creativity. Much of the research within this framework has used a mood induction paradigm. A specific mood state is induced by having participants watch a film, receive a gift, or think about a memory that is happy or sad. Mood induction provides a way of altering affect states so that the effect on cognitive processes can be observed.

A growing body of research has found that induced affect facilitates creative thinking. Alice Isen has carried out a series of important, carefully controlled studies in the mood induction area (Isen & Daubman, 1984; Isen et al., 1987). She and her colleagues found that positive affect induction resulted in more creative problem solving when compared with control groups (Isen, Johnson, Mertz, & Robinson, 1984). Other researchers found similar results with a variety of creativity measures (e.g., Green & Noice, 1988). Isen (1999) speculated that the underlying mechanism is that positive affect cues positive memories and a large amount of cognitive and affective content. This process results in defocused attention and a more complex cognitive context. This, in turn, results in a greater range of associations and interpretations.

What about negative affect? In general, induced negative affect has had no effect on creative problem solving. As researchers have pointed out, it is possible that the negative affect that was aroused (e.g., by a film of the Holocaust) was too extreme and that less extreme conditions of negative affect should be explored (Isen et al., 1987). A few studies have suggested that milder forms of negative affect could facilitate some kinds of problem-solving tasks (Vosburg & Kaufmann, 1999). Kaufmann and Vosburg (2002) found that positive mood facilitated early production of ideas, but negative mood facilitated superior idea generation in later idea production. This finding supported their satisficing/optimizing model. That is, negative moods could result in more constricted, but deeper, processing and facilitate problem solving that requires one best solution. Different types of affect may have different effects on various stages and dimensions of problem solving.

In a recent meta-analysis of 25 years of mood–creativity research, Baas, DeDreu, and Nijstad (2008) concluded that a number of variables are involved in this complex area of mood and creativity. Specific mood types (not just positive and negative) and aspects of those moods must be considered. The researchers concluded that positive moods produce more creativity than neutral moods. This is true for positive moods such as happiness that are activating and associated with approach motivation, but it is not true for positive but deactivating mood states such as relaxation. They pointed out that an interesting practical implication of this finding is that relaxing in a bathtub or on the beach may not be conducive to creative thinking. How the task is framed is also important. Positive moods lead to more creativity when the task is framed as enjoyable and intrinsically rewarding, and they lead to less creativity when the task is framed as serious and extrinsically rewarding. As for negative affect, in general, deactivating negative mood states (e.g., sadness) were not associated with creativity, but activating negative moods (e.g., fear) with avoidance motivation were associated with lower creativity. Baas et al. concluded that research should continue to investigate specific mood states on specific types of creativity tasks under various conditions. We need to learn about the underlying mechanisms that account for the mood–creativity link.

## Intrinsic Motivation

Intrinsic motivation is conducive to creativity (Amabile, 1983). *Intrinsic motivation* is defined as having to do with the intrinsic value of attaining a creative solution. Research has found that conditions extrinsic to the task, such as reward, evaluation, being watched, and having restricted choice, all have detrimental effects on creativity under certain conditions. Intrinsic motivation is important for task persistence, for seeing a project through, and for ensuring exploration of solutions.

Intrinsic motivation is also accompanied by positive affect. The love of the task is an important component of creative work. Love of the work has been mentioned as crucial by most creative individuals. Passionate involvement in the task is important for children as well. Anastasi and Schaefer (1969) found that passionate involvement in the area was an important characteristic of adolescent girls. Torrance (1988) concluded, "The essence of the creative person is being in love with what one is doing" (p. 68). Intrinsic motivation is a key element of all types of play. Children play because they want to. They can begin to experience the deep joy that comes with creative work.

## Tension and Creativity

Tension as an important factor in creativity was conceptualized by Mark Runco (1999b). He presented a variety of ways in which tension could be involved in the creative process. The anticipation of the resolution of tension could be an important motivating force in creative problem solving. The tension could be an internal conflict, similar to the psychoanalytic idea of conflict resolution. Tension could also develop from identifying a problem or sensing a gap in an area. Problem identification is important in creativity. Creative individuals could use the tension experienced in seeing the problem as both a cue and a motivator.

Affective pleasure in challenge could also be part of this process. There could be a mix of negative (tension) and positive affect in identifying a problem. The anticipation of the positive affect involved in solving the problem may act as a motivating force. However, there may be an inherent excitement in seeing the ambiguity in the situation that leads to problem identification, which is itself pleasurable. It may be similar to the pleasure that some children feel in discovering "what is wrong with this picture." The concept of optimal challenge is relevant here. An optimal amount of challenge is necessary for the experience of flow to occur (Csikszentmihalyi, 1990). *Flow* is a total involvement in the activity, a deep sense of enjoyment, and optimal challenge. Creative activities involve this sense of flow. Perhaps optimal challenge involves the best mix of tension in seeing the problem and the anticipated pleasure of the creative act.

## PLAY, AFFECT, AND CREATIVITY: RESEARCH EVIDENCE

All types of affect important in creativity are expressed in pretend play. Children express mood states, joy, affect-laden fantasy, and primary-process thinking, and they reenact tension and challenges. Children differ as to how frequently they express affect in pretend play. Children express both positive and negative emotion in play. In 1987, Fein proposed that the affect is represented in an *affective symbol system*. Information about affect-laden events and relationships is coded and stored in these symbols. These symbols are reflected in pretend play and are especially important for creative thinking. From a psychoanalytic perspective, play is a place where primary-process thinking as well as other kinds of affect can be expressed. What does the research say about the relationship between affect in play and creativity?

### Playfulness and Divergent Thinking

Early research on affect in play focused on the construct of playfulness. *Playfulness*, reviewed in Chapter 2, is defined as "an internal predisposition to bring a playful quality to interactions within the environment and across a variety of contexts and episodes" (Trevlas, Grammatikopoulos, Tsigilis, & Zachopoulou, 2003, p. 33). Lieberman (1977) found a relationship between playfulness, which included affective components of joy and spontaneity, and divergent thinking in kindergarten children. Lieberman postulated that playfulness mediated the relationship between play and creativity. She thought that the playfulness in play is a forerunner of the recombining of ideas involved in the creative act. The positive affect in playfulness should be an important component of the relationship between playfulness and creativity. D. G. Singer and Singer (1990) postulated that positive affect was related to imagination in play. D. L. Singer and Rummo (1973) also found a relationship between playfulness and creativity in kindergarten boys but not girls. Christie and Johnson (1983) concluded that there was a relationship between playfulness and creativity in children.

The findings of the mood induction research are relevant to the playfulness and creativity research. Positive affect facilitates creativity on a variety of measures. Pretend play involves a great deal of positive affect states for many children. Whether this positive affect in play has any long-term effects on creativity is an open question.

Affect themes in fantasy are another type of affect in play. J. L. Singer and Singer (1981) found that preschoolers rated as high-imagination players showed significantly more themes of danger and power than children with low imagination. Most of the support for the relationship between affect themes in fantasy play and creativity has come from our research with the APS (Russ, 2004). Before presenting the research findings, it may be useful to present samples of pretend play and their APS ratings.

**Play Samples From the Affect in Play Scale**

The following examples from the APS illustrate what imagination and affect expression in play actually looks like. These are actual transcripts from girls from 6 to 10 years of age from a research study. In the play session, all of these children displayed above average imagination, organization of the story, and emotional expression. In these examples of pretend play, one can observe divergent thinking, object transformations, cognitive flexibility, problem solving, expression of affect states and affect-laden themes. Positive and negative affect is expressed. What is harder to convey in written transcripts is the enjoyment and "fun" that these children experience in play in which they are truly engaged.

The scores on the APS were presented in Chapter 3. The main affect scores are frequency of affect expression in the play narrative, variety of affect themes, frequency of positive affect and frequency of negative affect. The positive affect score is derived from adding the instances of competition (COMP), happiness (HA), affection (N/A), oral references (O), and sexual references (SEX); the negative affect score is derived from instances of anal references (AN), anxiety and fear (A/F), aggression (AG), frustration and dislike (F/D), oral aggression (OAG), and sadness and hurt (S/H). Affect expressions include both actual feelings and affect themes. The comfort score rates enjoyment and pleasure in the play. Here, some of the affect scoring has been included to give a sense of the actual scoring system. Affect scores are noted where they occur. The tone and intensity of the affect expression, evident in the videos, influence the affect scoring as well. This dialogue is occurring between two human puppets. Four blocks were available for use.

*Child #1 (First Grade)*

This child had much positive affect in her play. She also had many different elements to her story and used the blocks to be different things.

> Hi, my name is Julie. Hi, my name is Fred. Do you want to be my friend? Sure! [N/A] Let's go play with the blocks. What are you building? I'm building the Eiffel tower. What are you building? I'm building a slide.

Um, I might build something tall. Do you want to go play with—like go play with something else? Sure. But I really like playing with the blocks. [HA] I bet it's almost time to go home. Well not really. [F/D] So I'll build something different. I don't know what I should call this. [F/D] Maybe the Julie and Fred building. Mm, I think I might just go with the Julie. I think I might build something too. What did you build? I build like sort of a stage with a background. I feel like taking a break on the bench. Yeah, good idea. [HA] I can't wait until the 100th day of school. Yeah! [HA] That's gonna be fun. [HA] I hope so. Said Julie. I really, really, really, really, really—I'm really, really, really, really tired. [F/D] I hope you liked playing with me. [HA] I have to go home. Bye! Bye! I think I might go over her house. Let me call her. Boop boop boop. Hello? Yeah, can I come over to your house? Well sort of—I'm kinda busy. You can help me. [N/A] OK. Hi! Let's play with blocks again. Sure! Or we can just color. Blocks. Hm. I might stand up here. I might take this off and stand right there. Let's put on a show! [HA] Hi, my name is Julie. Hi, my name is Fred and together we're best friends. [N/A] I hope you like this episode. Hi, my name is Julie. I am a really, really nice girl. [HA] Yes! [HA] She is a really, really nice girl. [HA] I hope you like this show. Is that it? [Experimenter: You have about a minute left.] We're back with the show. Let's go on. Hi! Let's eat some food. [O] Sure! Let's go. Yum, yum, yum. [O] Let's have a pie food race. [O, COMP] OK. Ready, get set, go. [COMP] Yum, yum, yum. [O] All done! [COMP] All done. [COMP] Come on. It's time for me to go back home. Let me just call my mom. OK. Hi, Mom, I'm coming back home. OK, honey. How was your play date? Good. [HA] Is your friend Julie nice? Yeah. [HA] She's really, really nice. [HA] I just went over her house. I think I might come over his house again. Boop boop boop. Hello? Yeah, can I come over your house? Sure. Hi! Do you want to color? Sure! I'm drawing a picture of a flower. What are you drawing a picture of? I'm drawing a picture of a rocket ship. All done! [HA] Here! Bye. Let me just go call my mom. Hi, Mom! Yeah. Oh. OK. Yeah. OK. Bye. She said I could stay over a little bit longer. OK, let's build. [Frequency of affect = 27, variety of affect = 5, positive affect = 24 (COMP = 4, HA = 13, N/A = 3, O = 4), Negative Affect = 3 (F/D = 3)]

*Child #2 (Second Grade)*

This child has both positive and negative affect expression in play. There are many imaginary elements as well.

Hello. Hello. Wanna build some blocks? Sure. Let's start with the green one, then we'll go on to red, and then yellow. I think I like the red first. [HA] Well then let's start with the yellow since we—wait, no. I wanna go with the yellow first [AG] and I wanna go with the red first. [AG] Well then, why don't we use the green first since that's the one we both agree on?

Sure. And then why don't we do the red one? But I like the yellow one. [AG] Well, the red one's more round, and the yellow one's more triangular and won't really [F/D]—we can't really put anything on it. [F/D] So let's put the red one on. OK. And then there's the yellow one. So ours was first, mine was second, and yours is first. Good! [HA] Here. Let's go tell our friends. Hi. Hi. Look at the tower we built. Oh my gosh! [HA] That is so tall! [HA] Um, you wanna go to the park? Sure. Hey, let's go. Hey, do you wanna go down the kind of weird slide? Sure. Whee! [HA] Now my turn. Whee! [HA] Hey, do you wanna go see a movie? I hear there's a really good movie called Bee Movie. That's a made up title by the way. Wait, no, it's a real title. OK. So let's go. Here's the bee, here's the hive, here's the big guy. OK. So, whoa! There's the bee, right there! [A/F] Oh my gosh, I'm gonna get stung! [A/F] Help me, help me! [A/F] Oh, phooey! It's just a TV screen. [F/D] Oh, right. Never mind. Oh, there's the big guy. I'm a little bit scared! [A/F] Eee! It's just a screen! [AG] Oh, yeah. Oh, there's the [unintelligible]. It's so cute! Boing. Don't forget it's a screen. Oh, yeah. OK. So wait, I know a good, um—here, do you want to come over to my house and have a sleepover? Sure. Let's go call our parents. Hi, Mom. HI, Dad. Can I have a sleepover at Jenna's house? Sure! OK. I'll be back tomorrow. OK. Hi, Mom. Hi, Dad. Um, Suzie's sleeping over at our house today. OK, sweetie, bye. Oh, and we'll be home at 8:00. OK, we're good. [HA] [Singing.] [HA] Kind of an awkward house but OK. Oh, let's go inside. OK. [Singing.] [HA] OK. Now do you want to go to my room? I have a bunk bed. Sure. Whoa! [HA] That's the coolest bunk bed! [HA] Can I go on the top? Sure. Whee! [HA] Whoa it's so cool up here! [HA] Oh, wait, I'm afraid of heights. [A/F] Ah! [A/F] [Experimenter: One minute left.] Never mind. Oh, well. OK. Let's go to sleep. Next day. Oh, I'll go back to my house. Well, see you tomorrow. Bye! Oh, and by the way, um, do you want to go to the park tomorrow? Sure. OK. And at the park. [Singing.] [HA] OK. Now. I want to—here, do you want to sleep over at my house today? Sure! Thanks, Mom. Bye. Well, she says we can sleep over. OK. Come on let's go. [Frequency of affect = 27, variety of affect = 4, positive affect = 14 (HA = 14), negative affect = 13 (A/F = 6, AG = 4, F/D = 3)]

### Child #3 (Fourth Grade)

Hello. Hello. Do you like building with blocks? Yes I do. [HA] OK, here's a green block. OK. What are we gonna do with it? I don't know. [F/D] Here's two more blocks. Let's play with them. Let's see what we can make. It's a house! [HA] Da da da! [HA] It's a horsie! [HA] Can I try to ride it? Sure just don't break the blocks. [AG] Whee! Whee! [HA] Can I try? Sure. That was fun! [HA] Yeah it was! [HA] Let's try to do some dancing on it. OK. Whee! [HA] Whoo! [HA] Oh no! [F/D] That one's hard to do. [F/D] Maybe we can stand on top of it. OK. Whee! It's a house again! [HA] Oh, cool! [HA] Maybe this can be a hat for you. It fell off of me! [F/D] OK. Maybe I can sit on this. Maybe I can sit on this. Maybe we could play a hand game. You lose. [COMP] I win! [COMP] Oh, no. [F/D] Can we play again? Sure. Whee! [HA] This time none of us won. [COMP] Both of us lost. [COMP] OK. Let's try to hold this up together and see if we can catch it. We caught it! [HA] We caught it! [HA] We dropped it. [F/D] It's a house. Again. Maybe it could be a table! It could be a table, and we could eat stuff on it. [O] See? Like this. [*Eating noises.*] [O]. Yeah! [*Eating noises again.*] [O] Yeah. OK. What do you want to do now? Hmmm . . . I don't know. [F/D] You want to play hide and seek? [COMP] OK. I love playing hide and seek! [COMP] OK. You hide. I'll seek. OK. 1, 2, 3, 4, 5, 6. Oh, no! [F/D] I found you! [COMP] There's not a lot of places to hide here. [F/D] OK, then we can jump up and down. My feet hurt now. [S/H] OK, well . . . I don't know what to do now. [F/D] Maybe we could hm. I have some dolls in my pocket. We can play with those. OK. It's in my very back pocket. Can you reach it? Sure. Nice doll! [HA] Thank you! Hi, my name is Cindy. Hi, my name is Bob. Let's go to the park. La, la, la. [HA] How are we supposed to climb this thing? [F/D] I don't know how we're supposed to climb it. [F/D] Ooh, look at there's a slide! [HA] We can use the triangle as the slide. Mine can go first. Whoosh! That was fun. [HA] Yeah, let me try now. Whoosh! Oh, no. [F/D] It's OK, we can put it back on [N/A]. Maybe the dolls can roll on this. Roll. Roll. Roll! [*Experimenter: One minute left.*] It's a house. And this is a seat. Maybe we can see what colors we can see in the house. I can't see much of it. [F/D] Maybe I can try. Ooh, I can't find anything. [F/D] OK. Well, let's see what's inside. This green block. All I see is green! [F/D] Well, let me try. Yeah, all I see is green. Maybe this red block. I see you! Me too! Hehe. [HA] This is fun. [HA] I wish this day would never end. Yeah! I wonder where my little sister is. Maybe we could go find her. [Frequency of affect = 49, variety of affect = 7, positive affect = 31 (COMP = 7, HA = 20, N/A = 1, O = 3), negative affect = 18 (AG = 1, F/D = 16, S/H = 1)]

## Child #4 (*Fourth Grade*)

OK. Hey, Sally. What do you want to do today? I don't know, Bessie. What do you? Let's wrestle. Ugh, ugh, ugh! [AG, AG] How about we do a cartwheel. Ah! [S/H] You fall. [S/H] This is what you're supposed to do. You fell too. [S/H] I really know what I'm doing. Hm. How about we solve a mystery? Which blocks should I put on next? Ow! [S/H] I touched my eye! [S/H] Ah! [S/H] Let me, let me try. [*Kiss.*] [N/A] You kissed a girl! [SEX] Eee! [F/D] How about we put this block on? We found something! [HA] Let's try—come on, let's try to go in it. Ugh, ugh, ugh. [F/D] I guess we didn't fit [F/D] Let's go to the circus. [*Singing.*] [HA] Wait! The circus isn't open. [F/D] Hmm. How about I be a teacher, and you be a student?

Sure. What is two plus two? Seventy-five! It is four. What is 10 times 10? Two million! One hundred! Now if you get this question wrong, I'll have to attack you. [AG] OK, teacher. Teacher Sally, what is 70 million times 70 million? Butter! Grrrr! [AG] Ahh! Grrr! [AG] Wow, that was sure fun! [HA] I broke all the bones in my body! [S/H] Hm, what should we do next? How about we read a book? Hm. Grr! [AG] Hm. I wonder what we should do. Hm. Let's be actors. We want to be in your next movie. Yeah, OK. Say the alphabet. Words, words, words, words, words! Eee! [HA] Ba! That is not the alphabet. [F/D] Now just pretend that she is fainting [S/H], that she is tied [A/F], and you have to rescue her. Help me! [A/F] Help me! Help me! I'm gonna fall into this rocky bottom [A/F] and get myself all hurt! [S/H] Da-da-da-da! Here let me untie that for you. [N/A] Thank you. [HA] Ah! [A/F] Er. No, not how you—you're fired. Let's be princesses. Look there's a prince! Oh, we're trapped in this castle! [A/F] Prince, save us! [A/F] Ah, er, don't hurt the dragon! [AG] That prince doesn't like us. [AG] Let's throw some blocks at him. [AG] Er, ah! Er, ah! [AG] Hm. How about we throw his horse at him? [AG] Er! [AG] Hm. What should we do next? Let's go and race cars. [*Driving noises.*] I won! [COMP] I won too! [COMP] Er er! [AG] Wait we just [*unintelligible*] and getting us away. What did we do? I don't know. Urgh! La-la-la. [HA] What should we do next? La la. [HA] Hm. Let's be done. Look, there's a mailman. Let us attack! [AG] [*Barking.*] Come [*unintelligible*]. Yes, the mailman's calling the police. [A/F] La la la. [HA] Jail happy. [HA] We're gonna go to jail. Yeah, yeah, yeah, yeah. [HA] Blah, blah, blah, blah. Boo! We are criminals, and we just broke out of jail. We are going to try to do stuff to entertain us. Be very careful! [A/F] La la la la. [HA] This is the end of the show! This is the end of the show! This is the end of the show! Yeah, yeah! [HA] I'm Sally. I'm Bessie. We switched our names and souls. Yeah, yeah, yeah, yeah. [HA] Bye, bye, bye, bye! Get out of here! [AG] Scram! [AG] You know what I mean! [AG] Let's wrestle. [AG] I'll wrestle you if you don't come! [AG] [Frequency of affect = 59, variety of affect = 8, positive affect = 18 (COMP = 2, HA = 13, N/A = 2, SEX = 1), negative affect = 41 (A/F = 8, AG = 19, F/D = 5, S/H = 9)

## Child #5 (Third Grade)

Hi. Hi. Do you want to go on the stepping-stones? OK. [*Uses blocks as stepping stones.*] That was fun. [HA] Do you want to do it again? Um, how about we skip some stones. OK. Whee! [HA] OK. I'm going to do this one. Good job. [HA] Thanks. Um, what do you want to do next? Do you want to play sword fighting? [COMP] OK. Boom, boom, boom. [*Clicks blocks together like swords.*] I won this time. [COMP] Oh, boy. [F/D] Let me try it. I won! [COMP] Hey, no fair! [F/D] Yes, it was. OK, never mind. So, what do you want to do now? Well, I don't know. Hmm, hmm. I'm not really sure. Well, we could play imagination. All right, what do you want to play? Um, let's not play imagination. How about we play something . . . how about we do stepping-stones again? Oh my, these are different stepping-stones. [A/F] We should go back. [A/F] That was nice. Maybe we should . . . but they're above the river; it is kind of dangerous to skip. [A/F] But I want to skip. [AG] It is very dangerous to skip! [A/F] But I want. [AG] No. Well, I am. OK, I will watch you. Ahh! [A/F] Oh, my. [A/F] Dive in. Whee! [HA] OK, thank goodness you saved me. [A/F] Maybe you were right. Yeah, mm-hmm. How about . . . we better go home. [A/F] We should? Yeah. My mom is cooking something really nice for dinner, she said. [O] Oh well, I better leave too. Bye! Do you know what happened today? Mom, do you know? Yeah, I skipped on step-stones. I went on these weird different blocks and I saved her. [N/A] Oh yeah, and can I tell you something? I saved her life. [N/A] It's like I'm a hero. [HA] Yeah, she was today. And do you know what the best part was? That she was saved, and now we can play together again. [HA] Even though she is . . . .Yeah, I am a little damp. Yeah, even though she's a little damp. Hi, friend. I told about the day yesterday. Me too. Awesome. [HA] Um, do you want to watch a show? OK. Awesome. [HA] That was a good show. [HA] Yay! [HA] Oh, my gosh, that was, wasn't it? [HA] Yeah. I better go home again. You gotta play piano, right? Yeah. OK, bye. Bye. Mom we watched this awesome . . . yeah, we watched this cool show. [HA] Really, oh, uh-huh. Awesome. It sounds fun to me too. [HA] Yep. What are you doing? I don't know. Today was much fun. [HA] We watched this show and it was about acting this fun way that was about like horses. Animals, yeah. Hmm-mm, animals. It was really good. [HA] I know wasn't it so good. [HA] Did you ever see it? It's a new show. Have you mom? It's a really good show. [HA] You really need to see it. There's only 3 more days. Yeah, only 3 more days. You've got to go to it. You've got to go. OK. And I have some extra tickets in my pocket. Here you go, Mom. [N/A] Now you can watch the show with my friend's mom. Oh, yes, you have to go, Mom. It's so much fun. [HA] [Frequency of affect = 37, variety of affect = 7, positive affect = 25 (COMP = 3, HA = 18, N/A = 3, O = 1), negative affect = 12 (A/F = 8, AG = 2, F/D = 2)]

## Child #6 (Kindergarten)

These are going to be about girls who lose their friendship [F/D], so they are not going to be nice to each other the whole story. [AG] You know what, you are my favorite person to play with. [HA] Yeah, you too. [HA] Should we have a play date? Yeah. And this is the girl who starts the fight. [AG] I'm going to play with this block. No, I'm going to play with this block. No, me, me, me. [AG] Put it down. I'm not going to be friends with you anymore. [AG] I am going to make a new friend. I am not going to be friend with you anymore. [AG] Try me. I want that one. No, I do. No, I do. No, I do. No, I do. [AG] Try the green block. Nope,

I want this block. No, I do. No, I do. No, I do. No, I do. No, I do. [AG] Very well then. I'm not going to talk to you again. [AG] [*Experimenter prompts more time.*] And this is going to be the new girl that she meets. And this is going to be the new girl that she meets. And this is going to be the new girl that she meets. Really, these are the same girls who meet up again, but then just because they look different is why they are going back together, but when she looks the same again to her and they go over to each other's houses again, then are going to get in a fight again. [AG] Oh, hello there. Hello. Do you want to play together? Yes. Do you want to come over to my house for a play date? Good idea. [HA] Now they are at each other houses and she is dressed the same as she looked. I am going to play with the red block. No, I am going to play with the red block. [AG] [*Struggle.*] [AG] Oh, dear! [F/D] No, me. No, me. No, me. No, me. No, me. No, me. [AG] And now, since they live next door, she gets the better house than she [COMP], because her house falls over and her house is very sturdy, and she is just talking to herself about the house. She says, "I am going to get a better house than you." [COMP] So she is thinking about it. And this is what her new house looks like. And she says it is big enough for me to sit on. So she sits on it, it fits her, and then a tornado came around where she lived, and then her house fell over because of the strong wind. [A/F] My house is big enough for me to sit on. Oh dear a tornado! [A/F] Aunty Em! The house fell over. [F/D] And that is the whole movie. [*Experimenter prompts more time.*] And then this is the mommy. This is the mom. Hey, what were you fighting about? This girl wanted the same things as I did, and her house never falls over, and my falls over because of the tornadoes. [F/D] Well, well, that is what you were fighting about? Yes it was! [*Experimenter: One minute left.*] And now she is leaving her mom's home. I am leaving you forever and never coming back home. [AG] Goodbye! She shut the door and is running away [AG], and the mom is running after her. Come back! Come back! Come back! Come back! Come back! Come back! Come back! Come back! Come back! [S/H] She ran off. Her mom can't find her. [A/F] How much more time do I have left? I'm all done. [Frequency of affect = 27, variety of affect = 6, positive affect = 5 (COMP = 2, HA = 3), negative affect = 22 (A/F = 3, AG = 14, F/D = 4, S/H = 1)]

### Child #7 (*Third Grade*)

Hi! My name's Sam! My name's Charlie! Ooh, let's build a sandcastle! Oh, cool! Let's go! Yeah! Stack! Stack! Hoorah! Yeah! We built the fort! Oh, hey, you got to put all the pieces on. No, you did. Blah, blah, blah! Hey, I think we should try to work this out. Let's build something else instead. Blocks-schmocks. Ooh, what should we build now? Uh, I don't know. Don't look at me. Ah! We don't know what to do! Ooh, look! Books! Let's read. And together they lived happily . . . wait. Two hours later. When the 16th hundredth book. Ooh! And they lived happily ever after! Five years later. The prom! Oh! [*Kiss.*] Now what? [*Experimenter: Keep on playing.*] Mah. Fine. Yee! That looks cool! Ooh, let's play dress up! What? That's just an example. I'm 40. Me too. Oh! Yeah, we fixed it. Wah! It broke! Wah! Ooh, let's fix it together. And perfect! Ooh, look! This, look! A brick is flying! Wait. Wait a second. They all [*unintelligible*]. Ooh, look this brick is falling from the sky. [*Hitting noise.*] Ahh! Well, now that we have casts on our arms and bodies, what should we do? Wait, we left out the legs. We have no legs! We can't walk! Ahh! What should we do master? Don't look at me. I'm not always the brightest person. Think! Use your imaginations! Ooh, yeah. Let's use our imaginations! Yeah, we just learned something new! At school. Patty cake, patty cake, bakers man. Bake me a cake as fast as you can. Roll it, pat it, mark it with a U. and put it in the oven for me and you. Yeah! I love you. I love you too. Let's promise never to fight again and always be best friends! Yeah! Hoorah! Whoo-hoo! Party! Party! Party! Party! Party! Party! Party! Party! Party! Party! Party! Party! Hoorah! And now for the curtain call! Hello, my name is Sammy. Hi, I'm Oozzie! Thank you! Thank you! [*Unintelligible.*] Thank you! Thank you! Thank you! Thank you very much! Ah! Thank you! Thank you! Thank you! Whoo! Our show ends. Hee hee! We did great on TV! Ah, ah, ah! Ah, ah, ah! Yeah! Oh boo! [*Unintelligible.*] [*Snoring.*] [*Unintelligible.*] Ooh, let's get a puppy! No, let's get a kitty! Let's get a puppy! Let's get a kitty! Let's get a puppy! Let's get a kitty! Let's get both! Kitty. Puppy. Roof! Meow! Roof! [Frequency of affect = 72, variety of affect = 7, positive affect = 45, negative affect = 27]

These samples of children's play illustrate how creative cognitive and affective processes occur in play. They show the richness of ideation and emotional expression that is possible in play. Children who have this ability in childhood should have an advantage in adulthood because they have these processes to call on in creative work. What does the research say about this hypothesis?

### Affect in Play and Divergent Thinking

In the first study with the APS, we were especially focused on affect in play. We investigated the relationships among the APS, primary-process thinking on the Rorschach, and divergent thinking in 60 first- and second-grade children (Russ & Grossman-McKee, 1990). Divergent thinking was significantly related to frequency of affect ($r = .42$, $p < .001$) and variety of affect ($r = .38$, $p < .001$). These correlations remained significant when verbal ability was controlled for. Verbal ability did not relate to any of the APS scores (see Table 4.1). Also, primary-process scores on the Rorschach were significantly related to the amount of affect in play. The amount of primary-process

## TABLE 4.1
### Pearson Product-Moment Correlations Among Primary Process and Affect Measures and Alternate Uses Test

| | Alternate Uses—# categories score | | |
| --- | --- | --- | --- |
| | Total sample | Boys | Girls |
| Rorschach[a] | | | |
| % Primary-process | .50*** | .72*** | .27 |
| AR | −.17 | −.09 | −.27 |
| AR x # primary-process responses | .10 | .34 | −.21 |
| Affect in Play Scale[b] | | | |
| Frequency of affect | .42*** | .40* | .44** |
| # Categories of affect | .38** | .56** | .29 |
| Comfort in play | .23* | .36* | .22 |
| Frequency of primary-process affect | .41*** | .38* | .48** |
| Frequency of nonprimary-process affect | .20 | .20 | .22 |
| Quality of fantasy | .30** | .48** | .32* |
| Imagination | .35** | .40* | .44** |
| Integration of affect | .42*** | .45** | .38* |

*Note.* AR = adaptive regression. From "Affective Expression in Children's Fantasy Play, Primary Process Thinking on the Rorschach, and Divergent Thinking," by S. W. Russ and A. Grossman-McKee, 1990, *Journal of Personality Assessment, 54,* p. 765. Copyright 1990 by Lawrence Erlbaum Associates, Inc. Reprinted with permission.
[a]$n = 46$ for total; $n = 22$ for boys, $n = 24$ for girls. [b]$n = 60$ for total; $n = 30$ for boys, $n = 30$ for girls.
*$p < .05$. **$p < .01$. *** $p < .001$.

thinking on the Rorschach was significantly related to cognitive scores of organization and imagination as well. This was true for both boys and girls (see Table 4.1). This is an important finding because it suggests that there is some consistency in the construct of affective expression across two different types of situations. The consistency was evident for both genders. It also supports Waelder's (1933) concept that play is a time to let go and allow primary-process thinking to occur.

We investigated the relationships among the APS, divergent thinking, and coping in school in first- and second-grade children (Russ & Peterson, 1990). The main purpose of this study was to obtain a large enough sample size (121 children) so that a sound factor analysis of the APS could be conducted. A second purpose was to replicate the results of our study (Russ & Grossman-McKee, 1990) that found a positive relationship between affective expression in play and divergent thinking. One hundred and twenty-one children (64 boys and 57 girls) were individually administered the APS and a Coping in School scale. In a separate testing session, with a different examiner, they were administered the Alternate Uses Test.

The main finding in this study was that the APS was significantly positively related to divergent thinking. These results replicated the findings of our study with children of the same age (Russ & Grossman-McKee, 1990). As in the previous study, there were no gender differences in the pattern of correlations. For the total sample, divergent thinking was significantly related to frequency of total affect, $r(115) = .26$, $p < .01$; variety of affect, $r(115) = .25$, $p < .01$; comfort, $r(115) = .37$, $p < .001$; quality of fantasy, $r(115) = .43$, $p < .001$; and imagination, $r(115) = .42$, $p < .001$. These relationships remained significant when verbal IQ was partialed out. On the basis of this study, we can say with more confidence that affective expression in fantasy relates to divergent thinking, independent of the cognitive processes measured by intelligence tests.

It is important to note that in both these studies (Russ & Grossman-McKee, 1990; Russ & Peterson, 1990) the significant relationship between play and divergent thinking occurred when the play task and the divergent thinking task were administered by different examiners. Scoring was done blind. Given Smith and Whitney's (1987) criticism that previous positive results that linked play and associative fluency were due to experimenter effects, these are important findings.

We also investigated the relationship between affect in play and creativity in 46 first- and second-grade children (Russ & Schafer, 2006). We found that frequency of affect in play related to originality of divergent thinking. Frequency of negative affect especially related to both fluency and originality. However, in a recent study we found only variety of affect, not frequency, to be related to divergent thinking in a group of 46 girls (Hoffmann & Russ, 2012). The cognitive play variables were related to divergent thinking.

In a study with preschool children ages 4 to 5, using the APS–P, we also found relationships between affect in play and divergent thinking (Kaugars & Russ, 2009). Frequency of affect expression was related to fluency and originality on a divergent thinking task. Affect in play also related to teachers' ratings of amount of make-believe in daily play in the classroom (see Table 4.2). A recent study by Fehr (2012) with a different sample of preschool children found a similar pattern of relationships between play and divergent thinking. In this sample, positive affect related to divergent thinking but negative affect did not. From these two studies, it appears that the relationship between affect in play and divergent thinking occurs as young as 4 years of age in typically developing children.

### Affect in Play, Affect in Memories, and Creative Narratives

One of the reasons expressing affect in play helps with the creative process is that the child develops more comfort thinking about emotions and processing emotions in memory. These memories are then available for creative work—especially in narrative art forms. There is some evidence that

TABLE 4.2
Correlations Between the Affect in Play Scale–Preschool and Creativity

| | APS–P | |
| --- | --- | --- |
| | Frequency of affect | Variety of affect |
| MSFM creativity scores | | |
| Total number of responses | .32 | .39* |
| Total number of original responses | .37* | .37* |
| Teacher ratings of daily play | | |
| Imagination | .43* | .47** |
| Use of make-believe | .42* | .46** |
| Enjoyment | .46* | .52** |
| Expression of emotions | .34 | .42* |
| Use of make-believe in dramatic play | .30 | .44* |

*Note.* $N = 33$. APS–P = Affect in Play Scale–Preschool; MSFM = Multidimensional Stimulus Fluency Measure. From "Assessing Preschool Children's Pretend Play: Preliminary Validation of the Affect in Play Scale–Preschool Version," by A. S. Kaugars and S. W. Russ, 2009, *Early Education and Development, 20*, p. 748. Copyright 2009 by Taylor & Francis Group, LLC. Adapted with permission.
*$p < .05$. **$p < .01$.

supports this hypothesis. In our 2006 study, affect in play related to affect expression in memories (Russ & Schafer, 2006). Frequency of affect in play was significantly related to the amount of emotion expressed in a memory task ($r = .28$, $p < .05$), as was variety of affect ($r = .32$, $p < .05$). These were small and medium effect sizes, respectively. Controlling for word count in the memory narratives did not significantly alter the correlations. The finding that affect in play related to affect in memory descriptions suggests a cross-situational ability in children. Children who are able to express affect in play are also able to include emotion when talking about a memory.

We investigated the relationship between affect in play and creativity of story narratives (Hoffmann & Russ, 2012; see Table 4.3). For the storytelling measure, using a consensus scoring system, the positive affect in play significantly related to story likeability, $r(44) = .30$, $p < .05$; creativity, $r(44) = .31$, $p < .05$; and imagination, $r(44) = .29$, $p < .05$. Children who expressed more positive affect during pretend play also tended to tell stories rated as more likeable, creative, and imaginative. As expected, imagination in pretend play also positively related to creativity in storytelling, $r(44) = .26$, $p < .05$. Children rated as more imaginative in pretend play were also rated as telling more creative stories. Affect in play also related to affect in storytelling. Direct affect expression in storytelling, tallied as instances in which the child used an affect-laden word (e.g., "The boy was mad") as opposed to implied affect (e.g., "The boy shook his fist"), related to affect expression in pretend play. Direct affect expression positively correlated with frequency of affect expression in play, $r(44) = .31$, $p < .05$; variety of affect expressed in play,

## TABLE 4.3
### Pearson Product–Moment Correlations Among Creativity and Pretend Play

| Creativity variables | Pretend play variables | | | | | | |
|---|---|---|---|---|---|---|---|
| | Org. | Imag. | Comf. | Freq. | Var. | Pos. | Neg. |
| Divergent thinking[a] | | | | | | | |
| Fluency | .32* | .38** | .18 | .15 | .25* | .22 | .01 |
| Flexibility | .28* | .36** | .16 | .14 | .22 | .21 | −.01 |
| Originality | .24 | .28* | .16 | .14 | .20 | .19 | .03 |
| Storytelling (Affect & fantasy scoring)[b] | | | | | | | |
| Fantasy | .02 | .20 | .20 | .25 | .20 | .20 | .19 |
| Direct affect | .08 | .15 | .18 | .31* | .27* | .51** | −.02 |
| Implied affect | .08 | .07 | .07 | −.01 | −.03 | .10 | −.12 |
| Total affect | .09 | .13 | .14 | .16 | .12 | .34* | −.09 |
| Variety of affect | −.05 | .03 | .02 | .06 | −.01 | .22 | −.12 |
| Storytelling[b] (Consensus scoring) | | | | | | | |
| Likeability | .13 | .19 | .06 | .11 | .06 | .30* | −.12 |
| Novelty | .19 | .21 | −.01 | .05 | .03 | .22 | −.14 |
| Creativity | .20 | .26* | .09 | .12 | .11 | .31* | −.12 |
| Imagination | .15 | .24 | .08 | .15 | .09 | .29* | −.06 |

*Note.* Org. = organization, Imag. = imagination, Comf. = comfort, Freq. = frequency of affect, Var. = variety of affect, Pos. = positive affect, Neg. = negative affect. From "Pretend Play, Creativity, and Emotion Regulation in Children," by J. Hoffmann and S. Russ, 2012, *Psychology of Aesthetics, Creativity, and the Arts, 6,* p. 180. Copyright 2011 by the American Psychological Association.
[a]$n = 46$. [b]$n = 44$.
*$p < .05$. **$p < .01$.

$r(44) = .27, p < .05$; and positive affect expressed in play, $r(44) = .51, p < .01$. Again, as in our 2006 study, there was support for a cross-situational ability to think about and express affect, in play, memories, and storytelling (Russ & Schafer, 2006). This cross-situational ability to access affect in ideation and in memories should be helpful in creating narratives in writing, poetry, film, videogames, and other art forms that involve telling stories.

### Factor Analysis of the Affect in Play Scale

There is growing evidence that there are two separate dimensions of play: a cognitive dimension and an affective dimension. Fein (1987) stated that affect is intertwined with fantasy in pretend play. This is true and presents a challenge for the measurement of pretend play. Can the two processes be separated when measuring play? The conceptualization underlying the APS was that there were two separate processes. Initial exploratory factor analysis, although with small samples, supported a two-factor structure, with correlated factors, in three separate studies (for a review, see Russ, 2004). These studies used a principal component analysis with oblique rotation. Organization and imagination loaded on the cognitive factor and frequency of affect, variety of affect, and intensity of affect loaded on an affective factor. It is notable that comfort loaded on the cognitive factor. The comfort score measures enjoyment and engagement in the play. Perhaps engagement in the play task occurs when imagination and narrative comes easily to a child.

In a study with a large sample of 519 Italian children from 6 to 10 years of age, a confirmatory factor analysis (CFA) was used (Chessa, Di Riso, Delvecchio, Salcuni, & Lis, 2011). The CFA supported a two correlated factor model as the best fit. Factor loadings were high with almost all variables. A cognitive and affective factor emerged, with comfort loading on the cognitive factor. Chessa et al. (2011) concluded that this factor structure supported my theoretical model of pretend play (Russ, 1987, 1993) as consisting of two distinct cognitive and affective dimensions that influence each other reciprocally. One implication of these factor analyses is that it makes sense to continue studying both cognitive and affective processes in pretend play. These processes may have different developmental trajectories and developmental correlates.

## CONCLUSION

A growing body of research supports a relationship between affect in play and creative thinking that is independent of intelligence. A positive relationship has been found between playfulness (that included the affective components of spontaneity and joy) and divergent thinking in kindergarten children. Similarly, a relationship has been found between the amount of affect expressed in play and divergent thinking in several samples of first and second graders and in preschool children as well. Affect in play has also been found to relate to creativity in storytelling. It is important to note that both positive and negative affect in play relate to creativity in most studies. In play, negative affect is well controlled in most children and is pretend, after all. The negative affect is not intense and is often enjoyable to the child.

There is also evidence that the tendency to access and express affect is a cross-situational ability. Affect in play has related to affect (primary process) on the Rorschach, affect in memory descriptions, and affect in storytelling.

The factor analyses of the APS, especially the recent CFA with an Italian sample, has found a two-factor structure of play—cognitive and affective—in which the two factors are related. Future research should identify different correlates of the factors throughout child development.

Play has been found to facilitate creativity in children, but there is no conclusive evidence that the affect expression in play is the causative factor.

That question needs to be investigated. One can speculate that expression of affect in play

- helps process emotions so that affective content can be coded and accessed,
- enables practice manipulating affect-laden images and memories,
- develops a broader memory system with affect-laden memories,
- helps the child become comfortable with emotions,
- develops an appreciation of the joy and engagement of the creative process, and
- develops an aesthetic sensibility.

During the past 25 years, there has been a resurgence of research in the affect and creativity area. As it should be in any science, the research is theory driven, theories are being developed and tested, measures and methods are being refined, and new lines of investigation are opening. I have identified key concerns for the future in the affect and creativity area (Russ, 2011): (a) identifying specific affective processes that are most important for creativity tasks; (b) discovering the underlying mechanisms that account for the relationships between affect and creativity; (c) exploring differential effects of various types of affect, such as positive or negative affect, on creativity; (d) understanding how affect and creativity relate to psychological adjustment and psychopathology; and (e) understanding the developmental processes involved in affect and creativity. Investigating affect in play and creativity should be a high priority.

The next two chapters focus on creativity in the sciences and the arts in adulthood. Examples of creative artists and scientists are presented, highlighting the similarities between the creative processes in children's play and the creative processes involved in adult creativity.

# 5

# CASE STUDIES IN SCIENCE AND TECHNOLOGY

What do the processes that we observe in play look like in adulthood? Ideally, we would follow children who demonstrate creative play into adulthood to determine the predictive power of play. Lacking these definitive studies, we can turn to case studies of creative individuals and catch some glimpses of these processes from their histories and from interviews with them.

The different domains of science and the arts require different abilities to achieve distinction in creative innovation. This chapter focuses on areas of science and technology. First, the processes and abilities important in science and invention are described. Then, case studies of scientists and inventors that illustrate some of these processes are presented. The final case study is of Miyamoto, a video game creator, who bridges the areas of technology and the arts. Abilities in both domains are necessary. Finally, personality characteristics of scientists, as compared with artists, are reviewed.

http://dx.doi.org/10.1037/14282-006
*Pretend Play in Childhood: Foundation of Adult Creativity*, by S. W. Russ

## CREATIVE PROCESSES IN SCIENCE AND TECHNOLOGY

The ability to generate ideas, to associate broadly, to think flexibly, and to feel passionately enough about a subject to be able to stay with it for long periods of time are all characteristics of the creative scientist and inventor. Feist (2011) concluded from the research literature that cognitive characteristics of the creative scientist are openness to experience, tolerance of ambiguity, and flexibility of thought. We have seen how pretend play can set the stage for divergent thinking, broad associations, and flexibility of thought. Play can also introduce the child to the experience of *flow*—the capacity for deep involvement in the task.

Rocke (2010) discussed the importance of deep immersion in a scientific field that then enables new combinations of ideas to emerge. He described the continuity of the work that comes before many scientific breakthroughs. He quoted Howard Gruber's (1981) extensive work in this area, which pointed to the need for a deep understanding of a domain and knowing it in different ways: "This multiplicity of perspectives grows slowly through hard work and sets the state for the re-cognition we experience as a new insight" (as cited in Rocke, p. 320). The continual reprocessing of information, images, memories, perspectives, metaphors, and so forth is a mental process that occurs both in and out of awareness and sets the stage for true creative ideas in an area. We can speculate how pretend play helps children develop the habit of this type of combinatory play with ideas and images. Good pretend play requires deep immersion, trying out ideas and combinations of ideas, and shifts in perspective taking.

There are several roles for emotion in scientific discovery. As we have reviewed, emotion can facilitate divergent thinking and remote associations. Also, emotion can serve as a motivating force behind the scientific pursuit. The scientist has a drive to cure cancer or prevent disease, perhaps for personal reasons. Love for the subject matter is also crucial. The ability to experience deep joy and passion to enable the individual to delve deeply into an area, with long concentration, is necessary for creative breakthroughs. The ability to experience joy as a child in play can whet the appetite, so to speak, for repeat joyful experiences. A playful approach to problems has also been noticed as common among scientists and inventors.

## BARBARA MCCLINTOCK—THE CAPACITY FOR JOY

Barbara McClintock was a plant biologist who discovered the transposition of genetic elements, for which she won the Nobel Prize in 1983. Her work went unrecognized for many years before she finally received recognition.

Evelyn Fox Keller (1983) wrote an excellent biography of McClintock that includes interview material. McClintock is open about memories and is articulate about her creative process.

McClintock experienced the feeling of joy as a young child, around the age of 6. She described loving to walk along the beach and then running in a special style: "You stood straight out with your back just completely straight, and you practically floated. Each step was rhythmically floating, without any sense of fatigue, and with a great sense of euphoria" (Keller, 1983, p. 22). This early experience of euphoria, as she called it, recurred through much of her creative work. In high school she loved solving difficult problems:

> I would solve some of the problems in ways that weren't the answers the instructor expected. . . . I would ask the instructor, "Please, let me . . . see if I can't find the standard answer," and I'd find it. It was a tremendous joy, the whole process of finding that answer, just pure joy. (Keller, 1983, p. 26)

The capacity for experiencing that joy in problem solving helps provide the passion necessary for scientific discovery but also serves as a cue for when the "right answer" occurs. Many years later, she experienced this joy in solving a major scientific problem. At Stanford, she was discouraged and realized that she was not solving the problem. She went for a walk and sat under eucalyptus trees for half an hour. "Suddenly I jumped up, I couldn't wait to get back to the laboratory. I knew I was going to solve it—everything was going to be all right" (Keller, 1983, p. 115). She recognized that she had the solution, even though it then took her 5 more days to work it out. McClintock used the word *ecstasy* in describing some of her reactions to insight and problem solving. "I don't understand ecstasy, but I enjoy it. When I have it. Rare ecstasy" (Keller, 1983, p. 204). One can speculate as to the similarity between this kind of affect and that of deep aesthetic appreciation.

McClintock described what happened under the eucalyptus trees as enabling her to "reorient" herself so that she could immediately integrate what she saw. Perhaps the experience permitted her to break out of an old way of thinking and think more flexibly. She spoke of the ability to resist dogma as being important in science. Theories and models become dogma and limit people's thinking. Investigators need to think freely: "I feel that much of the work is done because one wants to impose an answer on it. They have the answer ready, and they [know what they] want the material to tell them." Anything else, it tells them, "they don't really recognize as there, or they think it's a mistake and throw it out. . . . If you'd only just let the material tell you" (Keller, 1983, p. 179). This description is an excellent example of *cognitive flexibility*—the ability to shift ways of thinking and be open to new ways of thinking.

From an early age, McClintock had the capacity for deep absorption in a task. She would get lost in thought. In later years, in working with chromosomes, she found that

> the more I worked with them, the bigger and bigger [they] got, and when I was really working with them, I wasn't outside, I was right down there. I was part of the system. I was right down there with them and everything got big. I even was able to see the internal parts of the chromosomes— actually everything was there. It surprised me because I actually felt as if I were right down there, and these were my friends. (Keller, 1983, p. 117)

She went on to say that she had a "real affection" (p. 117) for the pieces that go together. This love of the work and the object of the work is evident in her comments. She really developed a love for the corn plant, which was so central to her work.

Keller (1983) referred to the work of Phyllis Greenacre, who thought that a necessary condition for the "flowering of great talent or genius is the development in the young child of what she calls a 'love affair with the world'" (p. 204). McClintock certainly described a childhood that developed that love affair. Psychoanalytic theories have also discussed the concept of *cathexis*— the capacity to attach and invest emotionally in a mental representation of a loved object or person (Brenner, 1974). This deep love and attachment to ideas, art, music, or in Barbara McClintock's case, the corn plant, needs to be nurtured and given time to develop.

The opportunity to find what you love and love to do can begin in childhood. The opportunity to experiment, play, and find different things that are enjoyable is important for creative development. McClintock described her request to her parents that she have "bloomers" made for her dresses "so that I could do anything that I wanted. I could play baseball, I could play football, I could climb trees, I could just have a completely free time, the same kind of free time that my brother and the people on the block had" (Keller, 1983, p. 24). Freedom of movement and exploration was important to her. At the time, in the early 1900s, girls had more limitations on their opportunities than today, but any culture imposes certain expectations and limitations. It is notable that, in her childhood, McClintock reported that her parents usually accommodated her requests. Her parents were respectful of who she was and her differences from others.

## GUGLIELMO MARCONI AND STEVE JOBS— PLAYFUL EXPERIMENTERS

Playfulness is an important characteristic of creative scientists and inventors and has been described as "an internal predisposition to bring a playful quality to interactions with the environment and across a variety of contexts and episodes" (Trevlas, Grammatikopoulos, Tsigilis, & Zachopoulou, 2003, p. 33). A playful attitude should help individuals stay with a task, delve deeply into it, and have fun with the task or problem. Damour (2009) discussed the importance of tinkering in learning to work with computers and mechanical objects. She cited a 2000 report by the American Association of University Women that proposed that boys saw computers as toys that were interesting in their own right. They could be played with, tinkered with, manipulated, and enjoyed. Because boys tinkered with these objects, they learned how they functioned. Girls, however, approached computers not as toys but as tools to accomplish something. Damour was concerned that girls were at a disadvantage because of this attitude. The concept of tinkering and having a playful approach to science and engineering is evident in many creative scientists.

Marconi, the inventor of wireless communication, exemplified playfulness and tinkering. The playful experimentation of Marconi's childhood is described in a biography by Trowbridge (2009). In Italy, Marconi had an early love of electricity and, in essence, "played" with the entire area of electricity. He also had "a lot of ideas in his head" (p. 4), which probably reflected his high degree of divergent thinking as a child. He engaged in many pranks, which also reflected his playful qualities. Trowbridge described how Marconi, as a child of 10, collected metals and other material that he then used to build various mechanical toys for his experiments. In this way, he played with ideas and manipulated objects and tested hypotheses. As he got older, the experiments became more sophisticated. In essence, he tinkered with the material.

At 20, Marconi had a secret workroom in his attic where he began his experiments on wireless communication. Trowbridge (2009) described an insight that Marconi had when he visualized wireless communication. In the obituary of the researcher Hertz, Marconi read about experiments that demonstrated that electricity could be sent in bursts across a room without wires. Marconi immediately visualized that electricity could be used to send signals through the air. Marconi was able to "see" the possibilities, the insight stage of Wallas's (1926) stages of creativity. Physical experiments then needed to be done to demonstrate what Marconi already knew. There is a similarity between this description of Marconi's insight and that of Barbara McClintock when she knew that she had the solution to a problem and then spent 5 days working it out.

Marconi's experiments involved working with transmitters and receivers and lengthening the distance that signals could be sent. He tried 500 different combinations of different shapes of tubes and different types of metals (Trowbridge, 2009). He continued to experiment outside, where he tested various distances by trial and error. He tried different parts, materials, and positions of the different components before achieving success. The patience and dedication involved in this verification stage is admirable. He had to have loved the process of experimentation to persevere.

In some ways, the playful childhood experimentation of Steve Jobs, developer of Apple computers, is similar to that of Marconi. As a child, he had his own space in which to work—his father gave him a workbench. On weekends, he and his father would go to various junkyards to look for parts (Isaacson, 2011). Later, a neighbor gave him electronic components to experiment with. Jobs said the neighbor "would bring me stuff to play with" (Isaacson, 2011, p. 11). A teacher gave him a hobby kit for making a camera. Adults in his life encouraged his creativity by giving him materials and components to play with and manipulate as he developed his talents.

As a high school student, he worked in an electronics store. While there, he explored electronic components and developed a knowledge of electronics. His affective engagement with these parts is evident in the following quotation in which he described the electronics store he worked in:

> Out in the back, near the bay, they had a fenced-in area with things like Polaris submarine interiors that had been ripped and sold for salvage. All the controls and buttons were right there. The colors were military greens and grays, but they had these switches and bulb covers of amber and red. There were these big old lever switches that, when you flipped them, it was awesome, like you were blowing up Chicago. (Isaacson, 2011, p. 18)

One can also hear his access to aggressive primary-process ideation in his blowing up Chicago fantasy. As reviewed earlier, research has found that access to aggressive fantasy is associated with creativity.

Jobs also had an early sense of aesthetics and knew what he loved. He "fell totally in love with" (Isaacson, 2011, p. 8) the first computer terminal he saw. Jobs experienced the early passion for a subject that is so important in driving creative work. As Barbara McClintock loved the corn plant, Steve Jobs loved the computer.

Jobs also demonstrated and could utilize remote associations. In his naming of the Apple computer, he combined the friendly concept of an apple (having just visited an apple orchard) with the technical computer (Isaacson, 2011). He made the association and then used his critical-thinking skills to evaluate the effectiveness of that name. Among other advantages, it would come before Atari in the phone book.

## POINCARÉ AND EINSTEIN—FLUID THINKERS

In the area of scientific creativity, the mathematician Poincaré's (1913/1952) essay "Mathematical Creation" is often quoted. This is because Poincaré so eloquently described how his mind worked when creating mathematical solutions. His introspection into the creative process is consistent with research and with observations of other scientists. In this essay, he described the fluid process of going back and forth between conscious and unconscious thought. He described the process of remote association and the importance of affect in the identification of useful ideas. Poincaré described the shifting images and ideas in the incubation stage of the creative process. He had been working on the problem of Fuchsian functions for 15 days. One night, after drinking coffee and being unable to sleep, "Ideas rose in crowds; I felt them collide until pairs interlocked, so to speak, making a stable combination" (Ghiselin, 1952, p. 36). By the next morning, he had the class of functions written out. What is evident is the loosening of cognitive control so that the ideation was spontaneous. He also recognized the correct combination that enabled him to develop the functions. Poincaré also discussed the importance of earlier working stages of concentrating on the problem at hand. This process gets the ideas moving, so to speak.

Affect helped him recognize the correct combination of ideas. Poincaré stated that the "rules which must guide the choice are extremely fine and delicate. It is almost impossible to state them precisely: They are felt rather than formulated" (Ghiselin, 1913/1952, p. 39). He wrestled with what determined whether a combination passed the threshold of consciousness. Combinations which affect one's "emotional sensibility" get attention. Affect cues the correct solution. He stated,

> It may be surprising to see emotional sensibility invoked apropos of mathematical demonstrations which, it would seem, can interest only the intellect. This would be to forget the feeling of mathematical beauty, of the harmony of numbers and forms, of geometric elegance. This is a true esthetic feeling that all real mathematicians know, and surely it belongs to emotional sensibility. (Ghiselin, 1952, p. 40)

He went on to say that the most useful combinations are the most beautiful, which enters the emotional realm. He suggested that affect guides the process of these associations. Useful combinations of ideas, at the unconscious level, stir the aesthetic sense and enter awareness, where they are then judged.

There has been a debate in the field as to whether the remote associations that are made in solving a problem are totally random or are guided in some way. Simonton (1999) argued from the framework of evolution that associations are random and the best solutions then emerge and are chosen. This is in support of Campbell's (1960) thesis that the generation of associations in creative problem solving is random. Therefore, the blind variation model of genetic mutations in the process of evolution applies to divergent thinking— the generation of many ideas and associations. Sternberg (1998) argued that divergent associations in creative problem solving is not blind variation but is sighted variation. Sternberg focused on cognitive processes in creative thinking and concluded that there are different kinds of knowledge that individuals use when generating ideas. Creative people consult these different kinds of knowledge when generating ideas, often without awareness of using these knowledge bases. He reviewed the findings from the study of expert–novice differences in many different domains.

Experts try better paths to solutions than do novices (Holyoak, 1990). For example, great chess players generate better moves from the start than do less creative chess players. I have argued that the associations are somehow guided by affective processes (Russ, 1999a). We know that access to affect in fantasy positively relates to divergent thinking ability in children and in adults. We also know that positive mood induction increases divergent thinking ability. The number of associations increases in a positive mood state. Various theoretical frameworks for understanding the relationship between divergent thinking and affect were reviewed in Chapter 4. They include psychoanalytic theory (Kris, 1952), associative network theory (Bower, 1981; Isen, Daubman, & Nowicki, 1987), and mood-related cognition (Rholes, Riskind, & Lane, 1987). What these theories have in common is the idea that affect activates a set of relevant cognitions that are mood related. A cognitive priming process occurs.

Affect could also guide the search process by making some ideas, associations, or images more salient than others. Consistent with Damasio's (1994) hypothesis of the somatic marker, there is a constant interaction between cognition and emotion in decision making. Affect guides the generation of associations and the continual evaluation of the associations that emerge. In Damasio's *somatic-marker hypothesis*, cognitive images become marked with physiological responses that affect emotions. Damasio applied his model to decision making, but it is also applicable to divergent thinking. As associations occur, they are highlighted (or made salient) by positive and negative emotional responses. These emotional and physiological responses are rapid and often out of awareness or are unconscious processes (Damasio, 1994; V. Simón, 1998). Damasio also referred to Poincaré's (1913/1952) description of a nonrandom search process of associations. Poincaré stated that to create involves making useful combinations of ideas. He implied that one sifts through a minority of useful possibilities after a preselection process. Poincaré actually described the guided process quite well in his essay.

Playing with combinations of ideas can use language or be entirely visual. Einstein described his use of visual combinatory play in his letter to Jacques Hadamard (Ghiselin, 1952, p. 43; Penrose, 1989). He stated,

> The words or the language, as they are written or spoken, do not seem to play any role in my mechanism of thought. The psychical entities which

seem to serve as elements in thought are certain signs and more or less clear images which can be "voluntarily" reproduced and combined. . . . this combinatory play seems to be the essential feature in productive thought—before there is any connection with logical construction in words or other kinds of signs which can be communicated to others. (Ghiselin, 1952, p. 43)

He then said that the elements of thought are visual and some "of muscular type" (Ghiselin, 1952, p. 43).

## TEMPLE GRANDIN—EMPATHIC VISUALIZER

It may be a surprise to think of Temple Grandin, an individual with autism, as an empathic visualizer, but that is how she described her development of the innovative method of slaughtering cattle humanely. This method and struc-ture had a major impact in the area and is now widely used (Sacks, 1995). Grandin is better known in our culture as a high-functioning individual with autism who has been quite articulate about the condition and about her inner life and mind. The invention of this device, and others, qualifies her as a big-C individual.

How can an individual with autism, given its symptoms, have such a creative mind? Some of the major symptoms of autism are severe problems with social interaction and understanding the perspective of other people, problems experiencing affect in relation to others, and lack of imagination. For example, Grandin has difficulty understanding metaphors. Yet, she has such a deep understanding of the mind of cattle that she was able to develop a humane way of handling them at the time of slaughter.

At the age of 3, she received early intervention in a nursery school with a speech therapist, which probably helped her development. We know that early intervention to help with language results in better prognosis for autistic children. By the age of 8, she was starting to achieve the pretend play level of 2- and 3-year-olds (Sacks, 1995). She began painting and building cardboard models and sculptures. Although she had much difficulty interacting with other children, she could connect with animals. She felt a deep empathy for them. She said, "I know what the cow's feeling" (Sacks, 1995, p. 268). So when she heard the cries and bellows of cows at the slaughterhouse, she was deeply affected and motivated to develop a more humane approach of slaughtering them. She developed a curved chute that cattle would walk through that prevented them from seeing distractions and that was also consistent with their natural tendency to circle.

In the documentary *The Woman Who Thinks Like a Cow*, Grandin (2006) described how she physically got down into the existing chutes and walked through them to see what the cattle experienced. She could put herself in their place and devised a system that would not agitate them. Grandin had excellent visualization ability and could combine that ability with her empathy for and understanding of the mind of a cow. She spoke of her deep love for cattle, which seems similar to Barbara McClintock's deep love of the corn plant and her description of being involved at the level of the cell to figure out what was going on.

In discussing her associative process, Grandin (2006) first referred to her mind as a computer where she could run visual simulations of an entire design. If an error occurred, she could detect it in the simulation and correct it. When it became clear in her mind, she made a blueprint of it. She said there is no emotion in it. This has been an advantage to her in the type of creative work that she does. However, the motivating force was her love of animals; she used her empathy with the cow to develop the ideal chute. Grandin claimed that she does not repress memories, that she has no blocked files. Her explanation for this is that "the amygdala locks the files of the hippocampus. In me, the amygdala doesn't generate enough emotion to lock the files of the hippocampus" (Sacks, 1995, p. 287). There is no memory painful enough to lock the files. This is an interesting hypothesis.

Sacks (1995) astutely pointed out that the particular affect system that is affected by autism is that of affect in relation to people and "allied ones— aesthetic, poetic, symbolic" (p. 288). He hypothesized that because of the concrete and fixed images and quasi-mechanical associations, individuals with autism have difficulty "letting go of fixities and definites in order to revise and reconstruct," which is so important in using imagination. He quoted Coleridge's description of imagination as something that "dissolves, diffuses, dissipates, in order to recreate" (p. 289). Grandin's ability to visually simulate various devices in the realm of engineering has enabled her to be highly creative in that domain. In the domain of literature or poetry, she would probably be at a major disadvantage. It is possible that without the usual affective valence to memories and processing of emotional experience, she would have difficulty transforming emotional memories into creative products in the arts.

## SHIGERU MIYAMOTO—A BLEND OF SCIENCE AND ART

The development of much technology is a blend of science and art. Video games are an example of this blend. One example of an artist–scientist in this domain is Shigeru Miyamoto, who is considered to be one of the great video game inventors. Miyamoto credits early play as important in his development. An article about him by Paumgarten (2010) described his ideal play experience in childhood. Because he did not have toys, he made his own from wood and string. He put on puppet plays, made cartoon flipbooks, and "pretended that there were magical realms hidden behind the sliding shoji screens in his family's little house" (p. 86). Miyamoto exemplifies many of the play processes research has supported as being important in creativity. He invented toys, made up stories, and engaged in fantasy. He created mystery for himself. Later, at around age 8, he played in caves, explored, and developed his imagination further.

Paumgarten (2010) described how his imaginary play in childhood carried over into adulthood and was incorporated into the many leading and innovative video games that he developed. For example, he included story-telling and narrative into video games. In his Super Mario video game, the goal is to rescue the maiden. In his cave exploration and play with friends, he faced down imaginary and some real dangers. He "filled his games with his childlike interpretation of the world as a carnival of quirky perils and hidden delights" (p. 92). He tried to have game players be active participants. He paid attention to the delicate balance between satisfaction and challenge. He seems to have incorporated Csikszentmihalyi's (1990b) maxim of optimal challenge for a joyful flow experience to develop. There are new challenges in the game, but they are well paced so that the participant can also do repetitive steps again. He used the word *joy* in describing that process for the participant.

Others have commented on his playful approach. Playfulness is an important ingredient in creativity. Will Wright, another important video game developer, stated, "He approaches the games playfully . . . but most people don't" (Paumgarten, 2010, p. 89). Miyamoto also concluded that using play in a transaction or task can induce people to do things they might not normally do. Play and fun are important developmentally for children's learning, but adults too can benefit from a playful approach.

## PERSONALITY CHARACTERISTICS: COMPARING SCIENTISTS AND ARTISTS

Creative individuals have been found to have certain personality traits that set the stage for creative thinking and production to occur. A number of research programs have investigated personality traits that occur in creative individuals in the sciences and the arts. A comprehensive review of the personality trait research with adults, with a specific focus on traits of creative individuals, is that of Barron and Harrington (1981). They concluded that there is a consistency in the findings of the different research programs of Barron (1969), Mackinnon (1965), Roe (1953), and Cattell and Butcher

(1968). Barron and Harrington listed a set of core characteristics of creative individuals that emerge in different domains: high valuation of aesthetic qualities in experience, broad interests, attraction to complexity, high energy, independence of judgment, autonomy, intuition, self-confidence, ability to accommodate opposite traits in one's self-concept, and a firm sense of self as creative.

Feist (1998) carried out a meta-analysis on personality studies of artists and scientists and concluded that creative individuals in both the arts and the sciences are open to experience, are less conventional, less conscientious, more self-confident, more self-accepting, more driven, more ambitious, more dominant, more hostile, and more impulsive than less creative individuals. Artists and scientists differed in that artists were more affective, more emotionally unstable, and less socialized than scientists, and scientists were more conscientious than artists. The finding that scientists tend to be high on conscientiousness is not surprising when one considers the importance of a focus on detail and close attention to the literature that is involved in scientific work.

Openness to experience has also been consistently related to creativity in both artists and scientists. Openness to experience includes intellectual curiosity, aesthetic sensitivity, liberal values, and emotional differentiation (McCrae, 1987). Openness to experience is one of the five factors in McCrae and Costa's (1987) five-factor model of personality. They conceptualized openness to experience as a mode of processing experience. Research has found that interest in a variety of experiences for their own sake, in a variety of domains such as fantasy, aesthetics, feelings, actions, and values, was related to divergent thinking and other creativity measures. Correlates of the openness to experience factor are being unconventional, perceptive, empathic, and flexible; having a high need for change, variability in mood, wide range of interests, variety of mood states, tolerance of ambiguity, and preference for complexity; and sensation seeking (McCrae, 1987). The openness to experience factor relates to divergent thinking with correlations around .40.

There is little research on the openness to experience construct and creativity in children. We did one study with a sample of first- and second-grade children and an adapted measure of the openness to experience scale (Cordiano & Russ, 2011). The adult measure was adapted for children by changing the wording to make it appropriate for children and by having it filled out by parents. As hypothesized, we found that openness to experience as rated by the parents related to imagination in pretend play on the Affect in Play Scale (Russ, 1987, 2004). Nine percent of the variance in openness to experience was accounted for by imagination in pretend play.

This relationship remained the same in a 2-year follow-up. This gives some preliminary evidence that openness to experience relates to creative thinking in children as well as adults. More research needs to be carried out, but it is a promising area to follow.

The personality differences that do exist between scientists and artists may reflect the differences in the domains of creativity. Divergent thinking is important in scientific problem solving and in artistic production. Breaking out of a set and creating new configurations is also important in both areas of creativity. Kuhn's (1962) concept of revolution in science involved the overthrowing of paradigms. This kind of paradigm shift requires the cognitive flexibility of breaking out of an old set or way of thinking. Openness to experience is important in all types of creativity. However, the role of affect appears to be a major difference in personality profiles and in what is required in the domains.

In science, the in-depth involvement in the affective processes themselves may not be as important. Going deeply into the affect states and affect themes in one's memories or unconscious material may not be important for scientific work to occur. The content of affective material does not emerge in scientific problem solving. Affective content is important in many artistic creations. Suler (1980) made this point and reviewed the work of Niederland (1973, 1976) that showed that artists incorporated early traumas and conflicts into their artistic products. In the next chapter, there are examples of this kind of affective influence in creative work. For scientists, the role of affect is different. As we have seen in the examples of scientists, aesthetic experience is important; love of the subject matter is important; passion and motivation, which can come from many sources, are crucial. Joy in problem solving and a playful, joyful approach to the work are frequent. But the nature of the affective involvement is different and less personal.

It is important to note that much of the personality research has occurred with male samples. There is some evidence that creative women may have different personality profiles than creative men. Helson (1990) did important research on creativity in women at Mills College. One of her findings was that creative women did not inhibit negative affect. Gough (1988) used his Adjective Check List for ratings by observers and found that creative women were rated as being different from creative men. The cluster of items for creative men fit the typical cluster of creative adjectives in the literature: adventurous, ingenious, artistic, versatile, original. For women, a different cluster emerged: thoughtful, playful, reliable, persevering, responsible, fair-minded, and logical. These creative women looked more conventional on the surface than did creative men. It is important to consider gender differences in thinking about the creative process in different domains.

## CONCLUSION

These case studies illustrate similarities in the processes that occur in children's play and in creative production in the sciences. Scientists experiment, manipulate ideas, associate broadly, become immersed in their area, and recombine images. They also love what they do, are often playful in their approach, and use affect to make decisions. They experience joy in creation. Research suggests they are relatively stable in their personality functioning. As we move to creativity in the arts, the role of affect comes to the forefront in the content of the creative production.

# 6

## CASE STUDIES IN THE ARTS

In the arts, affect plays a major role in the creative process. Memories of affect-laden experiences often provide the content of literature, poetry, plays, and the visual arts. Artists can use their art to express and resolve emotional experiences and conflicts. The memories are transformed into the particular domain of their expertise. Creative cognitive processes of divergent thinking, metaphor production, and flexibility are also essential. And affect aids the associative process. But the major way in which artistic creativity differs from scientific creativity is the use of affective material such as memories, images, and fantasy in the content of the art. This chapter focuses on creative processes in the arts, specifically the narrative arts and the visual arts. First, there is a review of the creative processes in play and the narrative arts, with brief case illustrations throughout. The importance of memory and emotion in the arts is discussed, and case studies are presented.

http://dx.doi.org/10.1037/14282-007
*Pretend Play in Childhood: Foundation of Adult Creativity*, by S. W. Russ

# NARRATIVE ARTS

Pretend play helps the child experience affect; manipulate images, memories, and representations; and perhaps, code the affect experiences in memory. Pretend play sets the stage for the arts that involve storytelling and evokes figural images of affect in the visual arts. Many processes that are important in creative storytelling occur in the play of childhood and are developed in the arena of pretend play. Pretend play involves imagination, fantasy, storytelling, emotional expression, absorption in the moment, spontaneity, risk taking, understanding the perspectives of others, and experiencing the joy of creation. Individuals who are able to engage in pretend play as children should be able to access these processes as adults during the creative process (Russ, 1993, 2004). The narrative arts include fiction, poetry, theater (acting and playwriting), and filmmaking. The ability to access memories and transform them is especially important to the artist who uses a narrative approach.

Creative writers often refer to and remember pretend play events in their childhood (Russ, 2009). Stephen King (2000) remembered that his earliest memory was "of imagining I was someone else. . . . the Ringling Brothers Circus strongboy" (p. 18). He was about 2½ or 3 years old. He was dragging a concrete block across the floor and imagined standing on it in the center ring and being dressed in an animal skin. He then fell, and the pain was intense. The memory stayed with him. Mark Twain engaged in make-believe play at age 7 with his friends. He would assign them roles and dialogue that he drew from books such as Robin Hood (Powers, 2005). He was practicing with dialogue and understanding different perspectives. Ingmar Bergman discussed the importance of playing with a magic lantern at the age of 9. He put on puppet productions of plays, which was an important part of his childhood (Rothstein, 2007).

Boyd (2009) conceptualized the similarities between play and engaging in the arts. Play is connected with the development of flexibility of cognitive processes in higher mammals and in children. Children learn to engage in cognitive play with patterns of information. This includes patterns of social information as well. Art is similar to play in that it involves cognitive play with patterns of information. Boyd conceptualized art as a playground for the mind: "A work of art acts like a playground for the mind, a swing or a slide or a merry-go-round of visual or aural or social pattern" (p. 15).

According to Boyd (2009), art has two functions. First, art is a stimulus and training for a flexible mind, which is important for functioning in many areas. Second, art is a system for calling forth creativity, which is crucial for thinking beyond the present. Boyd proposed that art evolved from animal play. In Chapter 2 of this volume, many theories of the evolution of play were reviewed and the continuity of development of children's pretend play from earlier forms of play was evident. Building on these conceptualizations, Boyd included art in the process of evolution. One important concept of Boyd's is that narratives in memory do not need language, but need representations of events. It is here that pretend play can be so important to the child. Pretend play helps develop and process those representations.

Fein's (1987) theories of affect and play, reviewed in Chapter 2, are especially relevant to this discussion. Fein conceptualized that play activates an affective symbol system. This affective symbol system stores information about emotional events and is manipulated in pretend play. These symbolic units represent affective relationships such as fear of, love of, or anger at. These symbols can represent real or imagined events. Fein thought that this affective symbol system was a key part of pretend play and was especially important in creative thinking. As children learn to process and manipulate these affective symbols, they develop the tools for narrative expression if they chose to use them.

Access to primary-process thinking is important to the artist. As we have reviewed, pretend play is an arena in which primitive, affect-laden primary-process thinking can be expressed. Creative writers have often described getting in touch with the primary-process mode of thinking. It can feel as if the writer is not in control of the process. A recent interview with the playwright Harold Pinter by Lahr (2007) presented another example of this process of being in control but not being in control. For the play *The Homecoming,* he began with one sentence: "What have you done with the scissors?" (p. 67). Pinter went on to say,

> I didn't know who was saying it. I didn't know who he was talking to. Now, the fellow he was talking to—if he had said, "Oh, I've got them right here, Dad," there would have been no play. But instead he says, "Why don't you shut up, you daft prat?" Once that's said, there's a spring of drama, which develops and follows its own course. I had no idea what the course was going to be. I hadn't planned anything. In the back of my mind, I think I knew there was another brother going to come back. I think I saw them quite early in a big house, with the doors being taken down, leading to a stairway. I saw them moving in that space. (p. 67)

In this passage, Pinter described the process of letting the material come to him without a tight evaluative or logical component. He was comfortable enough with that process to let it happen.

Jorge Luis Borges, the Argentine writer, also described the feeling of not being in control (Russ, 1993). As Beard (1983) pointed out, Borges often used the passive tense in discussing his writing:

> Suddenly I feel something is about to happen. Then I sit back and get passive, and something is given to me. I received a beginning and an end.

When I have a subject, the subject tells me the style that he needs. When I write, I forget my own prejudices, my own opinions. The whole world comes to me. (pp. 7–8)

## Access to Memories

Theoretically, children who can express affect content in play and who can think about and express affect-laden cognition in pretend sword fights, cake baking, feeding activities, running from monsters, and so forth, should have more access in general to memories with affective content. Children use play to process emotion and the events that happen to them that have emotional content.

One of our studies (reviewed in Chapter 4) found that expression of affect in pretend play, especially negative affect, related to amount of affect expressed in memory descriptions (Russ & Schafer, 2006). These findings support the many theories previously reviewed that would predict this finding, such as psychoanalytic (Kris, 1952) and affective symbol system (Fein, 1987) theories. It is possible that children who can use play well can store more emotional memories to begin with and also have better access to these memories than children who cannot use play to deal with emotion.

Paley (1990) viewed play as a story in action form. She thought that play and storytelling were closely related. Nicolopoulou (2007) studied play and storytelling in preschool children and proposed that play and storytelling are "complementary expressions of children's symbolic imagination that draw from and reflect back on the interrelated domains of emotional, intellectual, and social life" (p. 249). She concluded that, in young preschool children, in pretend play, character representation is the dominant process, whereas in storytelling, plot is dominant. As children get older, after 5 years of age, they begin to integrate plot and character representation in their pretend play enactments.

In a recent study of children from 6 to 10 years old, we found a significant relationship between pretend play (imagination and positive affect) and creativity in stories (Hoffmann & Russ, 2012). Affect expression in play also related to affect expression in the stories. Findings from Russ and Schafer (2006) and Hoffmann and Russ (2012) support affect expression as a cross-situational ability (in play, memories, storytelling) that is also important in creativity.

What advantage would having a rich store of affect-laden memories and having easy access to these memories give to the aspiring writer? The poet Stanley Kunitz (2005) beautifully described the importance of emotion in writing poetry: "The poem has to be saturated with impulse, and that means getting down to the very tissue of experience. How can this element be absent from poetry without thinning out the poem?" (p. 103). Many writers struggle to get to this "tissue of experience," which involves experiencing deep emotions and remembering experiences that might be painful or conflicted. Early play experiences in which the child learns to express, master, and contain emotions would help the child gain an early start in living fully. Of course, in the creative writing process, this personal emotional material is transformed into artistic productions. There too, the play experience may provide early practice with transformation of events.

Ingmar Bergman used his childhood memories in his screenplays. In a 1983 interview with Kakutani, Bergman said

> I have maintained open channels with my childhood. I think it may be that way with many artists. Sometimes in the night, when I am on the limit between sleeping and being awake, I can just go through a door into my childhood and everything is as it was—with lights, smells, sounds and people. . . . I remember the silent street where my grandmother lived, the sudden aggressivity of the grown-up world, the terror of the unknown and the fear from the tension between my father and mother. (Rothstein, 2007, p. A20)

Many writers have also had early losses of a parent or significant person in their lives (Morrison & Morrison, 2006; Pollock, 1962). Ideally, the intense emotion involved in early loss would be integrated, perhaps through play. Morrison and Morrison (2006) discussed writers who had experienced the pain of early loss but who had not been able to integrate the experience for a variety of reasons. They hypothesized that these intense early memories, if repressed, can serve as a motivation for creative expression in writing. They presented case conceptualizations of Emily Bronte, J. M. Barrie, Isak Dineson, and Jack Kerouac as examples of writers who were constricted in some ways by their unresolved mourning but who used their unresolved grief and identity issues in their transformative creative work. Transforming memories is often a part of the creative narrative.

John Updike (2008) thought that memories of life events in childhood and adolescence were the most important for the writer:

> Memories, impressions, and emotions from your first 20 years on earth are most writers' main material: Little that comes afterward is quite so rich and resonant. By the age of 40, you have probably mined the purest veins of this precious lode. (p. 38).

The richness and pathos of the early years are important.

The writer Colm Toibin (2012) spoke of the essential role of memory in writing fiction:

> If I tried to write about a lighthouse and used one that I had never seen and did not know, it would show in the sentences. Nothing would work;

it would have no resonance for me, or for anyone else. If I made up a mother and put her in another town I had never seen, I wouldn't bother working at all. I would turn to drink, or just sit at home, or run for election. If I had to stick to the facts, the bare truth of things, that would be no use either. It would be thin and strange, as yesterday seems thin and strange, or indeed today. The story has a shape, and that comes first, and then the story and the shape needs substance and nourishment from the haunting past, clear memories or incidents suddenly remembered or invented, erased or enriched. (p. 5)

Boyd (2011) pointed out that the great writer Nabokov thought that "imagination is rooted in memory" (p. 51) and entitled his autobiography *Speak, Memory*. He also concluded that Nabokov stressed that the use of memory in writing was directed by conscious search. Proust, on the other hand, focused on involuntary memory in the search process.

## Proust—Memory and Associations

In *Remembrance of Things Past*, Proust exquisitely delved into the process of association and memory. He thought that memory was the link between external and internal reality (Hirschberg & Hirschberg, 2003). In his famous passage about the Madeleine, he described how bodily sensations and sensory experiences trigger a deep-seated memory. His mother had offered the character Marcel some tea and then set out the Madeleine cake.

And soon, mechanically, weary after a dull day with the prospect of a depressing morrow, I raised to my lips a spoonful of the tea in which I had soaked a morsel of the cake. No sooner had the warm liquid, and the crumbs with it, touched my palate than a shudder ran through my whole body, and I stopped, intent upon the extraordinary changes that were taking place. An exquisite pleasure had invaded my senses, but individual, detached, with no suggestion of its origin. And at once the vicissitudes of life had become indifferent to me, its disasters innocuous, its brevity illusory—this new sensation having had on me the effect which love has of filling me with a precious essence: or rather this essence was not in me, it was myself. I had ceased now to feel mediocre, accidental, mortal. Whence could it have come to me, this all-powerful joy? I was conscious that it was connected with the taste of tea and cake, but that it infinitely transcended those savours, could not, indeed, be of the same nature as theirs. Whence did it come? What did it signify? How could I seize upon and define it? (Hirschberg & Hirschberg, 2003, p. 543)

Marcel tried to retrace the triggering event to get more detail but failed. Then he allowed his mind to rest and be distracted, describing an incubation period. Then the memory rose up, and he remembered that the Madeleine cake was what his aunt gave him on Sunday mornings. The smell and taste of the tea and cake brought back the feeling of joy. Then, when he remembered his aunt, it all came back.

> Immediately the old grey house upon the street where her room was, rose up like the scenery of a theater to attach itself to the little pavilion, opening onto the garden, which had been built out behind it for my parents (the isolated panel which until that moment had been all that I could see): and with the house the town, from morning to night and in all weathers, the Square where I was sent before luncheon, the streets along which I used to run errands, the country roads we took when it was fine. And just as the Japanese amuse themselves by filling a porcelain bowl with water and steeping in it little crumbs of paper which until then are without character or form, but, the moment they become wet, stretch themselves and bend, take on colour and distinctive shape, become flowers or houses or people, permanent and recognizable, so in that moment all the flowers in our garden and in M. Swann's park, and the water-lilies on the Vivonne and the good folk of the village and their little dwellings and the parish church and the whole village of Combray and its surroundings, taking their proper shapes and growing solid, sprang into being, town and gardens alike, from my cup of tea. (p. 545)

In this last passage, Proust used a beautiful metaphor to describe a recalled memory. The metaphor of dried paper shapes bursting into life of forms and shapes is an apt reflection of memories that come to life. The ability to invent creative metaphors such as this one requires the ability to recombine images and ideas into a new form. The affect that stirs the associations for Marcel is that of joy. A deep joy that he does not know the meaning of. Proust spent the rest of the book trying to identify the meaning of the memory.

### Bob Dylan—Poet and Musician

Bob Dylan is a creative poet, songwriter, and musician. He is recognized for the excellent poetry in his lyrics as well as for the music in his compositions. In the documentary, *No Direction Home*, directed by Martin Scorsese (2005), Dylan reflected on his early years and influences on his development. His passion for music began early. When he was 10, he got a guitar and also listened to records. He described how a particular record moved him and made him feel "like I was somebody else." Listening to the radio from places far away also stimulated him. He conveyed that there was a truth to the music that moved him. Later, as a teenager, when he listened to Woody Guthrie, he thought that one could "listen to his songs and learn how to live." Dylan was open to the deep emotions stirred by the words and the music and was motivated by it.

Dylan also described the carnivals that would come to the small town in which he lived in Minnesota. He was struck by the fact that the same person could do different things and have multiple roles. He could be a barker and then run the rides or be a clown. Later, as a teenager, Dylan took on multiple roles. He tried on different personas. He would pretend to be Bobby Vee, a popular singer of the time, and tell people he was Bobby Vee. He took on the characteristics of Woody Guthrie for quite a while, as he imitated his style. There seemed to be a quality of role-playing to what he was doing that had similarities to the role-playing that children do in thematic pretend play. This play-acting helped him to incorporate qualities of different musicians of the time.

This documentary beautifully portrays Dylan's brief period in Greenwich Village when he seemed to absorb everything and learn from everyone. When he returned to Minnesota, his creative production moved to a different level. That creative development was noticed by others as well as by himself. There seemed to be a kind of crystallization of his creative ability. The elements came together in a new way. He wrote a song for Woody Guthrie and discussed his need to write that song. He had imitated and then assimilated Guthrie. He stated that it was like he "went through Woody Guthrie." He did not want to, but it happened. He integrated elements from Guthrie's music and then went on to build on them in his own original work. And he wrote him a song.

What is also evident is the fluidity of Dylan's thinking and the broad associations he could generate. He said that he wrote quickly during those early years. Joan Baez remembered that he wrote one song overnight. He had been badly treated while checking into a hotel, so he stayed up and wrote a song. Baez speculated that his anger fueled the writing process. She also said that he did not always know what the words meant to a particular song. The poetry came fast to him and could be interpreted in multiple ways. Dylan also was motivated by the social injustices he saw around him. He wanted to make a difference, as Woody Guthrie had. He wrote about what he saw and, as he said, used all the elements within him to write about what was happening. And people responded to the truth of the music.

The documentary *No Direction Home* offers an excellent portrayal of the evolution of a creative artist. It captures the complexity of the process and the many variables that are involved. The seeds of musical talent were present, but music was especially important to Dylan's development in rural Minnesota. He had good divergent thinking ability but also read poetry and learned. He went to Greenwich Village, where he could learn from other musicians. He was able to deeply "take-in" and identify with others, like Woody Guthrie. He took risks. He found himself in a period of social unrest in which music became important to society. The time was right, and the audience liked his music and responded. A multitude of factors are involved in the development of the creative adult who makes major contributions. Early experiences such as play are important and perhaps necessary, but certainly not sufficient, for the emergence of creativity in the adult.

## VISUAL ARTS

From prehistoric times, visual arts have served a purpose for mankind. If only we could observe the play of children living in those ancient times and watch how they learned to engage in the arts, we might deduce what purposes those arts served. The earliest sculpture of a person, the *Venus of Hohle Fels*, is 40,000 years old and was found in a cave in Germany in 2008 (Curry, 2012). It is a figure of a woman but is more than just an imitation of a model. The breasts are huge, as is the genitalia. The figure involves imagination—and emotion. Conard, the archeologist who led the discovery team, thought that the art represents a larger meaning: "They're talking about something other than their daily lives" (Curry, 2012, p. 28). Artistic representation requires symbolic thinking, mental flexibility, and as Boyd (2009) conceptualized, cognitive play with pattern. Emotional expression and the representation of emotion is also important for many artistic productions. Two artists whose work illustrates these processes are Frida Kahlo and Alexander Calder.

### Frida Kahlo—Emotional Artist

Frida Kahlo was a Mexican artist in the early part of the 20th century whose paintings are increasingly appreciated. Kahlo had polio as a child and was confined to her room for an extended period. During this time, when she was 6 years old, she created an imaginary friend, who lived in the interior of the earth. Herrera (1983), in her biography of Kahlo, quoted from Kahlo's diary about this imaginary friend. Kahlo described how this creation was the origin of the double self-portrait called *The Two Fridas*:

> I must have been 6 years old when I experienced intensely an imaginary friendship with a little girl more or less the same age as me. On the glass window of what at that time was my room, and which gave onto Allende Street, I breathed vapor onto one of the first panes. I let out a breath and with a finger I drew a "door." Full of great joy and urgency, I went out in my imagination, through this "door." I crossed the whole plain that I saw in front of me until I arrived at the dairy called "Pinzon". . . . I entered the "0" of Pinzon and I went down in great haste into the interior of the earth, where "my imaginary friend" was always waiting for me. (pp. 14–15)

She described the great joy and happiness she experienced with this imaginary friend and the pleasure of using her imagination to enter this world and convey her "secret problems." Her imaginary friend knew everything about Frida. In this world, she was able to think her deepest thoughts and know her problems. Taylor (1999) studied the relationship between imaginary friends and creativity. Many creative adults had imaginary friends in childhood. For Frida Kahlo, this "magic friendship," as she called it, stayed with her throughout her life: "Thirty-four years have passed since I experienced this magic friendship, and every time that I remember it, it revives and becomes larger inside of my world" (p. 15).

As an artist, Frida Kahlo painted her emotions, conflicts, and life tragedies. She painted her miscarriage, divorce, physical pain, and thoughts of death. After a horrific bus accident when she was 18, she underwent many surgeries and experienced pain for the rest of her life (Donahue, 2011). After the accident, she began her serious artistic development as a painter. Her paintings are often described as surrealistic, with much use of symbolism and metaphor (Donahue, 2011). They are filled with intense primary-process content of a sexual and aggressive nature. She could easily access primary-process content and express that material in a creative way. One can speculate that she used painting to process emotions and resolve conflicts: "Thus, the accident changed my path, many things prevented me from fulfilling the desires which everyone considers normal, and to me nothing seemed more normal than to paint what had not been fulfilled" (Herrera, 1983, p. 75). Donahue (2011) described her as painting her inner reality: "She used art to reveal her internal experience and to heal and find meaning in her life" (p. 23). Kahlo certainly used her imagination as a child to express and work with problems in her life. She was able to continue using her imagination to transform her personal conflicts and distress into creative products with universal meaning.

## Alexander Calder—Playful Sculptor

Alexander Calder was one of the great sculptors of our time and was especially well-known for his abstract mobiles. The evolution of his work can be traced back to his childhood, when he made moving toys. As a child, Calder had a studio in the basement of his house. When he was 8 or 9, he made metal toys such as dogs or ducks. He built a castle with a drawbridge that he and his sister played in. He also made an animal zoo puzzle of metal and wood (J. Simon, 2008). His parents supported his early interests in art and also gave him the space and freedom he needed to develop. Later, he received a degree in engineering which gave him skills to integrate into his later moving mobiles.

As a mature artist, an intermediate step in the development of his mobiles was the creation of his miniature circus when he was in his 20s in Paris. He had continued to make wire toys and began to accumulate them.

He developed the circus "just for the fun of it" (J. Simon, 2008, p. 26). The circus eventually consisted of 268 objects. It has been preserved and was exhibited at the Whitney Museum in 2008 along with some film of Calder's actual performance. What is striking about the circus is that it was actually an adult puppet play. Calder voiced the ringmaster and was a puppeteer for the rest of the figures. He manipulated the movable figures and told the story. It was a circus for adults, not for children, and he entertained his friends with these performances.

The miniature circus consisted of moving animals made of wire, cloth, and metal; trapeze artists flying through the air; and lion tamers working with lions. The performances included a great deal of humor as well as emotional content, both sexual and aggressive. For example, the acrobat's penis would wiggle during the act, Fanni the belly dancer would swivel her hips, and the lion would be shot. A clown would blow up a balloon that would knock over the bearded lady. The action was unpredictable and would change from performance to performance. Calder developed different personalities for the figures. The impression one has in viewing what remains of this circus is that it was a joyful process to perform and to observe the action. Noguchi, who was present for the performances, wrote of the circus as a humorous but sad experience: The "combination of sadness and humor pervaded each performance" (Nagy, 2008, p. 204). Calder's invention of the circus, which he performed and focused on over a 5-year period, was really a playground for his mind. He began developing wire portraits of people. Later, his work evolved into moving abstractions, which were his mobiles. The mechanics of these mobiles had been developed partly through the intricacies of the miniature circus.


CONCLUSION

The artists discussed in this chapter illustrate the importance of access to emotional memories and images in their work. Be it in the form of storytelling or visual representation, affect is in the content of the artistic product. Early make-believe play was important to many of these artists, and they remember it as being important. For many, a search for associations and memories, either consciously or in an unconscious fashion, is a part of the artistic creative process.

# 7

# FACILITATING PRETEND PLAY AND CREATIVITY IN TRAINING PROGRAMS

Given all the evidence from research, case studies, and clinical observation that pretend play is associated with many forms of creativity and can facilitate creativity, what can we do to help children develop pretend play skills (i.e., to foster the processes that are important to creativity)? What do we know about developing pretend play processes in children? Are fantasy and emotional expression in play the results of careful nurturing over time, or can these processes be facilitated in briefer play interventions? These are key questions in child development, and the policy implications of the answers are important. Should we develop programs in schools to develop imaginative play ability, focus on creativity directly, or focus on general parenting practices that nurture play and creativity? Should we do all of these things? What does the research say about facilitating pretend play skills and using play to foster creativity?

This chapter first reviews the play-training studies in the area and then describes the research on play interventions emerging from my lab at Case

http://dx.doi.org/10.1037/14282-008
*Pretend Play in Childhood: Foundation of Adult Creativity*, by S. W. Russ

Western Reserve University. A pilot study with elementary school children is described in detail, then other recent play intervention studies from my research program are reviewed. Transcripts of play intervention sessions are presented for illustration purposes. After that, suggestions for future research on play interventions and creativity are presented. Finally, practical suggestions for improving play abilities are offered.

## IMPROVING PLAY ABILITY AND CREATIVITY

One way to foster creativity in children is through facilitation of pretend play ability. Because so many processes important in creativity occur in pretend play, play is an ideal venue in which to facilitate these processes. This is a challenging research area because one must demonstrate that a specific intervention improves play skills and also that this change accounts for improvement in creative performance on a different task. There have been previous efforts to improve children's play skills. Many of these play-training studies have been in an academic context. Much of the following review is based on our earlier reviews (Russ & Fehr, 2013; Russ, Fehr, & Hoffmann, 2013).

Smilansky's (1968) study was one of the first to demonstrate that teachers could teach play skills. She worked with kindergarten children from low socioeconomic status (SES) backgrounds in Israel for 90 minutes a day, 5 days a week, for 9 weeks. The children who engaged in sociodramatic play, with help from their teachers, showed significant cognitive improvement when compared with other groups. Their play skills were significantly improved. The teachers helped the children develop their play by commenting, making suggestions, and giving demonstrations. Hartmann and Rollett (1994) reported positive results with elementary school children in Austria, where teachers instructed low-SES children in play 4 hours per week. When compared with a comparable control class, the play intervention group had better divergent thinking and was happier in school.

In another study, Rosen (1974) found that, in addition to improving play skills, problem-solving skills also improved following 40 classroom-wide, hour-long play skills intervention sessions for African American children enrolled in two kindergarten and two day care classrooms primarily for children from disadvantaged backgrounds. Play training has also been found to be effective in populations with intellectual disabilities (Hellendoorn, 1994; Y. T. Kim, Lombardino, Rothman, & Vinson, 1989).

One of the methodological problems with many studies in the play facilitation area is the lack of adequate control groups. Smith (1988, 1994) has consistently raised this issue in reviewing the play intervention literature. Smith stressed that adequate research design requires the inclusion of a control group that involves experimenter–child interaction of a form other than pretend play. He concluded that when this kind of control group is included, usually both the play group and the control group improve. Dansky (1999) reached a different conclusion after reviewing the play-training literature. He concluded that many studies did have adequate control groups that controlled for involvement of the experimenter (Dansky, 1980; Shmukler & Naveh, 1984–1985; Udwin, 1983); there were consistently positive results in studies with adequate control groups that demonstrated that play tutoring, over a period of time, resulted in increased imaginativeness in play and increased creativity on measures.

In a recent review of the play literature, Lillard et al. (2012) raised a number of methodological issues that have challenged the conclusion that play facilitates creativity. They raised many of the methodological issues that were discussed by Smith (1988, 1994). They reached a different conclusion than Dansky (1999). They concluded that there is no evidence that play-training interventions facilitate creative thinking, but there is evidence that play training facilitates narrative expression. They did not consider narrative tasks to be in the creativity realm, but narratives and storytelling are one type of creativity.

Shmukler and Naveh (1984–1985) investigated the effect of the type of stories used in the play sessions by examining the play skills of 116 preschool-age children assigned to one of four groups: a play intervention where stories were unstructured (children were only given a general theme), a play intervention where stories were structured (children played out familiar fairy tales), an attention control (children played active games or structured activities with an adult, such as completing puzzles or art projects), or a no-contact control (children only met with researchers for baseline and outcome assessments). The results of this study indicated that the type of stories played out in the intervention was not important; children in either of the play intervention groups displayed significantly higher imagination, affect expression, and focus during the play after 12 sessions than children in either of the control groups.

Several studies targeted imagination in play and found that positive affect, focus during play, and cooperation with peers during social play improved for children involved in the group intervention play sessions. Imagination was also improved in comparison with those in active control groups who played with puzzles and building toys (Freyberg, 1973; Udwin, 1983). These two studies are also of note in that they were relatively brief. Although Smilansky (1968) required children in the sociodramatic groups to receive play intervention for 90 minutes each day for 5 days a week over 9 weeks, Freyberg's (1973) intervention involved only eight 20-minute sessions and, similarly, Udwin's (1983) intervention included ten 30-minute sessions over a 5-week period.

Barton and Wolery (2008) and Lang et al. (2009) reviewed the literature of play interventions for children diagnosed with developmental disabilities or autism and likewise found that targeted play interventions were effective at improving play skills. However, the play intervention approaches for children diagnosed with developmental disabilities, autism spectrum disorders, or cognitive deficits are typically much more time-intensive than the interventions for typically developing children (e.g., Kasari, Freeman, & Paparella, 2006; Nevile & Bachor, 2002; Stahmer, 1995; Thomas & Smith, 2004; Thorp, Stahmer, & Schreibman, 1995).

Kasari et al. (2006), in a randomized controlled study with young children (3–4 years of age) with autism, found that a play intervention resulted in increased symbolic play. This was a rigorous study that began the intervention at the child's current developmental level. The training involved modeling and prompting. Children received 30 hours of intervention weekly for 6 weeks on a daily basis. This was a rather intensive intervention. Children in the play group, compared with children in joint attention and control groups, had increased symbolic play that generalized to play with mothers. In a 5-year follow-up study, both the play group and joint attention group had better spoken language (Kasari, Gulsrud, Freeman, Paparella, & Hellemann, 2012).

The results of the studies examining play interventions are encouraging because they provide evidence that even brief play interventions led by adults can be effective at improving pretend play and theoretically related skills. Dansky (1999) pointed out that brief play interventions can have long-term implications for a child's development and play skills because children enjoy playing and are likely to incorporate improvements into their own play, which provides further opportunities to enhance their skills.

We concluded that studies have not examined the specific adult behaviors that are most effective in developing play skills (Russ et al., 2013). Two reviews of the literature have identified the elements most commonly used in play interventions for children with developmental disabilities (Lang et al., 2009; Trawick-Smith, 1998). Both reviews emphasized adults engaging in the child's play, following the child's lead, and using techniques such as asking questions, prompting, modeling, reinforcing, or giving suggestions to enrich the play. In addition, Trawick-Smith (1998) added the importance of adults withdrawing from the child's play over time and encouraging the child to continue playing without their direction. Nielsen and Christie (2008), in a study with typically developing children, found that imitated and novel pretend play increased following approximately 5 minutes of adult modeling in a dollhouse for children 2 and 3 years of age.

One of the problems in the field is that there is no play manual available for teachers and parents to use to facilitate play with children. We are attempting to develop an empirically based play intervention manual. What follows is a review of the play intervention studies that have been carried out at Case Western Reserve University in my play research program.

## DEVELOPMENT OF A BRIEF PLAY INTERVENTION FOR SCHOOL-AGE CHILDREN

### Pilot Study

In a pilot study, we developed a play intervention that attempted to facilitate specific cognitive and affective processes in pretend play (Russ, Moore, & Farber, 2004). We investigated whether cognitive and affective processes could be differentially affected by different types of play intervention techniques. The pilot study included a control group in which time and interaction with an interested adult were controlled. This study also developed a play intervention protocol that could be replicated in other studies and used as a manual in play intervention programs. In developing the play intervention, we followed guidelines from previous studies, described next.

In this pilot study, specific play intervention techniques were clearly spelled out and were based on common techniques used by play therapists. I previously outlined a number of techniques used by play therapists, such as labeling and reflection of feelings, empathy, and articulation of cause and effect (i.e., she is feeling sad because she lost her toy; Russ, 1998b). These techniques were the foundation of the intervention. Previous play interventions have used such techniques as modeling (Knell, 1993; J. L. Singer & Singer, 1999), positive reinforcement (Bodiford-McNeil, Hembree-Kigin, & Eyberg, 1996; Knell, 1993), reflection, and imitation (Bodiford-McNeil et al., 1996). This study used these methods as well, through the use of standardized prompts.

The pilot study investigated the effectiveness of two different play interventions on processes in play in comparison with a control group in a school-based population. One play intervention script focused on improving imagination and organization of the narrative. The other play intervention script focused on increasing affective expression in play. In addition, outcome measures of creativity, coping, life satisfaction, and classroom behavior were administered to explore the association of play with adaptive functioning. It was hypothesized that both play interventions would result in improvements in pretend play when compared with the control group. Of particular interest was whether affect expression techniques would be effective at improving affect expression in play and whether imagination expression techniques would be effective at improving imagination in play. In addition, it was expected that both play intervention groups would have higher scores on the outcome measures of adaptive functioning than the control group (see Table 7.1 for a description of the toys, stories, and prompts).

The study included 50 children, ranging from 6 to 8 years of age, who were in the first and second grades at an urban Midwestern elementary school. The children were all in mainstream classrooms. The ethnic minority composition of the school was 99% African American. The school reported that 92% of the families were at or below poverty level.

Children received a baseline measure of affect and fantasy expressed in play, the Affect in Play Scale (APS; Russ, 2004). The administrator of the APS was not involved in the intervention for that child.

Children were randomly assigned to one of three groups: imagination play intervention, affect play intervention, or control. There were 19 children in the imagination group, 17 children in the affect group, and 14 children in the control group. Each child participated in five 30-minute individual sessions that usually occurred over a period of 3 to 5 weeks. Specific instructions and stories were used for each group, and the toys, storylines, and prompts were standardized. In all cases the same play trainer carried out all five sessions with the child. There were four play trainers in the study. The trainers

TABLE 7.1
Play-Training Protocol

|  | Imagination group | Affect group | Control group |
|---|---|---|---|
| Activity | • Make up stories with beginning, middle, and end<br>• Use imagination | • Make up stories with feelings | • Puzzles<br>• Coloring sheets |
| Toys | • Dolls<br>• Animals<br>• Cars<br>• Clothes<br>• Lego | • Dolls<br>• Animals<br>• Cars<br>• Clothes<br>• Lego | • Puzzles<br>• Coloring sheets<br>• Crayons |
| Stories | • Boy getting ready for school<br>• Girl living in city underwater | • Sad—boy lost favorite toy<br>• Scared—girl goes to doctor<br>• Happy—girl goes to party | N/A |
| Prompts | • Reinforcement<br><br>• Modeling of pretend<br>• Different endings<br>• Summarizing | • Reinforcement for expressing feelings<br>• Modeling expression of feelings<br>• Labeling feelings<br>• Giving permission | • Praise<br><br>• Modeling<br><br>• Labeling of activity<br>• Examiner controlling amount of interaction<br>• Doing activity with child |

instructed each child to play out approximately four stories per session, and the children were instructed to make up their own story one time each session. The trainers attempted to limit discussion that did not follow the standardized prompts during the sessions. All trainers filled out session checklists at the end of each session indicating stories used, prompts used, and the child's reactions to the stories and prompts. Within 3 weeks of completing the intervention, outcome measures were given to assess a variety of cognitive and affective outcomes. Measures were given by a different investigator than the one who conducted the five sessions with the participant and who was blind to group assignment. First, the child again received the APS. In addition, each child received, in the following order, measures of divergent thinking, self-report coping, and life satisfaction.

## Intervention Groups

*Imagination Group.* Children in the imagination group were presented with a set of toys, including human-like dolls, blocks, plastic animals, Lego, and cars. They were asked to play out stories with high fantasy content (e.g., someone who lives on the moon) and high story organization (e.g., what someone needs to do to get ready for school). Children were encouraged to explore alternate endings for their stories, and they were reinforced for being creative and engaging in object transformations. During the 30-minute sessions, the trainer used standardized prompts to encourage the children to have stories with a beginning, middle, and end; they also encouraged the children to show details, to have the characters talk, to pretend something was there (e.g., using a Lego block as a milk bottle), to make up different endings, and to ask what happens next. The trainer used reinforcement, modeling, and praise.

*Affect Group.* Children in the affect group played with the same toys as the children in the imagination group. The instructions, stories, and prompts were different from the imagination play group. Instead of focusing on fantasy and organization, children were encouraged to express feelings and were asked to play out stories with affective content. For example, a child might have played out a story about someone who was happy because she was going to a birthday party or sad because he had lost his favorite toy. The trainers used modeling, reinforcement, and reflection of feeling states to encourage affective experimentation. Trainers used standardized prompts to encourage children to reflect and label feelings, ask how the dolls were feeling, have the dolls talk to each other about how they were feeling, state a reason for them feeling this way, and ask what happens next.

*Control Group.* Children in the control group spent their sessions putting together puzzles and coloring on coloring sheets. The puzzles and coloring sheets depicted neutral scenes, such as farms and flowers and butterflies.

Experimenter interaction was controlled for by using standardized prompts and encouragement unrelated to affect or imagination. Toy choice (i.e., being able to pick what toys to use, as in the intervention groups) was controlled for by allowing children to choose whether they wanted to start by doing a puzzle or by coloring. Children had the option of changing activities at their discretion. The prompts were asking what was in the picture, asking children to identify a puzzle piece, asking them to identify a color, and asking how many pieces were there. Examiners were also active in praising children for their effort and helping them with the puzzles.

Fidelity was difficult to establish in this particular sample because of limitations set forth by the school. Researchers were able to videotape the baseline and outcome play measures but not the five intervention sessions. However, the stories and prompts were standardized, and a session checklist was developed to monitor the stories and prompts used in each session. The affect play group had a different set of instructions and prompts used by the trainer than the imagination play group. Also, a totally different set of stories was used for the affect play group than for the imagination play group. Each trainer followed a script for the particular intervention group. An evaluation of the checklists for the intervention groups revealed that 86% of the time the prompt guideline was followed, and 89% of the time the story or feeling guideline was followed. No significant differences were found on the number of prompts given by the play trainers across the groups. As an additional exploration of intervention fidelity, mean differences between play trainers on the APS were investigated and no significant differences were found on children's play scores.

### Results

The major result of this study was that the play interventions were effective in improving play skills. The affect play condition was most effective in that, after baseline play was controlled for, the affect play group had significantly higher play scores on all play processes. These children had more affect in their play (both positive affect and negative affect), a greater variety of affect content, and better imagination and organization of the story than did the control group. The imagination play group also had significantly more positive affect and variety of affect than the control group. Although most of these individual group comparisons were no longer significant when the Bonferroni correction was applied, the effect sizes were medium or, for frequency of affect, large. Another major finding was that on the outcome measure of divergent thinking, there were significant effects for group. Although the individual contrast comparisons did not reach significance, inspection of the profile plots indicated that the play groups (usually the affect play group) had higher scores on the divergent thinking test. However, one limitation of this study was that no baseline measure of divergent thinking was obtained.

The affect play intervention was the most effective intervention in improving pretend play. By having children play out stories involving emotion, both positive and negative, we were able to improve play skills as measured by the APS. It is worth noting that the APS play measure was quite different from the play intervention situation in that there were only a few props (two puppets and a few blocks), whereas the intervention used a variety of toys. Also, the instructions for the APS are unstructured ("play any way you like"), whereas the play intervention was quite structured and the child was directed to make up stories with specific themes. Thus, the finding that play changed on the unstructured outcome play measure suggests that the effect of the play intervention would generalize to a natural play situation. Future research should investigate this issue.

The finding that the affect play group increased both affective expression in play and cognitive abilities of imagination and organization of the story suggests that involvement of affect also influences processes of imagination and fantasy. To express emotion, children called on storytelling and imagination. Developing a narrative around the emotion may be a powerful process for children. The imagination play group was significantly better than the control in frequency of positive affect and variety of affect. Similar results were found by previous researchers attempting to improve only imagination in play (Freyberg, 1973; Udwin, 1983). That the imagination play group improved positive affect and had a wider range of affect expression suggests that using one's imagination involves positive affect. This finding is consistent with results from the creativity research in which positive affect facilitates creativity and imagination (Isen, Daubman, & Nowicki, 1987). Another possible explanation for the overall greater improvement in the affect play group is that the instructions and prompts we used with this group were better at facilitating affect in play than the instructions and prompts in the imagination group were in facilitating fantasy and imagination. Perhaps if we had used other techniques or stories, they would have been more effective. Future research should explore this possibility.

The finding that both play groups increased their positive affect in play is important. Pretend play is fun for most children and may stimulate positive affect themes such as stories about having fun, being happy, and caring about others. This result could have implications for mood regulation in children.

In a follow-up study of these children 4 to 8 months later, the imagination group had improved play skills over time (Moore & Russ, 2008). The affect group did not maintain the play changes over this period. It may be that an increase in affect expression from a play intervention is temporary, whereas an increase in imagination and pretend in play could be longer lasting. In the follow-up study, there no longer was a significant group effect for divergent thinking. In fact, this time the control group had higher scores. Perhaps booster sessions would have been useful in maintaining the initial group effects.

## Refined Play Protocol Intervention Study

Given the promising results from this pilot study, a second pretend play intervention study for elementary school children was designed (Russ, Dillon, Fiorelli, & Burck, 2010). This study aimed to replicate the successful findings from the original intervention and incorporated several important modifications to the protocol. First, because both the affect play group and the imagination play group from the pilot study had yielded positive results, the two play intervention groups were combined into one play intervention group targeting both imagination and affect expression. Second, the number of sessions was reduced from five to four, making the intervention briefer.

This play intervention study took place at a private school for girls and enlisted 57 participants between the ages of 5 and 10 in kindergarten through fourth grade. Participants met individually with a researcher for four sessions, each 25 to 30 minutes long, in which the children practiced making up stories and acting them out with toys. Children enrolled in the control group also met with examiners for an equal number of sessions but completed puzzles and coloring sheets. This control group was designed to control for one-on-one time with a researcher but without the fantasy and emotional content included in the intervention sessions.

From the previous intervention study, a play intervention manual was developed so that all researchers administered the play intervention in a standardized way. The assortment of toys available for the children to play with always included human figurines, both predator and prey animals, blocks for building, vehicles (toy cars, snowboards, skateboards, jet skis), and props for the figurines (hats, shoes, books, instruments). During each play intervention session, researchers aimed to have the child create four to five stories, each approximately 5 minutes long. The manual provides story stems that elicit both emotional and fantastical content. For example, children are asked to tell "a story about a girl who lives in a city underwater" or "a sad story about a girl who loses her favorite toy." Over the course of the four sessions, story stems elicited more complex imaginative content. For example, a story stem from Session 1 might be "a girl who goes to school," whereas Session 4 might include "a girl who has superpowers." Thus, as children progress across sessions they are asked to expand their abilities to incorporate fantasy and emotional content into their stories.

The manual also outlines the types of intervention strategies to be used by the researchers facilitating the play sessions. Children are given praise and positive reinforcement for their use of creative ideas, including plot twists, adding characters, and transformation of objects. In addition, children are praised for expressing a variety of emotions and the ways in which they express these emotions through the dolls. Modeling is also used to help teach children ways of showing emotions or acting out ideas through the characters. Prompting and questioning are used to encourage children to think about what could happen next in their story or to think of alternate endings. Labeling of feelings and summarizing of events are used to emphasize the organization of the story and the cause-and-effect sequences that took place. Most children show clear strengths and weaknesses regarding their organization, imagination, comfort engaging in play, and ability to incorporate affect-laden themes. As the four intervention sessions progress, the researchers keep notes and can target sessions to meet the individual needs of each child.

In this second play intervention study, children's pretend play skills pre- and postintervention were assessed using the APS to determine whether the intervention had successfully improved children's pretend play abilities. In this particular high-SES sample, a majority of the children had already displayed good pretend play skills before the intervention, making it difficult to show an effect. However, when only the children who had shown poor pretend play skills at baseline (those children who had obtained the lowest scores before the intervention) were examined, significant results were found for improvement in both the organization and imagination of their play at outcome. We concluded from this study that the play intervention was promising for this group with play deficits. The intervention needs refinement and testing with other child populations.

The results of these two studies suggest that play interventions using this play protocol can successfully improve children's pretend play skills. In addition, the findings support the feasibility of short-term, school-based play interventions for improving children's fantasy play. The next step is to refine this intervention by identifying the kinds of prompts and guidance that result in an increase in creative processes in play. Hoffmann and Russ are analyzing the play sessions to identify effective prompting techniques by the play facilitator. This study is currently underway.

What follows are examples of several play intervention sessions with prompts by the researcher identified. Other examples of play sessions are in Appendix B. This purpose of this presentation is to give examples of the types of adult–child interactions in the play facilitation sessions. These are 20-minute sessions. For some of the adult prompts, labels are given to indicate the prompt category (modeling, labeling, praising, summarizing, asking for different ending). We also coded the child's responses for affect and imagination, though only the adult prompt coding is shown here. All the children in these transcripts are girls.

*Child #1 Session 2*

> Adult: OK, is your chair close enough? OK, so just like last time I have some toys for you to play with and we'll make up stories about different things by acting them out with the toys, OK? And let's tell a story with a beginning, a middle, and an end about a little girl who is getting ready for bed. OK? So it's almost bedtime. [INSTRUCTIONS]

> Child: This one. [*Picks up a toy, looks at toys on table smiling.*]

> Adult: Want me to move your chair in closer? [REDIRECTION]

> Child: No.

> Adult: No, you're good. [REDIRECTION]

> Child: [*Looking at toys.*]

> Adult: OK, so how should our story start? [ORGANIZATION PROMPT]

> Child: I don't know what her bed's going to be. [*Adult watching.*] This is her bed. [*Indicates blue block.*]

> Adult: You picked out her bed? [REFLECTION]

> Child: Mm-hmm.

> Adult: Well, what are some things she could do before she goes to bed? [ORGANIZATION PROMPT]

> Child: [*Looks at toys.*] [NONPLAY]

> Adult: Maybe our story could start with her coming home from school on the bus. Want to start that way? [MODELING ORGANIZATION]

> Child: Mm-hmm. [*Puts doll on bus.*] [NONPLAY]

> Adult: Is this going to be the girl in our story? [ORGANIZATION PROMPT]

> Child: This is her. [*Picks up different toy, then another one, bending them, puts hat on two. Adult watching.*] This is the mom.

> Adult: That's the mom. [REFLECTION]

> Child: And this is the little girl, and this is the little sister.

> Adult: OK, so they're coming home from school? Is that what's happening? [ORGANIZATION PROMPT]

| | |
|---|---|
| *Child:* | [*Putting toys in bus.*] |
| *Adult:* | So she's in the car and they're driving home. [SUMMARIZING] |
| *Child:* | [*Continues trying to get dolls all to fit in the bus.*] |
| *Adult:* | What could happen next in the story? [ORGANIZATION PROMPT] |
| *Child:* | [*Takes them all out of the bus.*] |
| *Adult:* | So they get home. [SUMMARIZING] |
| *Child:* | The mom. [*Plays with bendy toy. Adult watching.*] The dad is wearing this hat. |
| *Adult:* | Mm-hmm. [NEUTRAL RESPONSE] |
| *Child:* | [*Continues putting hat on doll.*] |
| *Adult:* | Who is the mom? [IMAGINATION PROMPT] |
| *Child:* | This is the mom. |
| *Adult:* | OK, so maybe the mom says, "OK, why don't you kids play while I cook dinner?" [MODELING ANIMATION + POSITIVE AFFECT] |
| *Child:* | Why don't you kids play while I cook dinner? |
| *Adult:* | You want to be the mom, or I could be the mom? [REDIRECTION] |
| *Child:* | I'll be the mom. |
| *Adult:* | OK, so here maybe she could cook at the table. [MODELING IMAGINATION + POSITIVE AFFECT] |
| *Child:* | This is here and here. [*Puts doll on top of blocks.*] |
| *Adult:* | Mm-hmm. We could just pretend she's sitting. [REDIRECTION] |
| *Child:* | The dad is playing with the car. |
| *Adult:* | OK. [NEUTRAL RESPONSE] |
| *Child:* | He's try to . . . uh-oh, I lost my toy car! I'm going to play the guitar. [*Adult watching.*] I feel like I want to read a book. |
| *Adult:* | So they are all doing different activities. Maybe the mom says it's time for dinner! [MODELING ANIMATION + POSITIVE AFFECT] |
| *Child:* | [*The next section occurred over time with the trainer observing the play.*] It's time for dinner! OK, Mom. Look at this book, Momma. It's a book, it's one of the oldest books in the whole wide world. Oh! I didn't know that. Mom, is it really time for |

dinner? [ANIMATION + POSITIVE AFFECT] Yes, darling. I am going to sit on the floor. [INSUBSTANTIAL SITUA- TION] Silly! You silly! That's the end.

Adult:  That's the end? [REFLECTION]

Child:  [Nods.]

Adult:  Well, we are going to make a story about her getting ready for bed, so she eats dinner and then what? [ORGANIZATION PROMPT]

Child:  She eats dinner and then she goes to bed.

Adult:  Then she goes to bed? [REFLECTION]

Child:  [The next section occurred over time with the trainer observing the play.] Time for bed! Goodnight. I'm going to sleep on the table. The end.

Adult:  The end? OK, good story. You started with them coming home from school and they all found different activities to do while the mom cooked dinner, and then they ate dinner and went to bed. Good story. [SUMMARY/PRAISE] So now let's use the toys to tell a story about feelings, so let's make sure people talk out loud so I can hear them so I know how they're feel- ing. Let's tell a story about a girl who hears a very scary noise. [INSTRUCTIONS]

Child:  I don't know what noise it could be.

Adult:  Well, you can think about it, or we can start telling our story and see what noise comes up. Which do you want to do? [REDIRECTION]

Child:  Hmm, think about it.

Adult:  You want to think about it for a minute? [REFLECTION]

Child:  I know. The window creaks!

Adult:  OK, that's a great idea. [ORGANIZATION REINFORCEMENT]

Child:  [Smiles.]

Adult:  So, maybe we should start by the little girl being in bed sleeping. [MODELING ORGANIZATION]

Child:  This is the big sister.

Adult:  OK. [NEUTRAL RESPONSE]

Child:  And this is her bed. [Adult watching.] And this is the mom and this is the dad.

Adult:  Mm-hmm. [NEUTRAL RESPONSE]

| | |
|---|---|
| *Child:* | [*Laughs.*] |
| *Adult:* | Do you want me to move your chair closer? [REDIRECTION] |
| *Child:* | Got to get the guitar! |
| *Adult:* | OK, so what should happen first in the story? The little girl is sleeping. [ORGANIZATION PROMPT] |
| *Child:* | Um, the little girl is sleeping. |
| *Adult:* | How's that? [REDIRECTION] |
| *Child:* | Good. [*Adult watching.*] And this is her favorite book, and this is her bedtime book, and this is her window held on a car. |
| *Adult:* | You could use this too if that's easier. [*Points to red block.*] |
| *Child:* | [*Puts window on red block.*] |
| *Adult:* | So maybe she is sleeping and she hears a very scary noise. |
| *Child:* | Creak! What was that? Scary! |
| *Adult:* | It's scary. [REFLECTION] |
| *Child:* | Maybe there is a monster in the house. I'm going to tell mommy. Mommy, there's a monster in the house! There isn't, dear, it's just the noise of the house. It's time to go to school. Get inside. [*Puts doll inside bus.*] |
| *Adult:* | So they're going to go to school. |
| *Child:* | Yeah. |
| *Adult:* | OK. |
| *Child:* | Vroom. Here's your teacher. He's wearing two hats. Come in! Ring, ring. School's over! How was school? Good, Mommy. Why don't you play while I make dinner? OK. Creak! [*Scared noises.*] I guess I have to go downstairs. That's better. Dinnertime. Creak. Uh-oh, Mommy, something is creaking. It's just your window, honey. Time to go to sleep. OK, Mommy. The end. |
| *Adult:* | The end? So they discover that it's the windows. And how does she feel now? |
| *Child:* | Sad. |
| *Adult:* | Sad? How come? |
| *Child:* | Uh, I mean happy? |
| *Adult:* | Happy because she's not scared anymore because she knows it's the window? |
| *Child:* | Uh-huh. |

| Adult: | OK, good, good. OK, now let's use our imagination to tell a story about a girl who has superpowers. OK? |
|---|---|
| Child: | [*Looks at toys.*] This is the girl. |
| Adult: | OK. |
| Child: | And her whole family has superpowers. |
| Adult: | OK. |
| Child: | And the doll is her little sister and this is her toys. She's sleeping. [*Puts doll on blue block.*] So she . . . |
| Adult: | Is that the girl's sister? |
| Child: | They're sleeping by each other, and this is their locker, this is their window and books. Ring, ring. Time to get up. Come on, sissy. Are you guys ready? Remember not to use superpowers at school. |
| Adult: | What kind of superpowers do they have? |
| Child: | She can run fast and she can turn herself into a monster. |
| Adult: | Turn herself into a monster? Wow. |
| Child: | And he can talk weird, and she can save her family. She's like strong and elastic. |
| Adult: | Oh, wow. |
| Child: | We remember! Mom, can I wear the hat? Yes, you may. Ah, time to go to school. Ring, ring. Class dismissed! |
| Adult: | Does that mean school is over? |
| Child: | Yeah. Ah, I guess today is not emergency day, but what? I know. Hmm, Mom, can we have dinner? Yes, that's what I'm doing. Make it fast because I am very hungry. OK, I'll make it. There. Now I am going to sit here up in my bedroom. Thank you! [*Sighs.*] We're the superpowers. The end. |
| Adult: | They didn't use their superpowers. |
| Child: | The mom used them to bring . . . when she wanted to cook dinner, she used her arms to give it to him. |
| Adult: | Mm, her arms stretch really far? |
| Child: | And she made the dinner very fast. |
| Adult: | Well, what is something that could happen in the story that lets the girl whose power is to run really fast use her power? |
| Child: | She made dinner really fast. |

*Adult:* Well, what about the little girl?

*Child:* This is the little girl. This is the little girl who can run really fast.

*Adult:* Mm-hmm.

*Child:* [*Picks up another doll.*] She doesn't have powers.

*Adult:* Oh.

*Child:* She can kick people, she's good at soccer, and she can stand on her head.

*Adult:* Well, what's another way for her to use her power to run really fast? What could happen that she needs to use her power?

*Child:* Her cat runs away, and then she has to get her.

*Adult:* OK, well, maybe let's act that out with the toys. So everyone is sitting around and they're talking, and we'll pretend this is the cat. So here's the family cat, and they're all playing and sitting and the cat . . .

*Child:* Runs away.

*Adult:* Runs away, just runs right out the front door that was left open.

*Child:* She caught it.

*Adult:* So she ran really fast to catch the cat.

*Child:* Then she went inside and put her in her cage.

*Adult:* Mm-hmm.

*Child:* And then everyone went to bed. The end.

*Adult:* And then everyone went to bed?

*Child:* Yeah.

*Adult:* OK, well, good story. You showed me a good way for her to use her superpowers. That was good. OK, let's tell one more story before you leave today, and this one will be another one about feelings, OK? But this will be a really, really happy story about a girl who has a birthday party.

*Child:* OK.

*Adult:* OK? So let's tell a story with a beginning, a middle, and an end about a birthday party.

*Child:* [*Moves toys around table.*]

*Adult:* You want this stuff out of your way?

*Child:* Mm-hmm, because these are her presents, and the people that bring the presents.

| Adult: | So is that her? It's her birthday today? |
|---|---|
| Child: | I don't have anything, but I wish I did. Oh, today is my birthday! I could probably get something today. Happy birthday! Thank you. I brought you presents. |
| Adult: | Maybe this could be her mom, and she says, "Guess what today is? Your birthday! And we are going to have a birthday party!" |
| Child: | [Looks at adult.] |
| Adult: | What would the little girl say back? |
| Child: | OK, Mommy. |
| Adult: | So who should we have over for your birthday party? Because we'll have to call and have them come over. |
| Child: | Can you come over for my birthday? Yeah. I am coming right away. Here's your birthday presents. Thank you! I've always wanted a book and . . . a . . . um, guitar. Well, I have other presents too. See? Thank you! |
| Adult: | Maybe we could . . . the mom could bring this in like a birthday cake. Look, it's time to blow out your candles and sing happy birthday. |
| Child: | It's time to blow out your candles and sing happy birthday. [Sings "Happy Birthday."] Time to blow out your candles. |
| Adult: | Remember to make a wish. |
| Child: | Yay! |
| Adult: | Did she make a wish? |
| Child: | I brought some toys for you. Thank you. |
| Adult: | Who is that? |
| Child: | The dad. A skateboard, a cat, a rock, and a car that I can balance on my head. Cool. But don't you know I can't drive a car yet. I know. Then why'd you buy me one? Well, I have no idea. The end. |
| Adult: | The end? Well, what's another way the story could end? |
| Child: | She plays with her toys. Time to play with your toys! Hey, can I go driving in the car with you? OK. [Puts dolls in car.] Vroom, vroom. Aah, we're driving without brakes! Whee, this is fun. Wah! [Car tips over.] That was fun! |
| Adult: | They crash in the car? |
| Child: | Whee! A rocking horse! Whee, whee, whee, wah! |

| Adult: | Then she fell off. |
|---|---|
| Child: | That's fun. Can I read a book? Ah, this is a good boy. I'm playing my guitar. Oh that's fun. Eating my birthday and putting my birthday cake on my head. |
| Adult: | That's silly. |
| Child: | Time to go to bed. The end. |
| Adult: | The end, and all her friends go home. Well, she had a great time at her party. Um, that was a great story. You started by her mom telling her that she was going to have a birthday party and then had her friends come over, bring her lots of presents, she played with the presents, ate cake, and then went to bed. |

## Same Child (#1), Next Session

| Adult: | Um, so thanks again for coming. We are going to play with toys just like the last couple times. So we have people and animals and a wagon and blocks. So let's use our imagination and tell a story with a beginning, a middle, and an end, OK? So make something happen about a girl who goes to the moon. OK? |
|---|---|
| Child: | Mm-hmm. [Picks up jet ski, puts doll on jet ski.] |
| Adult: | So how should our story start? |
| Child: | [Puts other doll on jet ski.] This is a little girl. |
| Adult: | That's a little . . . across the world? Well, maybe this is the flight attendant—you know, the people who are walking up and down the plane? And this could be the captain, flying the plane. |
| Child: | She's flying the plane. |
| Adult: | So is there anyone else on the plane? |
| Child: | No. |
| Adult: | Oh, OK, I'm sorry. So they're flying around the world? |
| Child: | She goes. |
| Adult: | So they're flying around the world, and then what happens next? |
| Child: | Whee! Uh-oh, we're coming in for a landing. We're on the moon. Oh, I didn't know we could go to the moon. Cool! Can you carry me on the moon? I don't know. Let's walk on the moon. But I can't get up. Then I'll carry you. I brought my wagon just in case. Whee! Uh-oh, I got a ah! Fell out of the wagon. I think we should fly around space just so we can get a better look. OK. |

[*Puts doll back on jet ski.*] Whoo! They fly around in space. I wanted to ride on the wagon. [*Doll falls over.*] Ah! Uh-oh.

Adult: So they're flying around in space. What could happen next in your story?

Child: I think we should get a spaceship. There, found a spaceship. Put on your helmet. Uh, are you sure this is right? Yeah, it protected my head when I was riding a bicycle once. That's silly.

## Child # 3, Session 3

Adult: OK, so, so, today . . .

Child: Today I am supposed to do a story about what?

Adult: About a girl going to the moon. [IMAGINATION PROMPT]

Child: The movies?

Adult: Moon. Going to the moon. [IMAGINATION PROMPT]

Child: What?

Adult: Make up a story about a girl who's going to the moon. [IMAGINATION PROMPT]

Child: OK.

Adult: OK? Use your imagination. [IMAGINATION PROMPT]

Child: I thought you said movies.

Adult: Going to the moon. [IMAGINATION PROMPT]

Child: Oh, moon. I am going to do this. First, that. I need the animals. I need the blocks.

Adult: The blocks. [REFLECTION]

Child: Put these way over. [*Adult watching.*] Don't need you, don't need you, don't need you. [*Building with Lego.*]

Adult: You're getting ready. [REFLECTION]

Child: [*Builds structure with Lego, and places at far end of table.*] Um. [*Moves other toys around table.*]

Adult: OK. [NEUTRAL RESPONSE]

Child: The bus is right there. [*Adult watching.*] That is the house.

Adult: Oh that's the house. [REFLECTION]

*Child:*    And the guy is right here. Car goes right there. Or . . . um . . .

*Adult:*    So what is going to happen next? [ORGANIZATION PROMPT]

*Child:*    In this story, and the horse has to be hiding.

*Adult:*    Ah. [NEUTRAL RESPONSE]

*Child:*    Oh, I'm gonna see what time it is. [*Adult watching.*] Oh, my gosh, I'm late for my trip to the moon.

*Adult:*    Hmm. [NEUTRAL RESPONSE]

*Child:*    Get my clothes on. Get my stuff. My space suit. Yep, I'm all ready.

*Adult:*    She's ready to go. [REFLECTION]

*Child:*    [*The next section occurred over time with the trainer observing the play.*] Lalala. [*Singing noises. Makes car noises.*] Beep, beep. Can you open this? Can . . . I'm just gonna. To the airport, please. [*Makes car noises.*]

*Adult:*    There she goes. [REFLECTION]

*Child:*    [*Takes doll out of bus.*] Whew, that was fun!

*Adult:*    Now what's going to happen? [ORGANIZATION PROMPT]

*Child:*    In the spaceship. One, two, three . . . blast off! [*Raises doll up in air. Adult watching.*] Oh, look at the space. I'm going to go outside. I'm floating, floating. I'm floating.

*Adult:*    [*Laughs.*] [POSITIVE RESPONSE]

*Child:*    Then, pretend they're on a planet.

*Adult:*    OK, they're on a planet. [REFLECTION]

*Child:*    Uh, the man. Nice, nice man. A house. [*Adult watching.*] Oooh. I want to look.

*Adult:*    What is it? A house, she found a house. [REFLECTION]

*Child:*    [*The next section occurred over time with the trainer observing the play.*] Nobody in here. [*Looks through window.*] I'm gonna go in. This is a very nice house. Woopsie. [*Walks man over.*] Oopsy. [*Doll falls over.*] You! [*Opening door noise.*] Why don't you get out of my house? [*Man hits woman.*]

*Adult:*    He kicked her out. How is she? [AFFECT PROMPT]

*Child:*    Don't have to kick that man. Then they start kicking.

*Adult:*    They get into a fight. [REFLECTION]

| Child: | [*Dolls kicking each other.*] |
|---|---|
| Adult: | They're angry. [REFLECTION] |
| Child: | I want to punch you. [*Woman hits man. Adult watching.*] Ha-ya! |
| Adult: | She's really mad. [REFLECTION] |
| Child: | [*The next section occurred over time with the trainer observing the play.*] There, that's what you get. No. [*More fighting.*] Are you an alien? No. Get out of here. [*Hits man across table.*] Neigh! |
| Adult: | Now what's going to happen? [ORGANIZATION PROMPT] |
| Child: | Ah! Horse! Ah, good thing it didn't go over me. |
| Adult: | So now what's going to happen? So now what's going to happen? |
| Child: | Oh, I didn't know there were horses on the moon. [*Adult watching.*] Neigh. I'm going to take you back. |
| Adult: | Can you put an ending on the story? [ORGANIZATION PROMPT] |
| Child: | [*The next section occurred over time with the trainer observing the play.*] Do you want to come? Sure, I've been stuck here forever. You just have to stand very careful. OK. Horsey will just wait. Whee! We're on the earth. Now you go over there. I'm going to go get horsey. Wah! [SUBSTITUTION] There you are. Horsey, get on. You get on! |
| Adult: | Can you put an ending on that story? [ORGANIZATION PROMPT] |
| Child: | I will. Once I get this thing set. [NONPLAY] |
| Adult: | That's going to be hard. [EMPATHY] |
| Child: | Wah! [*Adult watching.*] We're back. Now get in the bus. [*Puts horse, man, and woman in bus.*] |
| Adult: | Now they're going on the bus. [REFLECTION] |
| Child: | [*Drives bus around. Adult watching.*] Time to get out. [*Takes toys out of bus.*] Now to the farm. |
| Adult: | Mm-hmm. [NEUTRAL RESPONSE] |
| Child: | We're home. |
| Adult: | Good. [POSITIVE RESPONSE] |
| Child: | You can stay in this hotel. |
| Adult: | Whoops! [*In response to toy falling off table.*] |

*Child:* There is this very, very cool, very cool, cool car.

*Adult:* Can you make up another story? Make up an angry story. [AFFECT PROMPT]

*Child:* The end.

*Adult:* Can you make up an angry story where they both want the same toy? And put lots of feelings in it. They both want the same toy. [AFFECT PROMPT]

*Child:* This can be the toy.

*Adult:* And they're angry. [AFFECT PROMPT]

*Child:* [*Organizing toys, moves things around.*]

*Adult:* And put lots of feelings in it. [AFFECT PROMPT]

*Child:* [*The next section occurred over time with the trainer observing the play.*] Lalalala. [*Singing.*] Wah . . . beep, beep. Beep, beep. Oh, I want to buy that toy. Oh, I love that toy. I'm going to buy. No, I am. No, I am. Who likes you? I'm gonna buy it because I was here first. Who cares? I'm gonna buy it, OK? [*Hitting.*] Ow, that hurt.

*Adult:* Oh, it hurt. [REFLECTION]

*Child:* [*The next section occurred over time with the trainer observing the play.*] You are very mean. Now I'm buying this toy because, see, it only likes me. See? It'll let me sit down on it. It will let me too! Ah! Haha, sorry, I pushed it.

*Adult:* She's sorry. How does he feel? [AFFECT PROMPT]

*Child:* You did that by purpose. [*Adult watching. Child laughs.*] So? My toy! You go away, because it's mine. And I'm going to ride all the way to the cashier.

*Adult:* Oh, there she goes to the cashier. [REFLECTION]

*Child:* Now, how much money do you have? [*Adult watching.*] Two dollars. This thing costs lots of dollars. It costs four dollars. OK. Oh, money on the floor. Mine, mine, mine, mine. [*Picks it up.*] Now ten dollars. How many dollars do you have? Oops, I have 11. Sorry! I'm going to buy it.

*Adult:* So she gets it.

*Child:* Fine, then, fine. Then you know what? Then we both get to play with it. Which house are you in? I'm . . . OK? OK. What day? How about next Saturday? OK. Whee! [*Rides toys.*] I'd like to buy this toy. The bus. OK, goodbye. [*Puts toy in wagon.*] OK, let's play. The end.

*Adult:* That was a really good story. Another story about a girl with magic powers. Use your imagination. What kind of magic powers could she have? [IMAGINATION PROMPT]

*Child:* She could be invisible or . . . um.

*Adult:* That's good, invisible. [PRAISE]

*Child:* Or she could fly.

*Adult:* She could fly. [REFLECTION]

*Child:* And she is very flexible.

*Adult:* Yes, very flexible. So she can fly, and she's invisible. Very good. [PRAISE]

*Child:* She can turn invisible when she wants.

*Adult:* She can become invisible. That's good.

*Child:* You're not in the story. [*Moves toy.*] Lalala. [*Singing.*] I'm going to Cedar Point today.

*Adult:* Cedar Point. She's going to Cedar Point. [REFLECTION]

*Child:* Whee! Aw, shoot, stoplight. Oh, come on. It's taking forever. It's been an hour already. Thank you! We're there. Yay! I love this cotton candy. It looks really good. Mmm. I want to buy it. [*Eating noises.*] Hmm. Whoopsies. Achoo. Oh, my gosh, where am I? I can't see myself.

*Adult:* Oh, she's scared. [LABELING]

*Child:* Ahh. Let's run away before everybody gets freaked out. [*Running noises.*] Gets back in bus. [*Running noises.*] What happened to me? I do not want to be . . . I want to be invisible. This is fun. It's fun to be invisible. Yes, I'm very flexible.

*Adult:* She's flexible.

*Child:* Now what? I want to fly. I want to pretend that I'm a fairy and I put on my fairy wings. I can fly! I can fly! Look at me.

*Adult:* That's fun. [REFLECTION]

*Child:* I can fly.

*Adult:* It's really fun. [REFLECTION]

*Child:* I have secret powers, everybody. I have superpowers. Stop bragging! It's true, I have secret powers. See? I can fly, and I'm flexible and invisible. Haha. The end.

*Adult:* Very good. I think we'll stop today. I am going to see you next week. [PRAISE]

*Child # 3, Session 4 (Next Session)*

> *Adult:* OK, so just like the other times, I have some toys for you to play with, and we are going to make up some stories and then play them out with the toys? OK?

> *Child:* OK.

> *Adult:* And then when I say so, we will switch stories, OK? Have the dolls and the animals talk out loud. When they talk out loud then we know what is happening in the story and how they feel, OK? Try to make up a story using a beginning, a middle, and an end. So let's start by using our imagination and make up a story about somebody who lives in a city underwater. What would that be like?

> *Child:* I wish I could be a mermaid. Look, a shooting star. Yeah, I see a shooting star. Well, what are you going to wish? I wish I was a mermaid, that's what I wish. Oh, well, that's a good wish. Let's go to sleep. I am really tired. [*Brings over blocks for beds.*]

> *Adult:* Good idea.

> *Child:* Where am I? I'm underwater. The wish that I made yesterday has finally came true. I'm finally a mermaid. Now I can do whatever I want to. Superpowers. You wished that you had superpowers but you didn't, but now you do, so I bet you're happy. Oh what's this? Something to ride in. Nope. Who said that? Oh, me. Who are you? I'm . . . hey, who turned out the lights? Oh sorry. I didn't know what this is. Oh, it's hair. Oh, its weird hair, but that's OK.

> *Adult:* What could happen next in the story?

> *Child:* What is this? It's to go skiing on. So we can go skiing underwater. You don't have to get skis. Oh.

> *Adult:* Cool idea.

> *Child:* What are these little things? That's to steer. I think I know something better. Oh, what? Snowboard. A snowboard? I used to have one before I lived underwater. Hey, why did you take off your own hair? Because . . . why did you take off your own hair? Because it was hurting my head really a lot, so I wanted to take it off. [*Laughs.*] Oh, well, sorry to tell you this, but we do not take off our own hair. Oh, we don't. Sorry. I won't ever do it again. I bet you will like this. What is this? It's a guitar. Oh, here. Oh, I can. . . . Oh, sorry. . . . I got this and . . . look. It's, um, it's um, I can't answer.

> *Adult:* [*Laughs.*] Then they go to sleep again?

*Child:* Yeah.

*Adult:* So they see a shooting star and then. . . . OK, let's tell a story with lots of feelings this time, and let's make an angry story. So, an angry story.

*Child:* Here have it. No, I don't want it. Why? It's pretty. Because. But no buts! Fine, let's do something. A game. And whoever wins has to keep the hair. OK. Well, so what are we going to do? We have to skateboard, I'll skateboard. No, of course not. Hey! Don't call me that kid. Hey, don't call me kid. You're the one, you're the. . . . I don't want you to, just. . . . Why do you have to get so mad? Because. . . . Oh, no, that is not going to happen. Who turned out the lights? Take off that wig right now! And I have something else. You have to wear it for the whole time snowboard and skateboarding. I don't want to wear it. It's too girly. Oh, sorry, I wasn't paying attention. And I have something else. I have to wear something over my face so I can't see. I can't see! Well, I can't see either. Ready, get set, go. [*Skateboarding noises.*] Ready, get set, go. I won! Aw, you cheated! I bet you cheated, but you didn't. Go away. I have to keep the hat. You have to keep the wig. Ugh, that's what I don't like about . . . .

*Adult:* Good story. I could really tell that they were angry at each other, about a girl who can talk to animals.

*Child:* OK. Hey, hi. Oh trust me, it's awesome. You have to learn how to play. Yeah that's good. Sorry, I need this. Why? Because I need. . . . Do you know how to talk to animals? Yeah. Well, I don't want to be your friend, because I told my mother I would never, ever talk to people who have . . . who talk to animals. But, look, he is cute, but. . . . OK. So bye. OK, bye. Time to take it up to the zoo. Oh, I see you like that bag. I do like it. Time to go skateboarding.

## A Group Intervention Format

Recently, a group play intervention study was carried out in which the play intervention sessions were conducted in a group format consisting of four students and two cofacilitators, one teacher, and one psychology graduate student (Hoffmann, 2012). In this study, 40 female students were given the APS to determine their baseline levels of fantasy play. The children were then placed into groups of four on the basis of both their age and their baseline play ability, so that each group contained two children who were above-average players and two children who scored below average on the APS; these children were all within 1 year of age of each other. Groups were then randomly assigned to the intervention or control protocols. The intervention groups met for six 30-minute sessions and worked together to make up stories using a similar set of dolls and toys as those used in the individual interventions described previously.

The group format uses *peer modeling,* in which the children who are already strong players can act as models for those children showing more difficulty engaging in fantasy play. As each member of the group brings his or her own strengths and weaknesses to the intervention sessions, each participant's play skills are stretched and enhanced by peers' ideas. Facilitators continue to serve a similar role as in the individual intervention, offering positive reinforcement, prompting children to expand their repertoire of play skills, and modeling skills when necessary. Children in the control groups also met with their group for six sessions, where they constructed puzzles, completed coloring sheets, and made necklaces out of beads. These activities were meant to control for group social interaction and special time away from the classroom to work as a team on a project, without the fantasy or affective content that is included in the intervention groups' work.

Results were that children in the group play intervention had significantly more imagination, organization, and positive affect in their play at outcome than did the control group. The implication is that group play intervention may be an efficient way to include play experiences in schools. The divergent thinking scores for the play group increased slightly but not significantly. As research with play interventions continues, there may be different advantages to working with children individually or in small groups. Conducting interventions with groups allows for more children to be included in an intervention in less time; however, each child receives less individualized attention than can be given during individual play intervention sessions.

## DEVELOPMENT OF A PLAY INTERVENTION
## FOR PRESCHOOL-AGE CHILDREN

What about play facilitation for preschool children? Given the importance of the preschool years for development and the fact that pretend play peaks during this same developmental period, there is a need to adapt interventions to target play skills during this time. Interventions implemented during this key developmental period may have an even greater impact on children's development than those implemented later in childhood. Therefore, the intervention methods of the school-age play intervention were adapted for use with preschool-age children. A pilot study was conducted in a children's museum setting, with promising results (Christian, Fehr, & Russ, 2011). In addition, a randomized controlled trial was carried out with a larger sample in a preschool setting (Fehr, 2012).

## Pilot Study in a Children's Museum

When adapting the intervention protocol for preschool-age children, we thought that the most effective way to improve play would be to teach parents the intervention techniques. Parents frequently play with their children at this young age. Therefore, the pilot preschool play intervention included only three weekly 20- to 30-minute sessions with the play facilitator. During these sessions, however, parents observed the play facilitator, and parents were asked to conduct two 10-minute play sessions at home between each play session with the facilitator. All other procedures described in the play intervention manual for the school-age children were followed (e.g., types of toys, number and types of story stems per session, alternating stories targeting imagination and affect expression, behaviors of play facilitator), although adaptations for developmental level resulted in changes within the session interactions. For example, one main task of the play facilitator is to follow the child's lead.

When implementing the play intervention task with school-age children, children may be prompted to put an ending on a story if they change topic abruptly. However, with preschool-age children, following the child's lead means allowing children to have stories with loosely related events while still encouraging an overall organization (e.g., first the characters go to the moon, then a monster eats them all up, and then they go home). In this example, encouraging the child to come up with an ending after the monster eats everyone allows them to come back to the original theme of going to the moon. In contrast, having the monster eat everyone might be considered the end of a school-age child's story, or it may be seen as a change in the topic altogether if the monster is not on the moon. Being sensitive to normal development in preschoolers' play allows the play facilitator to maintain the difficult balance between encouraging improvements in play while also following the child's lead, even if the theme is not completely apparent to the adult facilitating the session.

With these changes, this approach was used in a pilot study with seventeen 4-to-6-year-old children who had not yet entered the first grade. Children and their parents were recruited from a local children's museum and randomly assigned to be a part of the play skill intervention or active control group that colored and played with puzzles or a building toy. Parents in both groups observed sessions and were asked to conduct play sessions at home modeled after the ones they observed. A handout was given to parents in both groups describing suggestions for toys to use and ways they could interact with their child consistent with the group they were in. Parents in the intervention group were encouraged to play out stories with their children and reinforce, model, or provide suggestions to enhance their children's play skills. Parents in the control group were encouraged to play with puzzles, build, or color with their children and praise their children for effort and ask questions about what they were doing (e.g., what color this is or which piece will go next).

Following the third play session, the children's play skills were evaluated with the Affect in Play Scale–Preschool version (APS–P; Kaugars & Russ, 2009). Given the small sample size, effect sizes were focused on in analyses, and preliminary results were that play skills improved for children in the play intervention group relative to those in the control group. Effect sizes were medium to large. Affect, organization, and imagination all increased relative to the control group. More detailed scoring and analyses to examine group differences are currently being conducted.

## Randomized Controlled Trial in a Preschool

Following these encouraging results, an additional examination of this protocol was developed with a larger sample size. On the basis of lessons learned during the pilot study, a number of changes were proposed for use in this second examination of the intervention. First, it became apparent during the pilot intervention that children interacted with the play facilitator differently when their parent was in the room. Many children became shy or would defer to their parents when prompted during play sessions, even when their parents were out of view or provided encouragement. In addition, parents were inconsistent in their approach to the play sessions at home, both in terms of whether they set aside time to conduct the sessions and in terms of the content of the play sessions. Therefore, it was decided the intervention should be tested with children without their parents present. Second, it was decided to conduct the intervention at a school rather than in the community to minimize difficulties in consistent scheduling of sessions. Third, on the basis of the experience with the children in the pilot study, a standard set of play stories was established for use with every child in an increasingly difficult order. Although play facilitators were encouraged to follow this order of stories, which seemed to work best with the pilot study children, they were allowed to deviate from the suggested order if the child rejected a story and requested an alternate story stem or if the play facilitator thought a particular story did not reflect the child's play development (e.g., a child who struggled to make up a story with familiar content was not given a more unstructured story with a theme that required a high use of fantasy).

In this study, the play intervention group was not significantly different from the control group on the APS–P. Perhaps at the preschool level, the play intervention should be more intensive (more than three times) or be more specifically tailored to each child's strengths and weaknesses. It is also possible that parental involvement and practice at home are important at this young age. The results with children in the museum setting were more promising when parents were involved in the play intervention. The home environment may be more important for preschool children in play facilitation.

## HOME ENVIRONMENT, CREATIVITY, AND PLAY

A classic longitudinal study by Harrington, Block, and Block (1987) tested the principles put forth by Rogers (1954), who stated that creativity in children was most likely to occur when three conditions were present: openness to experience, internal locus of evaluation, and the ability to toy with elements and concepts. He thought that these three internal conditions were fostered by two external conditions: psychological safety and psychological freedom. In the Harrington et al. study, 106 children and families were followed longitudinally. They categorized child-rearing practices on the basis of data collected when the children were preschoolers. The child-rearing practices data were based on parent questionnaires and observations of parent–child interactions. Relationships were investigated between child-rearing practices and a creative potential index of the child as a preschooler and as a young adolescent. The creative potential index was based on teachers' ratings and on personality Q sorts (a sorting of cards containing personality descriptors and behaviors that apply to the child). There was a correlation of .33 between the preschool creative potential score and the adolescent potential score, indicating some stability of the construct. The main finding of the study was that parents who used child-rearing practices consistent with Rogers's theory had children who were more creative. After using path analysis techniques, they concluded that Rogers's child-rearing practices approach contributed significantly to adolescent creative potential scores after gender, IQ, and preschool creativity scores were controlled for. They concluded that environments that foster the child's autonomy and self-confidence should also foster creativity.

These findings are consistent with those of Csikszentmihalyi and Rathunde (Adler, 1991), who found that a home environment that combined support and optimal challenge was essential for creative development.

Families of teenagers who promoted creative functioning exhibited five characteristics: clarity of expectations, interest in what the child was currently doing, availability of choices, commitment, and complex opportunities for action (challenge). Studies by Lubart and colleagues found that families with flexible rules have children with greater creativity than families with rigid rules, regardless of socioeconomic level (Lubart & Lautrey, 1998; Lubart, Mouchiroud, Tordjman, & Zenasni, 2003). D. G. Singer and Singer (1990) followed preschoolers and conducted home visits for an in-depth study of parents and home environment. They reported that imaginative children had parents who were more resourceful, adventuresome, and creative, on the basis of self-descriptions. They also used inductive child rearing, not physical discipline, had clear rules and orderly routines, and had more sitting down time and reading time with their children.

In a recent popular video on YouTube, "Caine's Arcade" (Nirvan, 2012), a 9-year-old boy builds a complex arcade out of cardboard boxes. This video is a wonderful illustration of the use of pretend play to foster flexibility of thinking and creativity. The boy, Caine, spends time in his father's auto parts store over the summer and uses cardboard boxes to start building an arcade for people to play with. He tinkers and becomes totally absorbed in the arcade. It also provides an observation of the father, who encourages the child's play and creativity. The father encourages him but also gives the child a lot of space, physically and psychologically. He stays out of his way as he builds his arcade. He also clearly enjoys what his son is doing. When the boy asks him for a specific tool, the father tells him to build it. He challenges him, and the boy responds with ingenuity.

## PRACTICAL RECOMMENDATIONS FOR FACILITATING PRETEND PLAY

Parents, teachers, and child care workers can help children develop processes that are important to creativity through play. There are no empirically supported play facilitation protocols that are ready to be disseminated for wide use. There are principles inferred from research studies that have implications for working with children to enhance processes through play. Adults can help children

- practice with divergent thinking in play—for example, they can encourage using objects in different ways or making up different endings to stories;
- generate different stories—for example, they can use different story stems to help the child develop different scenarios;

- express emotions in play—for example, they can suggest stories that would involve expression of emotions;
- label emotions that occur in play to help the child understand different emotions;
- by modeling telling stories and pretending;
- by providing unstructured toys such as blocks, cars, action figures, dolls, and plastic or stuffed animals—toys that are open-ended leave room for the child's imagination and challenge the child to come up with their own ideas;
- by following the child's lead, letting them determine what is happening, and by modeling and encouraging them when they "get stuck";
- enjoy the play—it is important that children not get the message that they are wasting time;
- enjoy their imagination and different forms of expression;
- by providing the space and time for them to play;
- by encouraging play with other children—in addition to developing social skills, they are also learning from the creative play of other children;
- by being sensitive to when children want adult involvement in play and when they do not; young children, 3 to 5, often want an adult to engage in the play with them, but older children often want to play by themselves or with other children.

There are also tools available for parents and teachers. For preschool children, J. L. Singer and Singer (1999) developed a video-based program for parents and other caretakers. The video and accompanying manual use play and learning games to strengthen school readiness. The tape and manual provide clear examples and instructions for parents and caregivers modeling how to use play to help children use imagination and to learn through play. D. G. Singer and Singer (2002) also published a book for parents and teachers that reviews games and activities for imaginative play. For preschool children especially, valuing and nurturing play in the home may be the best way to help them develop good play skills.

## CONCLUSION

The field is working to build an empirical base for play-training protocols that facilitate different processes and skills in pretend play. Lillard et al. (2013) raised a number of important methodological issues in this area. I agree with Dansky's (1999) conclusion that there are well-done studies that have resulted in improved pretend play and imagination. My own research program has developed a play-training protocol that improved play processes for first-and second-grade school children in a low-SES population, with some results that lasted in a follow-up study (Moore & Russ, 2008). This same protocol was less successful with a higher SES population of girls, but it did result in improved play in girls with below-average play skills at baseline. An adapted version of this play protocol for a group format did result in improved pretend play with a high-SES group of girls. A next step is to replicate the results with a larger sample of children and to continue to refine the protocol. In general, there is a need for development of empirically supported play intervention protocols.

# 8

# PLAY, CULTURE, AND THE MODERN WORLD

What is happening to the play experience in our modern Western world? Pretend play has remained a universal aspect of childhood throughout the ages. But is our society changing so much today that pretend play is endangered? If so, what are the implications for the development of creativity? This chapter reviews the area of culture and play. Does pretend play look different in different cultures? This chapter reviews a research study that used the Affect in Play Scale (APS; Russ, 1987, 2004) to compare pretend play in children in the United States and in Italy. On the basis of studies with the APS, changes in play in the United States during the past 23 years are then discussed. The chapter concludes with a review of the ways in which engagement in pretend play helps with the development of the self.

http://dx.doi.org/10.1037/14282-009
*Pretend Play in Childhood: Foundation of Adult Creativity*, by S. W. Russ

## CULTURE AND PLAY

What have we learned from other cultures about play in different contexts? A key question is whether the processes in play differ in different cultures. Although the toys and materials used vary in different cultures, does the underlying structure of the play reflect those differences? Do we find the same cognitive and affective processes in play? Does play relate to similar areas of adaptive functioning in different cultures?

L'Abate (2009) provided an excellent review of studies addressing these questions. One of the difficulties is separating educational opportunities and poverty from cultural differences in child rearing. He pointed to a study by Edwards (2000) that compared play in children from six countries. Edwards found that the lowest scores on quality of play were for children from Kenya and India, and the highest scores were for children from Japan and the United States. He concluded that cultural norms and opportunities determined whether children had the opportunity to explore and the motivation to practice adult roles. As L'Abate stated, the connection between culture and the play of the child is mediated in large part by the parents. What messages do the parents send about the value of play and about important tasks of childhood? Those messages and parental behaviors largely determine what occurs in play.

Jared Diamond (2012), in his recent book, *The World Until Yesterday*, viewed play as practice for adult civilization. He described tribal war games played by children in the New Guinea highlands that included play with pretend bows and arrows. He also referred to Karl Heider's observations of Dani children in the New Guinea Highlands pulling flowers with a string, pretending that the flowers were pigs (wars and pigs are important in this culture). In contrast, he described the play of Nani children in the Sudan, which involved building toy cattle enclosures out of sand, ashes, and mud. They filled these enclosures with mud figures of cattle and then played at herding the cattle. Cattle are important in that culture. Diamond saw this play as an educational activity that prepares children for adult life. He was struck by the self-invented play of children in traditional cultures such as the New Guinea Highland people and also by the frequency of multiage playgroups in these cultures. Young children play with older children routinely. Diamond saw advantages in the practices of children making their own toys and in playing with children of all ages.

Gaskins, Haight, and Lancy (2007) argued that although play is universal, it differs in content, social interaction, and available resources (toys, space, time). They concluded that there are both quantitative and qualitative differences in play across cultures. For example, symbolism seems to be universal, but it is valued differently. The authors also suggested that play may have different developmental outcomes in different cultures. For example, play has a smaller role in child development if it is not valued by the culture. Perhaps in cultures that are complex, with continual change, in which a high level of creativity is necessary in adulthood, pretend play would be more necessary in childhood. Pretend play activities would be valued by the culture that is dependent on creative innovation in adults.

Gaskins et al. (2007) discussed three different cultures that reflect different types of play cultures. *Culturally cultivated play* occurs in Euro-American families and other cultures of the urban, educated middle class. In these families, play—and especially pretend play—is highly valued and supported. Parents engage in play with their young children and enjoy it. Parents provide toys appropriate for pretending and help the children elaborate on play themes. *Culturally accepted play* occurs in cultures that accept and may value play but do not invest in it. Gaskins et al. reviewed Lancy's (1996) study of the Kpelle group in Liberia. The group was described as "slash and burn" horticulturalists. There is no public school and little access to the outside world. In this culture, older children tend younger children. Adults do not play with their children. At age 4 or 5, children start to engage in pretend play. This is later than the occurrence in Euro-American families. The play episodes incorporate scenes from adult behavior and are grounded in observations. The complexity of the play is limited. By ages 8 to 10, storytelling has become dominant. The children are also engaging in the work of the group. *Culturally curtailed play* occurs in work-oriented cultures in which play is viewed as a distraction and not valuable. Gaskins (2003) studied a Yucatan Mayan village where lives are structured around household chores. Opportunities for play are restricted by physical and social resources. Adults believe that children should not be stimulated. Pretense is often viewed as inappropriate and may be viewed as lying. Parents do not participate in the play. Even in this culture, in which play is not valued and is limited, children from 3 to 5 years of age spend 40% of their time playing. However, pretend play is never the dominant form of play. Gaskins et al. (2007) concluded that the Yucatan Mayan children's motivation for play differs from that for Euro-American children and that the play looks different. Play is mainly motor play and games with rules. When pretense does occur, it is repetitive and is a reenactment of daily life. Older children take charge of the content of the play. The children do not use dolls and figures. Also, the play is always public and anyone can participate and observe.

Gaskins et al. (2007) concluded that some features of play are universal. Joy and pleasure in play occurs in all cultures. Symbolism in play is also universal but is valued differently. Reality-based scenarios occur but vary in quantity and quality. The use of play to express emotions in a cathartic way does not occur in all cultures. Gaskins et al. concluded that play has less of a role in child development if it is not valued by the culture. In simple cultures, in which there are not many demands on children, learning to use play to cope with problems may not be necessary. In more complex societies, in which creativity in adulthood is important to the society and to adult functioning, play is valued more. Gaskins et al.'s important point is that different aspects of play may relate to different aspects of child development. For example, reality-based themes may be important for some aspects of development, and fantasy themes for other aspects. Parents, reflecting the values of the culture, shape the play. Play is used to develop processes and abilities that are important in adult functioning in that culture.

In modern societies, in which creativity is valued in adulthood, pretend play has been valued and encouraged in children. However, even in modern cultures with similar values on the surface, play may differ. One of the problems in studying play across cultures is that different measures of play have been used. Ideally, the same measure would be used to assess play in different cultures. The APS is a measure that has been used in studies in the United States and Italy. Comparisons have been made of play in the two countries using this same method of assessment (Chessa et al., 2013).

## PLAY IN THE UNITED STATES AND ITALY

The United States and Italy are modern Western cultures in which creativity in adulthood is valued and benefits the society. However, there are differences in child-rearing practices that influence the development of play in children. Chessa et al. (2013) reviewed the literature from which this summary is drawn.

Parental support helps to promote and encourage children's engagement in fantasy, imagination, and pretend play (Parmar, Harkness, & Super, 2004; Smith & Gosso, 2010; Taylor & Carlson, 2002). How that support is expressed differs across cultures. Differences in home environment and parental caregiving systems are linked with different pretend play experiences of children (Cote & Bornstein, 2005; Parmar et al., 2004). In the United States, play is thought to be a central component of the parental role, and parents are engaged as active partners to promote child self-skills (Bornstein, Cote, & Venuti, 2001). In contrast, in the Italian context, play is considered to be the child's own activity, not requiring parental intervention. Italian parental attitudes and caregiving goals are focused mainly on feeding and grooming. New (1988, 1994) found that in Italy toys were used more as distractions during caregiving tasks and parents did not encourage active and independent exploration of the environment. Play is considered as "a natural thing" (Emiliani & Molinari, 1995) more than a way of promoting competence, as in the U.S. context (Bornstein, Haynes, Pascual, Painter, & Galperin, 1999). Parmar et al. (2004) argued that in the U.S. middle-class, play is encouraged to improve cognitive and social abilities crucial for achievement goals in school. Comparing different samples of American and Italian parents, Oyserman, Coon, and Kemmelmeier (2002) found that American parental practices emphasized an individualistic and self-autonomy orientation, whereas Italian practices were linked to interpersonal interdependency and relatedness.

How parents engage with children also differs. Italian mothers perceive themselves as engaging in more social than didactic interactions compared with U.S. parents (Bornstein et al., 2001). Italian mothers engage in more frequent looking at and talking to their young infants than do U.S. mothers (Richman, LeVine, et al., 1988; Richman, Miller, & Solomon, 1988). Moreover, everyday caregiving practice by Italian mothers is characterized by a precise feeding schedule, co-sleeping (Owens, 2004), and not encouraging independent exploration of the environment for infants (Welles-Nyström, New, & Richman, 1994; Wolf, Lozoff, Latz, & Paludetto, 1996). By contrast, U.S. mothers prefer to feed their infants on demand, insist on a regular schedule and routine for their infants to sleep alone, and encourage their infants' independence in exploring (New & Richman, 1996). Although U.S. mothers attempt to establish a sense of independence and autonomy in their infants, Italian infants are expected by their mothers to "modulate their own needs in coordination with the rituals and routines of the family" (New & Richman, 1996, p. 398; Welles-Nyström et al., 1994).

Hsu and Lavelli (2005) reported one of the few studies that directly compared Italian and U.S. parenting practices. They observed mother–child dyadic interaction during the first months of life during feeding sessions. Italian mothers displayed significantly more open affect and physical contact during feeding. U.S. mothers did not respond and attend to their infants' social signals. Infants' involuntary behaviors (hiccupping, sneezing, drowsiness) aroused a less intense social response (looking, smiling, caressing) in U.S. mothers than in Italian mothers. Axia and Weisner (2002) reported that Italian parents demonstrated an open tendency for active affect expression. They stressed that the Italian parental attitude, starting from the first months of life, is "to grasp the notion of liveliness" (Harkness et al., 2001; p. 257), sometimes encouraging active attitudes or not regulating or inhibiting children's emotional and behavioral reactions. However, mothers in the United States encouraged a sense of autonomy, personal choice, and self-reliance in their infants (Harwood, Schoelmerich, Schulze, & Gonzalez, 1999; Miller & Harwood, 2002). Culture may influence the context in which emotions are experienced and expressed and the way in which children's play develops.

How might these cultural differences influence play behavior? On the basis of the different child-rearing parental practices and the previous cross-cultural findings in U.S. and Italian samples, one would expect differences in play processes in the two countries. First, on the basis of the more active attitude toward and valuing of emotional expression, it could be expected that Italian children would show a higher number of affective themes in play. Affect appears to be more valued in the Italian parent–child relationship. Second, higher scores on cognitive variables could be expected in the U.S. sample because of the educational and achievement role that play has in that culture. Because play studies in the United States and Italy used the same play measure, play processes could be compared. The main aim of the study was to explore differences and similarities in children's pretend play in U.S. and Italian samples. The APS (Russ, 2004) was used in both samples. The APS has been found to have good psychometric properties in both countries.

### Participants: U.S. Sample

Participants were 613 children mostly in the first and second grades, with 38 children in the third and fourth grades (for details, see Chessa et al., 2013). These children were from 10 different studies carried out from 1985 to 2008. All but one of the studies were carried out in school settings in the Cleveland, Ohio, area. Schools were either public or parochial and included typically developing children. There were different examiners and raters for the different studies; however, raters had been trained and checked for adequate interrater reliability on APS scoring.

### Participants: Italian Sample

Participants were 218 Italian children in the first and second grades who belonged to a community sample. Participants were recruited from six urban and suburban primary schools in Northern and Central Italy. All the subjects were Caucasian, and all were in mainstream classrooms. No participants had been referred for mental health or social services. Most of the children's families belonged to the middle class (Hollingshead, 1975).

### Procedure for the U.S. Sample

The U.S. sample was composed of 10 different studies that took place in the United States between 1985 and 2008. Studies were selected for inclusion in this sample on the basis of the following criteria: (a) there was standardized administration of the APS, (b) participants were in first and second grades, and (c) a random sample of normally developing school children was used. The specific procedure for each of the 10 studies varied depending on the research questions; however, in each study, the APS was administered by experienced raters who had established interrater reliability on the measure.

## Procedure for the Italian Sample

Data were collected for 6 years, from 2002 to 2008. All children completed the play task individually during their regularly scheduled classes. According to standard administration procedures for the APS, the examiners had a room where the children could be comfortable to play and to be video recorded. The standard instructions for the APS were used. Ten different examiners were trained for administration procedures according to the APS administration manual (Russ, 1987, 1993, 2004). Only 15 children were unable to complete the task, consistent with the literature on the APS (Russ, 2004). Scoring procedures for the APS included five independent judges who were graduate students in clinical psychology. All judges were trained by an experienced psychologist who was directly trained by me. No significant examiner effects were found.

## Results

### Interrater Reliability

For the Italian study, interrater reliability for the APS was assessed on 47 protocols. A random procedure was used to identify the protocols and to proceed with the scoring. Two of the independent judges, both graduate students in clinical psychology who independently scored the tapes according to the APS training manual (Russ, 1987, 2004), achieved intraclass correlation coefficients (ICCs) of frequency of affect expression (.93), frequency of positive affect expression (.94), frequency of negative affect expression (.92), organization (.93), imagination (.89), and comfort (.92). For the U.S. studies, each study had assessed interrater reliability. The ranges of interrater reliability were as follows: frequency of affect expression (.77–.99), variety of affect expression (.75–.99), organization (.70–.98), imagination (.74–.97), and comfort (.86–.99).

To verify the agreement on scoring procedures between the Italian and the U.S. research groups, one Italian rater was directly trained by me. ICCs were assessed between this Italian rater and an independent U.S. rater on 20 protocols selected from the original APS training (Russ, 2004). Results showed good interrater reliability between the two countries' raters, supporting the validity of the study. ICCs were frequency of affect expression (.85), organization (.83), imagination (.82), and comfort (.82).

*Comparison of Play Between the United States and Italy*

Means and standard deviations of the APS scores for the U.S. and Italian samples were compared. Not all studies included scores for all of the APS variables; thus, some sample sizes were lower. Only comfort was scored for all 613 children in the U.S. sample. Mean scores and standard deviations were calculated for the U.S. first- and second-grade sample ($n = 613$) by combining the means and standard deviations from the 10 different studies included. The following procedures were used to calculate these combined means and standard deviations. For each variable, means and standard deviations presented in each previous study were collected and then combined as a sum, weighted by the total number of subjects for which the variable was scored.

Student's $t$ for unpaired samples and effect size for the Student's $t$-test (Cohen's $d$) were calculated to compare the U.S. and Italian samples. According to the Student's $t$, the comparison between the two countries was significant for the variables variety of affect expression, positive and negative affect expression, and imagination. The total of affect expression and comfort showed a marginal trend of significance. By convention, $t$-test effect size values of 0.2, 0.5, and 0.8 are considered small, medium, and large, respectively (J. Cohen, 1988). According to this rule, all the considered variables had a small $t$-test effect size value ($0.05 < d < 0.28$), except variety of affect. The variety of affect score showed a high significance value for $t$ ($p < .001$) and a medium effect size value ($d = 0.51$). Italian children had a higher variety of affect categories score ($M = 3.83$, $SD = 2.18$) than U.S. children ($M = 2.77$, $SD = 1.99$). Italian children also expressed more positive and negative affect, although the effect size for the comparison was small. Moreover, American children showed a higher level of cognitive processes, particularly on imagination, but with a small effect size ($d = 0.23$).

To illustrate, a more qualitative overview of two narrative scenarios from the Italian sample are presented. These examples are from Chessa et al. (2013). The first is an example of a high imaginative level.

> Hi, I'm Minnie. Hi, I'm Mickey Mouse. We are going to a party in the castle tonight. [*Build a house with blocks.*] Did you bake a cake? No? Come on! Oh, yes, the cake is still inside the microwave. I want to eat it. It's a red strawberry cake. I like it. I'm very hungry. It's Minnie's birthday. After the party they go to sleep. Minnie is on the stairs waiting to blow the candles. Shh. They sleep all night and tomorrow. Good morning! Good morning! It's time for breakfast! They go to the supermarket. Mmm, a pumpkin donut. Nom nom. Too sweet. I don't like it. She opened all the gift packets. One yellow. Oh, it's a suitcase. One red; it's a dress. One blue; it's a chocolate bag. Then Minnie's nanny comes and tells her that it's time to go to school and gave her the books. She doesn't want to go because she wants to play with Mickey Mouse. They play colored chess.

Imagination was scored 4 out of 5 for the many transformations, the variety of events, the inclusion of some novel fantasy events, and the unusual twists that are removed from daily experiences, such as living in a castle, and the addition of other characters beyond the two puppets.

The following is an example of a narrative with a high variety and frequency of affect:

> The mother is fighting with Alex. [AGGRESSION] Why you don't want to take a shower? [ANAL] Oh, Mommy, no, no, no, I want to watch TV now! [ANGER] I went to a football game and won with his team. [COMPETITION] Yeah! [HAPPINESS] He was very excited, enjoyed very much [HAPPINESS] the game and did a goal. [COMPETITION] [*Singing.*] I am a champion. [COMPETITION] Oh, my God, what is going on? [FRUSTRATION] Suddenly, his friend Luke [NURTURANCE] broke his leg and start to cry. [SADNESS/HURT] Ooh eeh. [SADNESS] They were very preoccupied for him. [ANXIETY] Come on, Luke. Good luck. I will hug to make feel better. [AFFECTION] Luke went to the hospital. [SADNESS/HURT] Nurses gave him an ice cream [ORAL], and he felt better. [HAPPINESS]

In this sample, there were 16 total affect units spanning eight of the 11 affect categories, so this play would get a frequency of affect score of 16 and a variety of affect score of 8.

Results showed significant differences for both cognitive and affective processes consistent with the hypotheses. Only one result had a medium effect size: variety of affect. Italian children were more able to use a wider range of affective expressions in play than the American children. They also had more positive and negative emotion in play. The American children had more imagination in their play than Italian children.

These results are consistent with differences in child-rearing practices in these two countries. In the U.S. family and school context, play is used to improve children's skills, particularly cognitive and social abilities (Bornstein et al., 2001; Parmar et al., 2004). Although there was a small effect size, U.S. children did show more imagination. They were more able to use fantasy, to pretend, and develop transformations in the play session. One explanation for the greater imagination in the U.S. sample is that U.S. mothers use play to promote children's self-skills (Bornstein et al., 2001). Parents are more focused on cognitive development and achievement.

Italian children, however, were more able to express affect in the play narrative and to use a wider range of emotions. Previous studies on parental interactions with children have shown that Italian mothers express emotions openly to their children (Hsu & Lavelli, 2005). Their interaction is more focused on letting the child play without encouraging achievement. They also encourage more active affect expression (Axia & Weisner, 2002). If emotional expression is more valued and supported in the Italian culture, then play behavior could be influenced.

If these results are replicated in other samples, what are the implications of these differences in play behavior for child development? We know that children use imagination and affective expression in play for different purposes. An interesting difference can be detected between U.S. and Italian samples in similar studies with the APS that can contribute to understanding the cross-cultural findings of this study. We (Seja & Russ, 1999) administered the APS with the Kusche Affective Interview–Revised (KAI–R; Kusche, Greenberg, & Beilke, 1988), a measure of emotional understanding in a sample of 66 first- and second-grade U.S. children. Results were that emotional understanding was related to the quality of fantasy but not affective variables of the APS. Cognitive dimensions of play (organization, imagination, comfort) were directly related to the ability to describe emotional experiences and to understand others' experiences. That is, children with more sophisticated fantasy seemed to be better able to understand others' mental states and emotions.

Mazzeschi, Salcuni, Parolin, and Lis (2004) administered the APS and KAI–R in a sample of 50 Italian children ages 6 to 11. Correlations between the APS and the KAI–R were of medium effect size between the affective expression in the play and the ability to understand emotion and explore self and others' affects. Children in Italy were more able to understand emotions when they were more able to express them in play. In that study, organization and imagination in play did not relate to the KAI–R variables. For the U.S. and Italian population, different processes in play predicted emotional understanding when using the same measures.

These results are supportive of Gaskins et al.'s (2007) speculation that different aspects of play are related to different functions in child development in different cultures. Children in these two cultures may use play differently in their development. Italian children may develop sensitivity to others' emotions and their own emotions through play. They may be more comfortable with affect expression and affective ideation. U.S. children may use imagination in play to develop understanding of others' perspectives. In general, U.S. children may use cognitive aspects of play to develop resources to help them "face the world." Research on play and coping has found that the cognitive dimensions of play relate to coping measures, but affect does not (Russ, Robins, & Christiano, 1999). Italian children might use emotional processing that occurs in play to develop coping resources. Further research on the correlates of affective and cognitive processes in play is warranted in these two cultures.

There were several limitations to this comparison study (Chessa et al., 2013). First, it could be questioned whether the APS captured the full range of cultural differences in play. We do not know whether children in both cultures are equally familiar and comfortable with puppets or whether they spend an equal amount of time pretending during everyday play. However, although Italian children are not equally familiar as the U.S. children with puppets, the comparable means of the comfort variable suggests cultural appropriateness for Italian children. Second, the child populations used in the U.S. and Italian studies were not matched for SES, neighborhoods, backgrounds, and so forth. It is possible that these factors could have affected the results and accounted for the differences.

## STRUCTURE OF PLAY

Another important question when thinking about play in different cultures is whether the underlying structure of the play is the same. What is the underlying factor structure? Are there differences in different cultures? In a study by Chessa, Di Riso, Delvecchio, Salcuni, and Lis (2011) of Italian school children, the factor structure was similar to that found with the APS in U.S. samples. In this study, they carried out a confirmatory factor analysis on 519 Italian children from 6 to 10 years of age. These children had received the APS. They found a two-factor structure—one for the cognitive score of imagination, organization, and elaboration and one for the affect scores of frequency of affect and variety of affect. This is a similar factor structure to those I found using exploratory factor analyses (Russ, 2004). As in the U.S. studies, comfort loaded with the cognitive scores. Also, the two factors were correlated in both samples.

The implications of these findings are that, in two different Western, Euro-American cultures, the underlying structure of play is the same. Even though there were mean differences in cognitive and affective processes in the other Chessa et al. (2013) study between the U.S. and Italian samples, the underlying processes are similar. However, there may be different correlates of the different factors in the U.S. and Italian populations, and future research should investigate this question. Another crucial question is whether a similar factor structure exists in cultures where play is not valued or is curtailed or in cultures where affective processes are regulated more tightly but cognitive processes are valued.

## CHANGES IN PLAY IN THE UNITED STATES OVER TIME

### Decreasing Play Time

There is growing recognition that children have less time to play in the United States (Elkind, 2007). This decrease in play time has been widely documented. Over the past few decades, the amount of free play for children has decreased (Hirsh-Pasek & Golinkoff, 2003; Hirsh-Pasek, Golinkoff, Berk, & Singer, 2009). Children have less time to just play spontaneously and freely. Research examining how time is allocated in elementary schools confirms that play time is disappearing from many classrooms in the United States despite evidence suggesting that play time is essential. According to surveys conducted by the National Association of Elementary School Principals (NAESP), although 96% of school systems reported having at least one recess period in 1989, only 70% of school systems reported one recess 10 years later. More recently, a 2010 Gallup poll sponsored by the Robert Wood Johnson Foundation, NAESP, and Playworks surveying 1,951 schools found that 92% of schools reported having recess, but over half of the respondents reported their school had 30 min or less for recess each day, suggesting that children are receiving minimal or no time for unstructured or child-directed activities during the day (Robert Wood Johnson Foundation, 2010).

Yet although play time is reduced in schools, this same 2010 study found that eight out of 10 principals reported that recess had a positive impact on academic achievement, and two thirds of principals reported that students listened and focused better after recess (Robert Wood Johnson Foundation, 2010). Furthermore, 96% of principals reported believing that recess had a positive impact on both social development and students' overall well-being. Thus, there is a discrepancy between what is actually occurring in schools and principals' views. Despite an observed connection between recess and positive student socioemotional and academic achievement, 77% of principals reported that their school took away recess as a typical punishment, and 20% of principals reported that they had decreased recess time because of annual academic testing.

There are many reasons why children have less time to play. In the age of the No Child Left Behind Act of 2001, schools are under increased pressure to produce strong test scores and to pack every minute of the day with structured material. In addition, many schools struggle with funding for better playgrounds and enough teachers to monitor play time. The trend toward less play time is not solely the fault of schools or government regulations: Parents too seem oriented toward childhoods with less time for play. Children have less unstructured play time at home. After a review of the research in a report by the American Academy of Pediatrics, Ginsburg (2007) outlined a range of possible factors contributing to this reduction in play. Among the factors is the increase in single parents or households in which both parents work, leaving children in child care or after-school activities for more hours of the day or to spend more hours in front of the television or video game console. Furthermore, the American culture increasingly views good parenting as building a child's skills, especially academic skills, and producing as many opportunities for them as possible. Children are enrolled in a number of structured activities such as sports, music lessons, and volunteer activities, resulting in overscheduling. College admissions policies promote the pressure that parents feel to help their child be well-rounded and well-prepared. On the practical side, for some children, the communities in which they live do not allow them to play safely outside.

The Academy of Pediatrics has called for an increasing recognition of the importance of play in child development (Ginsberg, 2007). There is little research about what is happening to actual play processes and abilities in children during this period of decreasing play time. Is the decrease resulting in poorer pretend play ability? K. H. Kim (2011) reported some evidence that there has been a decrease in creativity. What about pretend play?

## Changes in Pretend Play Processes

We (Russ & Dillon, 2011b) were in the unique position of having samples of pretend play from various child populations over a 23-year period. The same standardized play task with standardized administration and scoring was used in all studies. Therefore, over a 23-year period we could compare samples of children who had received the same play task, individually administered, which was scored in the same way. The purpose of this investigation was to compare play ability in children from 6 to 10 years of age over a 23-year period to determine whether play processes were improving, staying the same, or decreasing.

We (Russ & Dillon, 2011b) carried out an analysis of the 14 studies conducted during this 23-year period from 1985 to 2008. These included published studies as well as unpublished master's theses and dissertations. All were carried out in my research program at Case Western Reserve University. All the studies included in this comparison used the APS with school-based populations and used the same props, administration, and scoring manual. Only minor scoring changes have been made over the years. There were a number of different examiners and raters. All raters had been trained and checked for adequate interrater reliability.

Possible data points for the analysis were included or excluded on the basis of specific inclusion rules. To be included in the analysis, a study had to meet the following criteria: (a) participants were children between the ages of 6 and 10; (b) participants were taken from school-based samples, not clinical groups or at-risk populations; (c) means were reported for unselected groups of participants, not those chosen for scoring in any particular way on the APS or any other measure; and (d) the study had used the original version of the APS, not the brief rating version or the preschool version.

We analyzed how the five main APS scores may have changed over time. This was done by performing a cross-temporal meta-analysis and examining correlations between mean scores and year of data collection. The means were weighted by the sample size of each study to give better estimates of the population mean. This data analytic procedure followed that used by Jean M. Twenge in examining similar changes in test scores over time (Twenge, Konrath, Foster, Campbell, & Bushman, 2008; Twenge, Zhang, & Im, 2004). We also calculated the magnitude of the change in APS scores by using regression equations and the averaged standard deviation ($SD$) of the individual samples. To find the mean scores for specific years, we used the regression equation produced by the statistical analyses to draw the regression line. The regression equation follows the formula $y = Bx + C$, where $y$ is the predicted mean APS score, $B$ is the unstandardized regression coefficient, $x$ is the year, and $C$ is the constant or intercept. This formula yielded the position of the regression line for certain years. We then calculated the difference between a score's predicted value in the earliest year that score was obtained and the predicted value in the most recent year that score was used, obtaining a number representing the predicted amount a score would change across those years.

We also calculated the average $SD$ by averaging the within-sample $SD$s reported in the data sources; thus, this reflected the average variance of the measure in a sample of individuals. The previously calculated predicted amount that a score would change across years was divided by this average variance across those years to determine the number of $SD$s a score was predicted to shift across time. This too was the exact procedure used by Twenge et al. (2008). In the following sections, we discuss the results of our analyses.

*Organization*

There was no evidence of a change in organization scores on the APS across time. No significant correlation was found between APS organization scores and the year of data collection when weighted by sample size ($\beta = .146$, $p = .707$, $k = 9$). No correlation between organization score and time suggests that there has not been a significant change in how well children are able to organize their pretend play over time.

*Imagination*

Children were found to score progressively higher on imagination in pretend play between 1985 and 2008. There was a significant and positive correlation between APS scores of imagination and year of data collection when weighted by sample size ($\beta = .663$, $p = .026$, $k = 11$). Thus, more recently, children were more imaginative in their play.

The following is the regression equation produced by the statistical analysis: Predicted APS mean imagination score = $.028 \times$ year $- 53.65$. The regression equation yielded a score of 1.93 for the year 1985 and 2.57 for the year 2008. The average *SD* reported for the individual samples (from all the studies collected) was 1.25. Thus, APS scores of imagination increased 0.51 *SD*s from 1986 to 2008. This is a medium effect size using J. Cohen's (1977) guidelines.

## Comfort

Children also scored progressively higher on scores of comfort between 1985 and 2008. There was a significant and positive correlation between APS scores of comfort and the year of data collection when weighted by sample size ($\beta = .710$, $p = .014$, $k = 11$). More recently, children displayed more comfort engaging in fantasy play. The regression equation (Predicted APS mean imagination score $= .041 \times$ year $- 78.87$) yielded a score of 2.52 for the year 1985 and 3.46 for the year 2008. The average *SD* reported for the individual samples (from all the studies collected) was 1.40. Thus, APS scores of comfort increased 0.67 *SD*s from 1985 to 2008. This is a medium-to-large effect size (between .50 and .80) according to J. Cohen's (1977) guidelines.

## Frequency of Affect

Children ages 6 to 10 showed no clear directional change in their scores on frequency of affect on the APS across time. No significant correlation was found between APS scores of frequency of affect and year of data collection when weighted by sample size ($\beta = -.132$, $p = .659$, $k = 11$). Thus, there was no evidence of a change in how much affect children express during their pretend play over time.

## Positive Affect

No evidence of changes in scores of positive affect across time was found. No significant correlation was found between APS scores of positive affect and the year of data collection when weighted by sample size ($\beta = -.627$, $p = .183$, $k = 6$). Thus, there has not been a change in the amount of positive affect that children express during their pretend play across time.

## Negative Affect

No significant correlation was found between APS scores of negative affect and the year of data collection when weighted by sample size ($\beta = -.472$, $p = .345$, $k = 6$). However, the regression equation (Predicted APS score of negative affect $= -.496 \times$ year $+ 999.02$) yielded a score of 9.50 for 1995 and a score of 3.05 for 2008. The average *SD* reported for the individual samples was 9.29; therefore, APS scores of negative affect have decreased .69 *SD*s from

1995 to 2008, a medium-to-large effect size (between .50 and .80) according to J. Cohen's (1977) guidelines.

An examination of the data revealed that one data set (Goldstein, 1999) had an unusually high negative affect score, whereas the rest of the data points showed a relatively linear decrease in negative affect scores over time. To explore this further, the Goldstein (1999) data point whose score was unusually high was removed from the analysis. With this study removed, the regression equation was recalculated, showing a significant negative relationship between time and negative affect expression ($\beta = -.318$, $p = .01$, $k = 5$). This result suggests that the amount of negative affect that children express during pretend play is decreasing over time. The regression equation (Predicted APS score of negative affect = $-.318 \times$ year + 640.63) yielded a score of 6.22 for 1995 and a score of 2.09 for 2008. Because the average $SD$ reported for the individual samples changed to 7.35, APS scores of negative affect have decreased .56 $SD$s from 1995 to 2008, again producing a medium-to-large effect size (between .50 and .80) according to J. Cohen's (1977) guidelines. Similar analyses excluding Goldstein (1999) did not change results for the other APS scores.

*Implications of Study Findings*

The main findings of this study were that there was no evidence of change in some aspects of children's pretend play, and that there were improvements in other areas. There has been no evidence of change in children's pretend play from 1985 through 2008 in terms of organization of the play story and amount and range of affect expression. The surprising and important finding was that imagination has increased in recent play samples, as has comfort engaging in the play task. It is encouraging that these cognitive and affective processes in play have remained the same or have improved, given the decline in unstructured time for children.

There are several possible explanations for these results. First, children are resilient and may be finding ways to develop imagination and make-believe abilities other than through play. These abilities are then reflected in the pretend play task. For example, D. G. Singer and Singer (2005) explored whether the use of video games and computer games could enhance imagination in some ways. It is also possible that children are finding time to play in spite of their heavily structured schedules. Elkind (2007) suggested that children maintain the same desire to play, even though there are fewer opportunities to play. Children continue to play games and create learning experiences. It is also possible that the complexities and challenges of modern culture require creative problem solving and imagination to function from day to day.

Second, it is possible that the play task used in these studies is not sensitive to aspects of play that are in decline. For example, the imagination scale is a 5-point Likert scale that is a global measure of imagination in play. Perhaps if we looked at specific imagination behaviors, such as number of transformations of the blocks, the results would differ. However, this global rating is on the basis of consideration of a number of specific indicators of imagination and has related to measures of divergent thinking in a number of studies.

Third, it is possible that the results were confounded by other differences between the most recent samples of children and earlier samples. More recent samples were from parochial schools compared with earlier public school samples. However, the type of neighborhood was similar in both samples. Because there are only 14 studies, it is possible that these samples are not representative of the larger population.

The finding that negative affect expression in play decreased (after removing one outlier) is suggestive of a downward trend and should be explored in future research. If this finding is supported with more play studies, then the implications are important. The expression of negative affect themes in play has been shown to be related to divergent thinking (Russ & Schafer, 2006). We (Russ & Schafer, 2006) also found that positive and negative affect themes are related to expression of emotions in memory narratives, and we (Russ & Grossman-McKee, 1990) identified a relationship between affect-laden primary-process thinking on the Rorschach and affect in play. The results of these two studies suggest that expression of affect and affect-laden themes is a cross-situational ability. As discussed in earlier chapters, access to affect-laden imagery could be especially important to creativity in the arts (Russ, 2009). Constriction of negative affect expression in play, if supported in future research, could have consequences for creative expression.

These results are not consistent with recent findings reported by K. H. Kim (2011) that creativity scores, as measured by the Torrance Tests of Creativity (Torrance, Ball, & Safter, 1992), have significantly decreased since 1990. K. H. Kim reported that this decrease was especially clear in younger kindergarten through sixth-grade children. K. H. Kim analyzed a large database of normative samples for the figural version of the Torrance test. Given the large body of research that shows that pretend play ability correlates with creativity—and with the APS as well—how do we account for the finding that play ability is either stable or increasing? One explanation could be that even though children are finding ways to develop different abilities in play, they are not transferring these abilities to creativity tasks. Or perhaps creativity is still occurring in play or narrative but decreasing in divergent thinking.

Creative production in adults is driven by a variety of factors, and there are many different creative profiles of creative individuals. The abilities to imagine and use fantasy and think divergently are important ingredients, as are a strong work ethic, motivation, tolerance for failure, risk taking, and opportunity. Cultural changes may affect these different creative processes in different ways.

## IMPACT OF VIDEO GAMES

The results of our 2011 study (Russ & Dillon, 2011b) suggest that children are finding pathways in addition to pretend play to develop creative processes such as imagination. Video games, so often criticized, may actually facilitate fantasy and imagination. Although no studies to date have specifically investigated the effect of specific video games on creativity, there are studies that suggest that video games facilitate some types of cognitive functioning. More sophisticated video games require problem-solving skills. Although not demanding the total generation of a story, as in natural pretend play, many games do involve partial story generation from the child.

Henry Jenkins (1998) conceptualized game design as narrative architecture, viewing many video games as having narrative elements. Jenkins discussed video games as being virtual play spaces that compensate for disappearing backyards. Often, the narrative focuses on the struggle to explore and master spaces. Games involve world making and spatial storytelling. He outlined four ways in which the narrative experience is involved in video games. First, spatial stories can use preexisting narrative associations to design elements. Second, narrative events can be enacted by the characters in the game; the gamer witnesses or performs narrative events. Third, there is embedded narrative information that the gamer must use in playing the video game. Fourth, the child generates part of the narrative. The game provides resources for the emerging storyline. The Sims game (Wright, 2000) is an excellent example of this kind of game. The child writes a large part of the story, and there are many narrative possibilities that involve conflict and romance. The story is open-ended, although there is structure provided by the design and the rules. Playing these storytelling video games could enable children to develop imagination and feel comfortable with make-believe and fantasy. This area is ripe for investigation.

## PLAY AND THE DEVELOPMENT OF THE CREATIVE SELF

Pretend play is a place where children can be themselves, a place where they can "let go" and not censor their thoughts and feelings. Because the expressions in play are slightly distanced or symbolically transformed, the child can experience full expression of the self. This must be an experience of authenticity for the child. Play is one vehicle for this experience. From a different perspective, play is a place where the child can experience *flow*. Csikszentmihalyi (1990) introduced the concept of flow as an integral part of creative expression. Joy and love of the task frequently accompany the flow experience. In the play experience, a child can learn to seek out the experience of flow. She or he may learn through play to enjoy creative acts and creative production. Memories become consolidated, and the narrative of the self is formed. Engaging in creative acts could become part of the child's identity and help give a sense of purpose to life. Play and the development of the creative self is an important area for future study. Most important, as a culture we need to value play and convey that value to children.

## CONCLUSION

The culture shapes the play of children. Through parenting and exposure to the cultural context, cognitive and affective processes in play develop in different ways in different cultures. Gaskins et al.'s (2007) work showed that many aspects of play are universal, such as joy in playing and reality-based scenarios. The type and quality of pretend elements vary. Observations of play in different cultures have suggested that play is used to develop processes and skills that are important in adulthood in that culture.

In Western cultures, in which creative functioning as adults in a complex world is important, pretend play in children is valued. But we can see from the Chessa et al. (2013) comparison of play in the United States and Italy that there are differences in pretend play even in Western cultures. And there is some evidence of different correlates of pretend play as well (Chessa et al., 2013). The comparison of pretend play in different cultures with standardized measures of play is an important area for future research.

It is encouraging that, at least for the play processes measured by the APS, pretend play abilities in U.S. children have remained stable and, in the case of imagination in play, increased over the past 23 years. This finding is in spite of well-documented decreases in unstructured play time for children. My opinion is that children are resilient, are still finding ways to play and use their imagination, and that many video games and other forms of media and technology may be aiding the process of imagination. How these abilities transfer to the actual production of creative products in adulthood remains to be seen—and it is hoped—investigated.

# AFTERWORD: CONVERGING EVIDENCE

The thesis of this volume is that pretend play in childhood is where many of the cognitive and affective processes important in creativity occur. In pretend play, the child expresses a number of cognitive and affective processes that are unique to the creative process. Evidence for the importance of pretend play in the development of creativity comes from multiple sources. Research from the animal literature, theories of evolution, theories of child development, studies of different cultures, correlational research, longitudinal research, experiments, play training studies, case studies of the lives of creative adults, and observations of creative children all point to the importance of pretend play for developing processes important in creative production. Converging evidence supports the importance of pretend play for the development of creative processes.

Pretend play itself is a creative act. It is a creative production for children that illustrates Richard's (1990, 2007) concept of everyday creativity. Also, it is an example of little-c or mini-c creativity. As we investigate the correlates of pretend play, we should keep in mind that pretend play itself is also a creative production. Perhaps we should consider using pretend play as an outcome variable in some studies of creativity.

The correlational evidence that supports an association between pretend play and some of the processes important in creativity is strong. Correlational studies from different research labs and with different measures of play have consistently found associations. Some of these studies were quite rigorous. Intelligence, a major possible confounding variable, was controlled for and usually did not account for the relationship. Many of the studies used measures of divergent thinking, a key process in creative thinking. In addition, the abilities to generate ideas, to have a broad search process, to think flexibly and recombine ideas, and to access memories and affect in memories are all important in different ways in different domains. Case studies have illustrated the many different profiles possible in creative individuals. There are many routes to creativity, and pretend play is a way for many processes to be expressed and refined. Not all children use pretend play to develop these processes. They grow in other ways. But many children do engage in pretend play and express these processes and practice with these processes. The variety of ways in which creativity can develop poses a challenge for longitudinal research.

There is no consensus in the field about the robustness of the evidence that supports play as a facilitator of creativity. I agree with Dansky's (1999) conclusion that there are well-done studies that do support play as having a facilitative role in developing imagination and creativity. Lillard et al. (2013) concluded that there is not convincing evidence that play enhances creativity. However, they did conclude that there was evidence that pretend play could have a causal role in narrative development. I would argue that the ability to tell stories is a major form of creative thinking.

Research from my lab at Case Western Reserve University with school-age children is promising in that a play intervention did increase imagination and affect in play in several studies (Hoffmann, 2012; Moore & Russ, 2008). There were transfer effects on a divergent thinking task in one study. Play intervention studies are challenging. First, they must be effective in improving processes in play such as imagination and affect in fantasy. Second, they must then result in improved performance on tasks such as divergent thinking, insight, storytelling, and so forth. Finally, they must demonstrate increased creativity over a long period, ideally to adulthood. To carry out this kind of systematic research inquiry requires large samples, multisite studies, continual refinement of the play intervention, and funding sources. In addition, Weisberg, Hirsh-Pasek, and Golinkoff (2013) called for the use of statistical models and methods that are appropriate to the complexity of the play area.

Another issue is whether we should be focusing on specific processes in play or have a global play measure. My opinion is that we need to focus on specific processes that occur in play and identify the mechanisms that enhance different types of creativity. The development of the Affect in Play Scale (Russ, 1987, 2004) was one attempt to identify and measure specific play processes. There is a need for more measures of play with a specific focus. Different pretend play processes are important in different domains of creativity and may have different developmental trajectories. Forthcoming is a special issue of the *American Journal of Play* that will present the views of a variety of leading researchers in the play area on the state of the science of play research (Golinkoff, Hirsh-Pasek, Lillard, & Russ, in press). Developing optimal next steps for research in the play and creativity area is essential.

Children are resilient. They can develop cognitive and affective processes that are important in creativity in many ways. Pretend play has the advantage of being a place where many of these processes can be expressed. In that sense, play is a global activity: It leaves room for unique individual expressions in children's development. It is natural to children and a valuable asset and resource. As a culture, we should study play and learn from it. Most important, we should protect it and make sure that each child has the time and space to create through pretend play.

# APPENDIX A: AFFECT IN PLAY SCALE

The Affect in Play Scale (APS)[1] consists of a standardized play task and a criterion-based rating scale. The APS is appropriate for children 6 to 10 years of age, which includes children in Grades 1 through 4. The APS measures the amount and types of affect expression in children's fantasy play. The scale rates the frequency and intensity of affective expression, variety of affect categories, quality of fantasy, organization, imagination, comfort in play, and integration of affect. Play sessions are 5-minute, standardized puppet-play periods.

## The Affect in Play Scale Play Task

The play task consists of two human puppets—one boy and one girl—and three small blocks that are laid out on a table. The puppets have neutral facial expressions. Both Caucasian and African American versions of puppets are used, depending on the child population. The blocks are brightly colored and of different shapes. The play props and instructions are unstructured enough that individual differences in play can emerge. The task is administered individually to the child and the play is videotaped. The instructions for the task are as follows:

> I'm here to learn about how children play. I have here two puppets and would like you to play with them any way you like for 5 minutes. For example, you can have the puppets do something together. I also have some blocks that you can use. Be sure to have the puppets talk out loud. The video camera will be on so that I can remember what you say and do. I'll tell you when to stop.

The child is told when there is 1 minute left with the instruction, "You have 1 minute left."

## Prompts and Special Circumstances

- If the child does not know to put on the puppets, tell him or her to put them on. Let the child know when they can start, and start timing from that point.
- If the child does not start to play, prompt the child after 30 seconds by saying, "Go ahead, have the puppets do something together." Two prompts of this sort can be given. After 2 minutes of no play, the task should be discontinued.

---

[1]Anna Grossman-McKee, Zina Rutkin, and Amir Jassani contributed to the development of the scale. Larissa Niec, Astrida Kaugars, and Ethan Schafer contributed to a refinement.

- If the child plays but does not have the puppets talk, prompt with, "Have the puppets talk out loud so I can hear," after 30 seconds. Two prompts can be given, spaced about 1 minute apart.
- If a child has been playing, but then stops before time is up, prompt with "You still have time left; keep on playing." Prompt a second time, if needed, with, "Keep on playing; I'll tell you when to stop." Most children who have already played will be able to continue with prompts. If they cannot, then discontinue after 2 minutes of no play.
- Be sure not to give any verbal reinforcement during the child's play. It is important, however, to be attentive and watch the child and be interested. After the child has finished, say, "That was good" or "That was fine."
- Be sure to stop after 5 minutes. A wristwatch with a second hand is adequate. Time in an unobtrusive manner.

## THE AFFECT IN PLAY SCALE RATING SCALE

The APS measures the amount and types of affective expression in children's fantasy play. The scale measures affect themes in the play narrative. Both emotion-laden content and expression of emotion in the play are coded. The APS also measures cognitive dimensions of the play, such as quality of fantasy and imagination. Holt's (1977) scoring system for primary process on the Rorschach and Singer's (1973) play scales was used as models for the development of the scoring system. In addition, the work of Izard (1977) and Tomkins (1962, 1963) was consulted to ensure that the affect categories were comprehensive and covered all major types of emotion expressed by children in the 4-to-10 age group.

There are three major affect scores for the APS:

- *Total frequency of units of affective expression.* A unit is defined as one scorable expression by an individual puppet. In a two-puppet dialogue, expressions of each puppet are scored separately. A unit can be the expression of an affect state, an affect theme, or a combination of the two. An example of an affect state would be one puppet saying, "This is fun." An example of an affect theme would be "Here is a bomb that is going to explode." The expression can be verbal (e.g., "I hate you") or nonverbal (e.g., one puppet punching the other). The frequency of affect score is the total number of units of affect expressed in the 5-minute period. If nonverbal activity, such as fighting, occurs in a continuous fashion, a new unit is scored every 5 seconds.

- *Variety of affect categories*. There are 11 possible affect categories: happiness/pleasure, anxiety/fear, sadness/hurt, frustration/disappointment, nurturance/affection, aggression, competition, oral, oral aggression, sexual, anal. The variety of affect score is the number of different categories of affect expressed in the 5-minute period. Affect categories can be classified as positive affect (happiness, nurturance, competition, oral, sexual) and negative affect (anxiety, sadness, aggression, frustration, oral aggression, anal). Another classification is primary-process affect (aggression, oral, oral aggression, sexual, anal) and nonprimary-process affect (happiness, sadness, anxiety, frustration, competition, nurturance).
- *Mean intensity of affective expression* (1–5 rating). This rating measures the intensity of the feeling state or content theme. Each unit of affect is rated for intensity on a 5-point scale.

Because scoring intensity is time consuming, we score this only when there is a specific interest in the intensity dimension.

## CRITERIA FOR AFFECT CONTENT AND INTENSITY RATINGS

An affect unit is scored when there is an expression of an affect content theme, emotion word, or nonverbal expression of emotion in the play narrative. All of the affect intensity ratings are based on the expression of affect content themes, emotion words, and nonverbal expressions of emotions. "I like this hot dog" has both an affective content theme ("hot dog"—oral) and an emotional expression word ("like"). It could also be accompanied by a nonverbal expression of positive affect (e.g., voice tone, clapping). In general, combinations of emotional expression and emotion word and content themes get higher intensity ratings than the theme alone or emotional expression alone. The general criteria for the intensity ratings are

1. Reference to affect content.
2. Reference to affect content with special emphasis, which implies experiencing (e a personal referent).
3. Current experiencing, which includes (a) moderate action alone, (b) emotion with a conversational voice, and (c) a primary-process theme plus mild feeling state.
4. Stronger current experiencing, which includes (a) mild action plus a mild feeling state; (b) strong action alone; (c) strong affect alone; (d) for primary-process categories, an unusual and strong emotion or strong theme word, and (e) primary-process theme and moderate affect.

5. Strong feeling state, which includes (a) action plus a strong feeling state, (b) an extreme primary-process theme word, (c) extremely strong affect, and (d) extremely strong action.

In general, affective theme, emotional expression (emotion word, tone, facial expression, etc.) and action are additive components.

## SPECIFIC CRITERIA FOR AFFECT CATEGORIES AND INTENSITY RATINGS

### Aggression

Expression of anger; fighting, destruction, or harm to another character or object; or reference to destructive objects (guns, knives) or actions (breaking).

1. Reference to aggressive content (e.g., "Here's a toy gun," "Here's a knife," "This is broken").
2. Personalized references to aggressive content; mild bickering (e.g., "I have a knife," "I'll break it," "Let's fight," "No, I don't want to do that").
3. Actual fighting, hitting, tussling; destroying another's property; aggressive dialogue with feeling; angry feeling statements (e.g., "I am mad," "I don't want to do that—that's stupid" [with feeling], "I'll punch you," "I don't like you," "Let's fight" [with feeling]).
4. Action plus dialogue, strong feeling state, strong theme word (e.g., hitting plus "You're stupid," "I hate you," "Here is a bomb that is going to explode").
5. Strong action and strong dialogue, extreme emotional theme (e.g., "I'll kill you," "I'm going to beat your brains to pulp," actions of shooting or stabbing).

### Nurturance/Affection

Expressions of empathy or sympathy with another character, affection, helping, and support.

1. Reference to nurturing, affectionate themes (e.g., "Sally and John are friends," "Yesterday, my mom helped me").
2. A personalized nurturing theme or theme with special emphasis (e.g., "Are you OK?" "I'll help," "Don't forget your sweater," "Sally and John are best friends").

3. Nurturing activity, current feeling state of affection (e.g., "I like you," "You are my friend," gift giving, patting, helping).
4. Action plus dialogue, strong verbal statement, or strong action (e.g., hugging, dancing together, "I really like you," "You're my very best friend").
5. Strong action plus strong dialogue, strong nurturing action or word (e.g., "I love you," "I really like you" [while patting or hugging]).

## Happiness/Pleasure

Expression of positive affect that denotes pleasure, happiness, having a good time, enjoyment, and contentedness.

1. Reference to content involving happiness, pleasure, and satisfaction; general preference statements (e.g., "This is nice," "Saturday is the best day of the week").
2. Reference with special emphasis; personalized, affective content distanced by past or future or third person; subjective reference to fun and amusement (e.g., "Johnny looks happy," "That was fun," "Oh boy, the circus is in town, That's good").
3. Current affect experiencing or activity involving happiness or pleasure; happiness themes plus feeling state (e.g., "I feel happy" [conversational tone], "This is fun," hand clapping, "I love to get presents," "I like this" [with strong tone], "This is fun").
4. Activity plus affective expression; strong feeling state; strong action alone (e.g., jumping up and down with happy expression, "I feel happy" [with feeling], "Whee, this is fun," singing happily, dancing happily, "I really like this").
5. Combination of two of the following: emotional expression, theme, or action (at least one at extreme level or two at strong level). Extreme emotional words are also scored (e.g., "I love this" [with action], jumping, laughing).

## Anxiety/Fear

Expressions of fear and anxiety; content such as school anxiety, doctor visits, concern about punishment, and worry; and actions of fleeing and hiding or agitation.

1. Reference to a fearful theme (e.g., "Oh, it's time for school," "It's time to go to the doctor").

2. Mild anticipation with a hint of negative consequence (e.g., "Oh, no—I broke the teacher's ruler," "Uh-oh, I dropped my book").

3. Fearful theme with mild affect, more direct reference to consequences, withdrawal or fleeing activity (e.g., "We're going to get in trouble," "Let's hide from them," "There's a monster over there," "I see a ghost").

4. Clear expression of fear or anxiety, a combination of theme and strong affect (e.g., "I'm scared," "The monster's coming after me," "Mom's gonna spank me" [with feeling]).

5. Withdrawal activity plus fear, strong theme plus fearful affect (e.g., "I'm scared he'll kill us," "Don't let him hurt me" [while hiding]).

### Sadness/Hurt

Expression of illness, physical injury, pain, sadness, and loneliness.

1. Nonpersonalized reference to sadness or hurt in a conversational tone (e.g., "Sally got hurt yesterday," "Joe was in the hospital").

2. Personalized reference to sadness or hurt (conversational) or nonpersonalized reference with an exclamation (e.g., "Sally was crying yesterday," "Sometimes I cry").

3. Current experience of sadness or hurt state in conversational tone, actions of sadness or hurt (e.g., "That's sad," "That hurts," "I'm sad," "I have a headache," "Please don't leave me alone").

4. Statement of sadness or hurt action, stronger verbal statements, more intense sad action (e.g., "Ouch, that hurts," "Boy, I am sad," [whimpering, whining], "I don't want you to go").

5. Strong verbal statement of sadness or hurt with action, use of strong sad or hurt words, intense current experiencing of sadness or hurt (e.g., "I don't want the shot" [while crying], "This hurts" [while crying], moaning in pain).

### Frustration/Disappointment/Dislike

Expressions of disappointment and frustration with activities, objects, and limitations.

1. Reference to frustration or disappointment, nonpersonalized statement of frustration or disappointment in a conversational voice (e.g., "It fell," "Math is boring," "She seems bored").

2. Personalized statement of frustration or disappointment (conversational tone), current action of frustration or disappointment (e.g., "I'm not good at building," "It fell" [with affect]).
3. Current experience of frustration or disappointment (conversational tone), current action of frustration or disappointment (e.g., "This is hard," "I'm bored," "I can't do this," making noises such as clicking tongue).
4. Statement of frustration or disappointment with an action, statement of current experience of frustration or disappointment (exclamation), stronger action (e.g., "I can't get this" [while knocking down the blocks], "Boy, this is hard," "This is a rotten day," "Oh, darn, I can't get this").
5. Stronger statement of frustration or disappointment with an action, strong experiencing statement, strong action (e.g., slamming down the blocks while saying, "I can't do this"; swearing; "I hate this").

## Competition

Expressions of wanting to win, competitive game playing, pride in achievement, and striving for achievement.

1. Reference to competitive games (e.g., mentioning cops and robbers, checkers, hide and seek).
2. Personal reference to competitive games (e.g., "Let's play tag," "Let's see who can run the fastest").
3. Game playing with action, competitive themes with mild affect (e.g., playing hide and seek, "I want to win," "Mine is the best").
4. Action plus affect, strong feeling state (e.g., playing tag and saying, "I win"; "I'm going to beat you" [with feeling]; playing tag and saying, "Got you").
5. Action plus strong feeling state (e.g., playing tag and saying, "I'm king of the mountain"; jumping up and down and saying, "I win").

## Oral

Expressions of oral content of food, cooking, eating, and drinking. Affect expressions are positive about oral content.

1. Reference to oral content of food, cooking, mouth (e.g., "Here's an ice cream shop," "This is a new special cheese").

2. Personalized reference to oral content or content with special emphasis (e.g., "Let's eat dinner," "I'll feed you," "Johnny is hungry").
3. Current experiencing that includes eating behavior or an emotional word in addition to oral content (e.g., "I like candy," "I am hungry," "That food looks good," actual eating behavior).
4. Eating behavior plus affective content, oral-themed words plus moderate affective expression in voice or facial expression (e.g., "Mmm, this is good candy," "I really like cake").
5. Strong eating behavior plus strong affective expression (e.g., "Wow, this is great" [while eating]).

## Oral Aggression

Expressions of oral aggressive themes, such as biting, or food that has negative affect associated with it.

1. Reference to oral aggressive themes (e.g., teeth, dentist, poison, Dracula).
2. Personal reference to oral aggressive themes, a more intense theme word, special emphasis (e.g., "Let's go to the dentist," "That dog might bite me").
3. References plus mild affect, activity such as vomiting (e.g., biting activity, "This food tastes terrible").
4. Reference plus strong affect, activity plus affect (e.g., biting with feeling, "This is poison—yech").
5. Strong affect and activity (e.g., eating people, Dracula attacks puppet and bites).

## Anal

Expression of anal content includes dirt and making a mess.

1. Reference to anal content (e.g., "This is a mess," "That's dirty").
2. Personalized reference to anal content or impersonal reference with special emphasis (e.g., "I made a mess," "I'll get dirty," "Be careful not to make a mess," "We have to clean up").
3. Reference to anal content plus mild affect (e.g., "That's a real mess," "I don't like dirt," "This is muddy").
4. Anal activity plus feeling state, anal theme plus strong feeling state (e.g., "Yech—this is a mess," "This is gross," "Look at his butt").

5. Strong anal theme word, strong expression of disgust around dirt, inappropriate word (e.g., "Look—he pooped," "This is an awful mess").

### Sexual

Expressions of sexual content.

1. Reference to boyfriend or girlfriend (e.g., "That's his girlfriend").
2. Personalized reference or special emphasis (e.g., "I'm getting undressed," "He's my boyfriend," "She's going on a date").
3. Mild activity or sexual content with a feeling state (e.g., "I like to kiss," hugging with sexual overtones).
4. Sexual activity plus feeling or strong sexual content (e.g., kissing, dancing with sexual overtones, looking under dress).
5. Extreme sexual content or strong activity (e.g., strong kissing, blatant sexual jokes, reference to genitals).

## QUALITY OF FANTASY

The quality of fantasy rating is the mean of the following three dimensions of fantasy.

### Organization

This rating scale measures the quality of the plot and the complexity of the story.

1. Series of unrelated events, no cause and effect, disjointed.
2. Some cause and effect, series of loosely related events.
3. Cause and effect, organized in a temporal sequence, but no overall integrated plot.
4. More cause and effect, close to an integrated plot.
5. Integrated plot with beginning, middle, and end.

### Elaboration

This rating scale measures the amount of embellishment in the play. One should consider theme, facial expression, voice tones, and character development.

1. Simple themes with no embellishment, few details.
2. Minimal embellishment.

3. Much embellishment in one or two dimensions.
4. Moderate embellishment across many dimensions.
5. Much embellishment across many dimensions—many details, high activity, sound effects, changes in voice, and lots of facial expressions and verbal inflection.

## Imagination

This rating scale measures the novelty and uniqueness of the play and the ability to pretend and use fantasy, as well as the ability to transform the blocks and pretend with them.

1. No symbolism or transformations, no fantasy.
2. One or two instances of simple transformations, no novel events, few fantasy events in the story.
3. Three or more transformations, some fantasy and pretend events such as "Let's play house," some variety of events, no novel events or events removed from daily experience.
4. Many transformations; variety of events; some novel fantasy events; some fantasy with unusual twists or removed from daily experience, such as living in a castle or building a space ship; other characters in addition to the two puppets are included in the story.
5. Many transformations and many fantasy themes, novelty of ideas is evident, fantasy has new twists and often has elements outside of daily experience.

The organization, elaboration, and imagination scores can be used separately or combined into a mean quality of fantasy score for each child.

## Comfort

A global rating for the child's comfort in play measures the involvement of the child in the play and the enjoyment of the play. The lower end of the scale rates comfort more than enjoyment, and the higher end of the scale weighs pleasure and involvement.

1. Reticent, distressed, stops and starts.
2. Some reticence and stiffness.
3. Child is OK but is not enjoying and not involved. Continues to play.
4. Comfortable and involved.
5. Very comfortable, involved, and enjoying the play.

## Affect Integration Score

The affect integration score is obtained by multiplying the quality of fantasy score by the frequency of affect score. This score taps how well the affect is integrated into cognition.

To summarize, the nine major scores on the APS are total frequency of affect, variety of affect categories, intensity of affect, organization, elaboration, imagination, quality of fantasy, comfort, and affect integration.

Practically, the APS is easy to administer and takes only 5 minutes. The scoring system takes time to learn but then takes about 15 to 20 minutes per child. We have found that about 8% of children will not be able to engage in the play task. They are not able to make up a story or play in any way. For those children, we score 0 for frequency and variety of affect and 1 for the fantasy scores. The comfort score is based on what was observed. The inference is that lack of ability to do the task reflects low levels of the construct that the task is measuring. There is a videotape available for training and administration of the APS.[2]

---

[2]To obtain a copy of the videotape, contact the author at sandra.russ@case.edu

# APPENDIX B: TRANSCRIPTS FROM PLAY FACILITATION SESSIONS

## Child 2, Session 1

*Adult:* OK, so, I have a bunch of toys for us to play with, and what we're going to do is we're going to make up different stories with the toys. So then we'll make up a story with the toys and we'll play it out with the toys however you want, and then when I tell you to, we'll switch stories. OK, how does that sound? [INSTRUCTIONS]

*Child:* OK.

*Adult:* And we can have the dolls or the animals talk out loud so that we know what's happening in the story and we can know how they feel. [INSTRUCTIONS]

*Child:* OK.

*Adult:* OK? And you can use your imagination and make up new things of pretend, and we are going to start by making up a story about a girl or a boy who gets ready for a day at school. What might a story like that look like? Need some of the people? [ORGANI-ZATION PROMPT]

*Child:* Well, should I do it now?

*Adult:* Yeah, you can play it out however you want. You can be who-ever you want. I can be this guy. So let's see—a story about a day at school. Daughter, time to get up. [MODELING FANTASY]

*Child:* OK.

*Adult:* Don't want to be late for school. [MODELING FANTASY + NEGATIVE AFFECT]

*Child:* I know, I'll walk to school today.

*Adult:* Oh, OK, good idea. Do you have all of your stuff with you? [MODELING FANTASY]

*Child:* Um. [*Gets the wagon.*]

*Adult:* Good idea. [PRAISE]

*Child:* Yes.

*Adult:* Oh, OK, you have all your books and everything? [MODELING FANTASY]

*Child:* Yes.

*Adult:* OK, well, have a good day. [MODELING ANIMATION + POSITIVE AFFECT]

*Child:* Bye.

*Adult:* Then what could happen next in your story? [ORGANIZATION PROMPT]

*Child:* She could find an animal on the way.

*Adult:* OK. [NEUTRAL RESPONSE]

*Child:* [*Picks up moose toy.*]

*Adult:* What would that look like? [IMAGINATION PROMPT]

*Child:* Walking along and then she sees an animal and then takes it to school.

*Adult:* OK, show me. [DIRECTION]

*Child:* [*Singing. The next section occurred over time with the trainer observing the play.*] Ooh, a horse . . . I mean, a donkey! I don't think he has a home, so I will take him. But first I should go to school, so he can just sit in my wagon with all my things while I go to school. And then . . . now he's thinking, where is she taking me? OK, I am at school, so you can stay in the wagon, and I'll be gone for, like, a while. Ohhh.

*Adult:* Glad you made it to school on time. [ANIMATION + POSITIVE AFFECT]

*Child:* I found a donkey on the way.

*Adult:* You found a donkey! [MODELING FANTASY]

*Child:* Yeah.

*Adult:* Do you want to bring it inside?

*Child:* OK.

*Adult:* Maybe you could use it for show and tell. [MODELING FANTASY]

*Child:* Oh, we have show and tell today? [ANIMATION]

*Adult:* Sure, if you want to. [MODELING FANTASY]

*Child:* I'll come in to school now.

*Adult:* These could be, like, all the kids. [MODELING CHARACTER ATTRIBUTION]

*Child:* Hi, friends at school.

*Adult:* Hi. [MODELING FANTASY]

*Child:* This is a donkey, and I found him on my way to school, so I am going to talk about him to you. [*Adult watching.*] Well, I named my donkey Brownie.

*Adult:* Oh, that's a cool name. [MODELING FANTASY]

*Child:* Well, he's a . . . well, I don't know where he is from—I just found him on my way to school, so I thought he didn't have a home, so I'll keep my donkey and then show him to my dad at home.

*Adult:* Good presentation. [MODELING FANTASY]

*Child:* Thank you.

*Adult:* Can we make up an ending to this story? [ORGANIZATION PROMPT]

*Child:* She could go home and then show her dad.

*Adult:* OK, yeah, let's do it. [REDIRECTION]

*Child:* [*Gets wagon.*]

*Adult:* School's over. See you tomorrow. [MODELING FANTASY]

*Child:* Hi, Dad.

*Adult:* Oh, this is Dad again? Hi! How was your day at school? [MODELING FANTASY]

*Child:* I found a donkey.

*Adult:* Oh, wow. [MODELING ANIMATION]

*Child:* His name is Brownie.

*Adult:* Was he with you at school all day? [MODELING ANIMATION]

*Child:* Yeah, I showed him at show and tell.

*Adult:* Oh, neat. What did the other kids think? [AFFECT PROMPT]

*Child:* They thought that was a good presentation.

*Adult:* Oh, very good. [MODELING ANIMATION + POSITIVE AFFECT]

*Child:* Well, I'll go to bed now.

*Adult:*  OK, you had a busy day. [MODELING ANIMATION]

*Child:*  [*Doll lies down.*]

*Adult:*  All right, good story. She gets up, she walks to school, finds a donkey, shows it at show and tell, and then brings it home and tells her dad about her whole day. [SUMMARIZING]

*Child:*  Yeah.

*Adult:*  I like how that story had lots of pretend. This guy was two people, right? Because we didn't have quite enough characters. OK, now let's switch stories, and this time we are going to try to make up a story with lots of feelings in it, so we'll have everybody talk out loud so we know how they feel—we did a little bit of that in the last story. This time we are going to try to do a sad story. So it's going to be sad because a girl loses her favorite toy. [DIRECTIONS]

*Child:*  OK.

*Adult:*  Show me what that might be like. [FANTASY PROMPT]

*Child:*  OK, well, in this story she is going to have a farm, and these are her farm leaders, but this one likes to eat stuff, so . . .

*Adult:*  OK. [NEUTRAL RESPONSE]

*Child:*  [*Giraffe keeps falling over.*]

*Adult:*  Sometimes we stick him on a block so he stays. [REDIRECTION]

*Child:*  Her favorite toy is a tire here, so. [*Adult watching.*] OK, well, goodnight.

*Adult:*  Goodnight. [MODELING ANIMATION]

*Child:*  I love my toy, and it's a tire. It's so squishy and helps me fall asleep.

*Adult:*  I like your bed; that's good pretend. [PRAISE]

*Child:*  Goodnight.

*Adult:*  Goodnight. Sleep well. [ANIMATION]

*Child:*  Then she falls asleep, and then she wakes up because she gets up at night. [*Adult watching.*] Oh, no, where is my tire toy? I can't fall asleep without it.

*Adult:*  Why are you awake? It's the middle of the night. [ANIMA-TION + NEGATIVE AFFECT]

*Child:*  My tire toy isn't here, so I can't fall asleep.

*Adult:*  Oh, no. I guess we have to look for it. Hmm, it's not over here. [MODELING ANIMATION]

*Child:*  Is it under here? No, it wouldn't fall. [*Adult watching.*] It's not in the wagon either. It's not in here. Well, I'll try to fall asleep now.

*Adult:*  OK. [MODELING ANIMATION]

*Child:*  We'll find it tomorrow. Goodnight.

*Adult:*  Goodnight. [MODELING ANIMATION]

*Child:*  [*Looks at toy.*]

*Adult:*  How does she feel now? Can she say how she feels? [AFFECT PROMPT]

*Child:*  I feel so sad. I lost my favorite toy. [*Adult watching.*] Everyone else probably has their toys and they're sound asleep.

*Adult:*  I feel bad for you because you feel sad. [MODELING ANIMATION + NEGATIVE AFFECT]

*Child:*  I feel like I'm not hungry anymore. [ANIMATION + POSITIVE AFFECT]

*Adult:*  Yeah, how does he feel? [AFFECT PROMPT]

*Child:*  Guys, I just ate some food, and I was going to share it with you, but you probably don't like eating tires. They're really yummy. [*Adult watching.*] Oh, I like eating tires. Where is it? Oh, the tire's in my stomach right now.

*Adult:*  How does he feel? [AFFECT PROMPT]

*Child:*  I feel starved.

*Adult:*  Aw. Good story! [PRAISE] So she's sad because she loses it, but he's pretty happy because he gets to eat it, and he's not hungry anymore, and then he's kinda jealous, right? Because he's still hungry. [*Laughs.*] [LABELING FEELINGS] That one was fun. OK, so we are going to switch back to one with lots of imagination and pretend like how you pretended that this was a bed and that kind of thing. And like this is their whole farm, right? You're good at that. Let's do one about somebody getting ready to go to bed. Make it any kind of story you want. [IMAGINATION PROMPT]

*Child:*  I'm home from school now.

*Adult:*  Oh, welcome home. [MODELING ANIMATION]

*Child:*  Um, well, yesterday you said I was going to get a new bed, and I can't fall asleep without a bed because I can't sleep on the floor.

| Adult: | That's right, we bought you a new bed while you were at school. [MODELING ANIMATION] |
|---|---|
| Child: | OK. [*Moves toys around.*] Know where it is? [ANIMATION] |
| Adult: | It's a surprise. It's in your wagon outside. |
| Child: | I'm going to go see it. [*Adult watching.*] Whoo hoo! It's a new bed. I don't feel tired. I don't want to go to bed now. |
| Adult: | What could you do to make yourself more tired before bedtime? |
| Child: | Well, usually my tire makes me feel sleepy because it's so tired. |
| Adult: | [Laughs.] Oh, OK, well, then maybe you should play with your toy for a while then. [MODELING ANIMATION] |
| Child: | I'll go get it. [*Adult watching.*] Hmm, this doesn't seem to be working. I am going to go watch TV, but I am not supposed to go out of the room until I fall asleep, but I will bring the TV upstairs. |
| Adult: | Oh, good idea. Have that be the TV. [PRAISE] |
| Child: | I'll put it in the wagon. |
| Adult: | Oh, it's really heavy. [REFLECTION] |
| Child: | There, this will help. [*Adult watching.*] Now I am asleep. |
| Adult: | Oh, good, she fell asleep in her new bed. [ANIMATION + POSITIVE AFFECT] |
| Child: | Now take it down. |
| Adult: | Now I should take the TV back downstairs so that I can watch TV. We should buy another TV. [MODELING ANIMATION] |
| Child: | [*Puts TV on top of block.*] |
| Adult: | Oh, is that the TV stand? [REFLECTION] |
| Child: | Yeah. |
| Adult: | OK, good one. That one had lots of pretend. I liked how you thought of that as the TV. That was a good idea. OK, let's try another story with lots of feelings in it this time, but this time it can be a happy story. How about a happy story when someone gets a new present. |
| Child: | Um, OK. Just . . . |
| Adult: | Don't need those for this one. [REFLECTION] |
| Child: | Hi, Dad. |
| Adult: | Hi. [MODELING ANIMATION] |

*Child:*   Um, well, can you drive me to the zoo today?

*Adult:*   Sure.

*Child:*   Let's get in your motorcycle-slash-car.

*Adult:*   OK.

*Child:*   You know, I'm, like, old enough to have a car now. Should I be able to get one?

*Adult:*   Uh, sure.

*Child:*   Well, how about instead of the zoo we go to the car store?

*Adult:*   OK, I think you are old enough.

*Child:*   Hi. Are you looking for a car today?

*Adult:*   Yes, we are looking for a car for my daughter. She is old enough to drive now.

*Child:*   Well, I have the perfect car.

*Adult:*   OK, well, show us where it is.

*Child:*   I have to go get it.

*Adult:*   OK.

*Child:*   [*Puts Lego together to build a car.*]

*Adult:*   We can make it be anything because it's all pretend.

*Child:*   Here's your car. This is a nice car. I will drive it home. Here is the money for it. I feel so happy that I just got a new car.

*Adult:*   I am glad that you are happy.

*Child:*   Well, you can drive home in your car, and I will drive home in mine.

*Adult:*   OK, see you at home. Be careful.

*Child:*   Home.

*Adult:*   Hey, where did you get a new car?

*Child:*   I got a new car from the car place.

*Adult:*   Wow, you are really lucky. I don't have a new car.

*Child:*   Well, are you old enough to have a car?

*Adult:*   Yeah, but my dad didn't get me one yet. Your dad must really like you.

*Child:*   Yeah, 'cause he's my dad.

| | |
|---|---|
| *Adult:* | [*Laughs.*] Can I go for a ride? [MODELING ANIMATION] |
| *Child:* | OK. |
| *Adult:* | Great! [MODELING ANIMATION + POSITIVE AFFECT] |
| *Child:* | [*Car noise.*] OK, well, let's drive. |
| *Adult:* | Wow, cool. |
| *Child:* | OK, well, we're back home. |
| *Adult:* | Thanks for the ride in your new car. |
| *Child:* | You're welcome. I feel so happy I got a new car. |
| *Adult:* | Good story. OK, we are going to do one more story, and this time it can be about anything you want. |
| *Child:* | OK. In this one there is no people. |
| *Adult:* | No people. |
| *Child:* | Just animals. |
| *Adult:* | Can they talk? |
| *Child:* | Yeah. It can be a fun story. I am so tired. We've been walking for so long. I'm just hungry. Um, well, here's some things over here. What can we do with these? Eat them. No, we're not hungry. We should build somewhere to live in. Well, I am really good at building, so I'll start building, and you guys look for food. Found some. We'll go look for some more food. So now they're, like, gone. |
| *Adult:* | Now they're looking for food. |
| *Child:* | This will be hard to build this, right? Yeah, it'll be really hard. Well, this could be our refrigerator. It is really good for refrigerating things. OK, well, build that there, and then this could be our toy. But this might have to be a small house. This could be our beds, and over here could be another bed and another bed. Hey, but that's not fair—that bed has a pillow. Well, then you can sleep on the one with the pillow. I'll sleep on something. [*Moves all the toys around the table, organizing.*] Wow, this is a good house. We couldn't find much food. That's OK because we made a refrigerator, and we already had some good food in there. Oh, that's great. This is a pretty big house. I'll sleep on the one with the pillow. Hey, but that's where I was going to sleep. Well, I'm asleep now so . . . Hmm, I'll just sleep here. I'll sleep here. I changed my mind. I'm probably going to sleep in here, in the fridge. So I can sleep in here. I can sleep here, and yeah, now we all have a bed. Goodnight! Goodnight! |

*Adult:*  Good story. That had lots of pretend in it, didn't it? Because all the animals go and build a house, and I liked you pretended that this was the refrigerator and all the animals had beds. That was a good one. And it had lots of feelings in it like when he stole his pillow. We are all done for today.

## Child # 3, Session 1

*Adult:*  Somebody who's getting ready for a day at school. How could we start that story?

*Child:*  [*Picks up doll puts in bus. Puts doll on jet ski.*] It's time for school. [*Puts doll in the wagon.*]

*Adult:*  Are you bringing your wagon with you to school today?

*Child:*  Yeah.

*Adult:*  Oh, good idea. Do you still need a ride?

*Child:*  No.

*Adult:*  OK, have a good day at school.

*Child:*  OK. [*Puts doll on Jet Ski.*] Please sit down, class. Today we are gonna learn about subtraction, and it's almost time for lunch. Wash your hands, everybody. There you go. Now let's go to the cafeteria. I don't want to go to the cafeteria, I feel like. . . . You can read a book. OK.

*Adult:*  [*Laughs.*]

*Child:*  You're not allowed to be snowboarding on the school property. OK.

*Adult:*  [*Laughs.*] Oh, cool trick!

*Child:*  How about skateboarding? No skateboarding either. Fine, well, I'm going to the park. Aw, look at this baby horse. Neigh. Maybe they won't mind if I pet it. Can I borrow a pet from the park? OK, sure. This horse. Thank you. You're gonna have to take lots of good care of it. OK. [*Puts horse on jet ski.*] Where have you been? I was at the farm looking at a horse and they let me take it home. Oh, what a nice horse. Are we going to. . . . Yes! They have . . .

*Adult:*  Oh, good idea!

*Child:*  Now we're at the skateboarding park. Do you know how to skateboard?

*Adult:*  You could use these.

| Child: | You can just stay here and watch. [*Doll skateboards around.*] Jump onto my snowboard. |
|---|---|
| Adult: | Wow, you can do really good tricks. |
| Child: | Yep, I might be able to do some many in the Olympics. |
| Adult: | What could be a really cool ending to the story? |
| Child: | Maybe I should return the horsey. Bye, bye, horsey. The end. |
| Adult: | Good story! So she went to school and snowboarded and skateboarded and went to a farm first and then the skate park, and at the end she returned the horse and went back to school. Right? |
| Child: | Yep. |
| Adult: | Great story. OK, let's do a different story. This time we are going to make up a story with lots of feelings in it. So you can have them talk out loud and do stuff so you can tell how they feel. We are going to start by doing one that's a sad story about a girl who loses her favorite toy. How would a sad story begin? |
| Child: | I'm going on the bus. [*Puts doll in bus.*] Oh, no, I just noticed I lost my toy. [*Sighs.*] I'll just go out and try to find it, but if I can't find it by noon, I'll be super sad. |
| Adult: | Oh, I hope you can find it. I can help you look. |
| Child: | OK, well, it's not in the trunk of the bus. Maybe I left it at the farm. |
| | OK, let's go look at the farm. No, I don't see it anywhere. Teacher, I lost my favorite toy. What does it look like? It's red or fuchsia. When did you last have it? At home. Did you check at home? Yeah, maybe I should go check at home. Let me go skateboard over to my house. You have a skateboard? Yeah, I skateboard. Here, you can use my snowboard. Well, Teacher, it's not at home. Look more. OK. I feel really bad for you that you can't find it. Yeah, but I'm not giving up. Wow, you're a good skateboarder. You're good at snowboarding, Teacher. Did you check on the bus? That's where I lost it. Did you check on the trunk? Yep. How about the motorcycle? Nope. Nope, not on my motorcycle. So where will we find it? Well, maybe I'll search over town, and you search all around the city, and you search all around the whole state, OK? Got it. |
| Adult: | Not over here. |
| Child: | Not over here at the skateboard park. Well, perhaps I could do a little bit of skateboarding. Hey, you're not supposed to be skateboarding. You're supposed to be. . . . Well, start finding it. |

OK. I checked everywhere all along the city. Well, I checked everywhere all around the town, and it's still not there, so what are we going to do? How about we go back to school and forget all about it? But I can't. It's my favorite toy. We gotta keep on looking. If we can't find it before midnight, it looks like we'll have to search tomorrow. OK, let's search. I just wanted to see if I could get my foot in.

Adult:    What is an ending to the story?

Child:    Oh, I think I might have left it on the bus. Oh, I did. I left it on the front seat.

Adult:    How does she feel now?

Child:    Now I can go back to school. The end.

Adult:    Good story. She was really sad that she lost it, but everyone was really helpful, and then she found it and she's happy again. All right. Let's switch again, and this time let's do a story with lots of imagination and make up a new thing about somebody who's getting ready to go to bed.

Child:    Hmm, it's almost nighttime, but I don't want to go to bed, Teacher. You have to, or else you won't have enough sleep for the day. OK, I'll go to bed but only if I get to go skateboarding before. OK, go skateboarding. Time to get in your pajamas. OK, let me go get in the bus. Now it's the morning. OK, night-night. Goodnight. OK. I'm going on the bus to see what's . . . Let me just . . .

# REFERENCES

Adler, T. (1991, September). Support and challenge: Both key for smart kids. *APA Monitor, 22*(9), 10–11.

Amabile, T. (1983). *The social psychology of creativity*. New York, NY: Springer-Verlag. doi:10.1007/978-1-4612-5533-8

Anastasi, A. (1988). *Psychological testing* (6th ed.). New York, NY: Macmillan.

Anastasi, A., & Schaefer, C. (1969). Biological correlates of artistic and literary creativity in adolescent girls. *Journal of Applied Psychology, 53*, 267–273. doi:10.1037/h0027810

Arieti, S. (1976). *Creativity: The magic synthesis*. New York, NY: Basic Books.

Arlow, J., & Brenner, C. (1964). *Psychoanalytic concepts and structural theory*. New York, NY: International Universities Press.

Ashley, J., & Tomasello, M. (1998). Cooperative problem-solving and teaching in preschoolers. *Social Development, 7*, 143–163. doi:10.1111/1467-9507.00059

Astington, J. W., & Jenkins, J. M. (1995). Theory of mind development and social understanding. *Cognition and Emotion, 9*, 151–165. doi:10.1080/02699939508409006

Axia, V., & Weisner, T. S. (2002). Infant stress reactivity and home cultural ecology. *Infant Behavior and Development, 25*, 265–268. doi:10.1016/S0163-6383(02)00099-1

Baas, M., De Dreu, C. K. W., & Nijstad, B. A. (2008). A meta-analysis of 25 years of mood-creativity research: Hedonic tone, activation, or regulatory focus? *Psychological Bulletin, 134*, 779–806. doi:10.1037/a0012815

Bandura, A. (1965). Influence of models' reinforcement contingencies in the acquisition of initiative responses. *Journal of Personality and Social Psychology, 1*, 589–595. doi:10.1037/h0022070

Barnett, L. A. (2007). The nature of playfulness in young adults. *Personality and Individual Differences, 43*, 949–958. doi:10.1016/j.paid.2007.02.018

Barron, F. (1969). *Creative person and the creative process*. New York, NY: Holt, Rinehart & Winston.

Barron, F., & Harrington, D. (1981). Creativity, intelligence, and personality. In M. Rosenzweig & L. Porter (Eds.), *Annual review of psychology* (Vol. 32, pp. 439–476). Palo Alto, CA: Annual Reviews.

Barton, E., & Wolery, M. (2008). Teaching pretend play to children with disabilities: A review of the literature. *Topics in Early Childhood Special Education, 28*, 109–125. doi:10.1177/0271121408318799

Batey, M., & Furnham, A. (2006). Creativity, intelligence and personality: A critical review of the scattered literature. *Genetic, Social, and General Psychology Monographs, 132*, 355–429. doi:10.3200/MONO.132.4.355-430

Beard, D. (1983, May 22). Jorge Luis Borges: What else can I do but write? *The Plain Dealer*, 1–7.

Beghetto, R. A., & Kaufman, J. C. (2007). Toward a broader conception of creativity: A case for "mini-c" creativity. *Psychology of Aesthetics, Creativity, and the Arts, 1*, 73–79. doi:10.1037/1931-3896.1.2.73

Belsky, J., & Most, R. (1981). From exploration to play: A cross-sectional study of infant free-play behavior. *Developmental Psychology, 17*, 630–639. doi:10.1037/0012-1649.17.5.630

Berk, L. E., Mann, T. D., & Ogan, A. T. (2006). Make-believe play: Wellspring for development of self-regulation. In D. Singer, R. Golinkoff, & K. Hirsh-Pasek (Eds.), *Play=learning: How play motivates and enhances children's cognitive and social–emotional growth* (pp. 74–100). New York, NY: Oxford University Press. doi:10.1093/acprof:oso/9780195304381.003.0005

Berlyne, D. E. (1966). Conflict and arousal. *Scientific American, 215*, 82–87. doi:10.1038/scientificamerican0866-82

Blatt, S. J., Allison, J., & Feirstein, A. (1969). The capacity to cope with cognitive complexity. *Journal of Personality, 37*, 269–288. doi:10.1111/j.1467-6494.1969.tb01744.x

Bodiford-McNeil, C., Hembree-Kigin, T. L., & Eyberg, S. (1996). *Short-term play therapy for disruptive children*. King of Prussia, PA: The Center for Applied Psychology.

Bornstein, M. H., Cote, L. R., & Venuti, P. (2001). Parenting belief and behaviors in two groups of Italian mothers of young infants. *Journal of Family Psychology, 15*, 663–675. doi:10.1037/0893-3200.15.4.663

Bornstein, M. H., Haynes, M., Pascual, L., Painter, K. M., & Galperin, C. (1999). Play in two societies: Pervasiveness of process, specificity of structure. *Child Development, 70*, 317–331. doi:10.1111/1467-8624.00024

Bower, G. H. (1981). Mood and memory. *American Psychologist, 36*, 129–148. doi:10.1037/0003-066X.36.2.129

Boyd, B. (2009). *On the origin of stories*. Cambridge, MA: Harvard University Press.

Boyd, B. (2011, Autumn). The psychologist. *The American Scholar*. Retrieved from http://theamericanscholar.org/the-psychologist/#.UVsPYqvwK8s

Brenner, C. (1974). *An elementary textbook of psychoanalysis*. New York, NY: International Universities Pres.

Brownell, C. A., & Carriger, M. S. (1990). Changes in cooperation and self-other differentiation during the second year. *Child Development, 61*, 1164–1174. doi:10.2307/1130884

Brownell, C. A., & Carriger, M. S. (1991). Collaborations among toddler peers: Individual contributions to social contexts. In L. B. Resnick, J. M. Levine, & S. D. Teasley (Eds.), *Perspectives on socially shared cognition* (pp. 365–383). Washington, DC: American Psychological Association. doi:10.1037/10096-016

Bryant, B. (1982). An index of empathy for children and adolescents. *Child Development, 53*, 413–425. doi:10.2307/1128984

Burgdorf, J., & Panksepp, J. (2001). Tickling induces reward in adolescent rats. *Physiology & Behavior, 72*, 167–173. doi:10.1016/S0031-9384(00)00411-X

Burghardt, G. (2005). *The genesis of animal play.* Cambridge, MA: MIT Press.

Campbell, D. T. (1960). Blind variation as selective retention in creative thought as in other knowledge processes. *Psychological Review, 67*, 380–400. doi:10.1037/h0040373

Carson, D., Bittner, M., Cameron, B., Brown, D., & Meyer, S. (1994). Creative thinking as a predictor of school-aged children's stress responses and coping abilities. *Creativity Research Journal, 7*, 145–158. doi:10.1080/10400419409534520

Carson, S. H., Peterson, J. B., & Higgins, D. M. (2005). Reliability, validity, and factor structure of the creative achievement questionnaire. *Creativity Research Journal, 17*, 37–50. doi:10.1207/s15326934crj1701_4

Cattell, R., & Butcher, H. (1968). *The prediction of achievement and creativity.* Indianapolis, IN: Bobbs-Merrill.

Chessa, D., Di Riso, D., Delvecchio, E., Salcuni, S., & Lis, A. (2011). The Affect in Play Scale: Confirmatory factor analysis in elementary school children. *Psychological Reports, 109*, 759–774. doi:10.2466/09.10.21.PR0.109.6.759-774

Chessa, D., Lis, A., Di Riso, D., Delvecchio, E., Mazzeschi, C., Russ, S. W., & Dillon, J. (2013). A cross-cultural comparison of pretend play in U.S. and Italian children. *Journal of Cross-Cultural Psychology, 44*, 640–656. doi:10.1177/0022022112461853

Chethik, M. (1989). *Techniques of child psychotherapy: Psychodynamic strategies.* New York, NY: Guilford Press.

Christian, K. (2011). *The construct of playfulness: Relationship with adaptive behaviors, humor, and early pretend play* (Unpublished doctoral dissertation). Case Western Reserve University, Cleveland, OH.

Christian, K., Fehr, K., & Russ, S. (2011, August). *Effects of play intervention on play skills in preschool children: A pilot study.* Poster session presented at the meeting of the American Psychological Association, Washington, DC.

Christiano, B., & Russ, S. (1996). Play as a predictor of coping and distress in children during an invasive dental procedure. *Journal of Clinical Child Psychology, 25*, 130–138. doi:10.1207/s15374424jccp2502_1

Christie, J. (1994). Academic play. In J. Hellendoorn, R. Van der Kooij, & B. Sutton-Smith (Eds.), *Play and intervention* (pp. 203–213). Albany: State University of New York Press.

Christie, J., & Johnson, E. (1983). The role of play in social–intellectual development. *Review of Educational Research, 53*, 93–115.

Clark, L., & Watson, D. (1991). Tripartite model of anxiety and depression: Psychometric evidence and taxonomic implications. *Journal of Abnormal Psychology, 100*, 316–336. doi:10.1037//0021-843X.100.3.316

Clark, P., Griffing, P., & Johnson, L. (1989). Symbolic play and ideational fluency as aspects of the evolving divergent cognitive style in young children. *Early Child Development and Care, 51*, 77–88. doi:10.1080/0300443890510107

Cohen, I. (1961). Adaptive regression, dogmatism, and creativity. *Dissertation Abstracts, 21*, 3522.

Cohen, J. (1977). *Statistical power analysis for the behavioral sciences* (rev. ed.). New York, NY: Academic Press.

Cohen, J. (1988). *Statistical power analysis for the behavioral sciences* (2nd ed.). Hillsdale, NJ: Erlbaum.

Cohen, J. (1992). A power primer. *Psychological Bulletin, 112*, 155–159. doi:10.1037/0033-2909.112.1.155

Cordiano, T., & Russ, S. (2011). *Pretend play, openness to experience, and divergent thinking in children*. Manuscript submitted for publication.

Cote, L. R., & Bornstein, M. H. (2005). Japanese American and South American immigrant mothers' perceptions of their own and their spouses' parenting styles. In H. Grietens, W. Lahaye, W. Hellinckx, & L. Vandemeulebroecke (Eds.), *In the best interests of children and youth: International perspectives* (pp. 47–76). Leuven, Belgium: Leuven University Press.

Cramond, B., Mathews-Morgan, J., Bandalos, D., & Zuo, L. (2005). A report on the 40-year follow-up of the Torrance Tests of Creative Thinking: Alive and well in the new millennium. *Gifted Child Quarterly, 49*, 283–291. doi:10.1177/001698620504900402

Csikszentmihalyi, M. (1990). *Flow: The psychology of optimal experience*. New York, NY: Harper & Row.

Culbane, J. (1988, January 10). Throw away the script. *The Plain Dealer*, 1–5.

Curry, A. (2012). The cave art debate. *Smithsonian*. Retrieved from http://www.smithsonianmag.com/history-archaeology/The-Cave-Art-Debate.html

Damasio, A. (1994). *Descartes' error: Emotion, reason, and the human brain*. New York, NY: Penguin Books.

Damour, L. (2009, November). Teaching girls to tinker. *Education Week*, 25.

Dansky, J. (1980). Make-believe: A mediator of the relationship between play and associative fluency. *Child Development, 51*, 576–579. doi:10.2307/1129296

Dansky, J. (1999). Play. In M. Runco & S. Pritzker (Eds.), *Encyclopedia of creativity* (pp. 393–408). San Diego, CA: Academic Press.

Dansky, J., & Silverman, F. (1973). Effects of play on associative fluency in preschool-aged children. *Developmental Psychology, 9*, 38–43. doi:10.1037/h0035076

Diamond, J. (2012). *The world until yesterday*. New York, NY: Viking.

Donahue, K. (2011). Frida Kahlo. In M. Runco & S. Pritzker (Eds.), *Encyclopedia of creativity* (Vol. 2, pp. 21–26). London, England: Elsevier.

Drewes, A. (2006). Play-based interventions. *Journal of Early Childhood and Infant Psychology, 2*, 139–156.

Dudek, S. (1968). Regression and creativity. *Journal of Nervous and Mental Disease, 147*, 535–546. doi:10.1097/00005053-196812000-00002

Dudek, S., & Verreault, R. (1989). The creative thinking and ego functioning of children. *Creativity Research Journal, 2*, 64–86. doi:10.1080/10400418909534301

Dudek, S. Z. (1975). Regression in the service of the ego in young children. *Journal of Personality Assessment, 39*, 369–376. doi:10.1207/s15327752jpa3904_7

Dudek, S. Z. (1980). Primary process ideation. In R. H. Woody (Ed.), *Encyclopedia of clinical assessment* (Vol. 1, pp. 520–539). San Francisco, CA: Jossey-Bass.

Dudek, S. Z. (1984). The architect as person: A Rorschach image. *Journal of Personality Assessment, 48*, 597–605. doi:10.1207/s15327752jpa4806_4

Dunn, L., & Herwig, J. (1992). Play behaviors and convergent and divergent thinking skills of young children attending full-day preschool. *Child Study Journal, 22*, 23–38.

Edwards, C. P. (2000). Children's play in cross-cultural perspective: A new look at the Six Cultures study. *Cross-Cultural Research: The Journal of Comparative Social Science, 34*, 318–338. doi:10.1177/106939710003400402

Elkind, D. (2007). *The power of play: Learning what comes naturally.* New York, NY: Da Capo Press.

Emiliani, F., & Molinari, L. (1995). *Rappresentazioni e affetti: Carattere e interazione nello sviluppo dei bambini* [Representation and emotion, character and interaction in child development]. Milano, Italy: Cortina Editore.

Erikson, E. (1963). *Childhood and society.* New York, NY: Norton.

Fehr, K. (2012). *A brief pretend play intervention to facilitate play and creativity in preschool children* (Unpublished doctoral dissertation). Case Western Reserve University, Cleveland, OH.

Fein, G. (1987). Pretend play: Creativity and consciousness. In P. Gorlitz & J. Wohlwill (Eds.), *Curiosity, imagination and play* (pp. 281–304). Hillsdale, NJ: Erlbaum.

Feist, G. (2011). Creativity in science. In M. Runco & S. Pritzker (Eds.), *Encyclopedia of creativity* (Vol. 1, pp. 296–302). San Diego, CA: Academic Press.

Feist, G. J. (1998). A meta-analysis of personality in scientific and artistic creativity. *Personality and Social Psychology Review, 2*, 290–309. doi:10.1207/s15327957pspr0204_5

Feist, G. J. (1999). The influence of personality on artistic and scientific creativity. In R. J. Sternberg (Ed.), *Handbook of creativity* (pp. 273–296). New York, NY: Cambridge University Press.

Feitelson, D., & Ross, G. (1973). The neglected factor—Play. *Human Development, 16*, 202–223. doi:10.1159/000271276

Fiorelli, J., & Russ, S. (2012). Pretend play, coping, and subjective well-being in children. *American Journal of Play, 5*, 81–103.

Fisher, E. (1992). The impact of play on development: A meta-analysis. *Play and Culture, 5*, 159–181.

Folkman, S., & Lazarus, R. (1980). An analysis of coping in middle-aged community sample. *Journal of Health and Social Behavior, 21*, 219–239. doi:10.2307/2136617

Freud, A. (1965). *Normality and pathology in childhood. Assessment of development.* New York, NY: International Universities Press.

Freud, A. (1966). *The writings of Anna Freud* (Vol. 2). New York, NY: International Universities Press.

Freud, S. (1958). The unconscious. In J. Strachey (Trans. & Ed.), *The standard edition of the complete psychological works of Sigmund Freud* (Vol. 14, pp. 159–215). London, England: Hogarth Press. (Original work published 1915)

Freud, S. (1959). Inhibition, symptoms, and anxiety. In J. Strachey (Ed. & Trans.), *The standard edition of the complete psychological works of Sigmund Freud* (Vol. 20, pp. 87–172). London, England: Hogarth Press. (Original work published 1926)

Freud, S. (1966). Project for scientific psychology. In J. Strachey (Ed. & Trans.), *The standard edition of the complete psychological works of Sigmund Freud* (Vol. 1, pp. 283–413). London, England: Hogarth Press. (Original work published 1895)

Freyberg, J. (1973). Increasing the imaginative play of urban disadvantaged kindergarten children through systematic training. In J. Singer (Ed.), *The child's world of make-believe* (pp. 129–154). New York, NY: Academic Press.

Furnham, A., Crump, J., Batey, M., & Chamorro-Premuzic, T. (2009), Personality and ability predictors of the "consequences" test of divergent thinking in a large non-student sample. *Personality and Individual Differences, 46*, 536–540. doi:10.1016/j.paid.2008.12.007

Gamble, K. R., & Kellner, H. (1968). Creative functioning and cognitive regression. *Journal of Personality and Social Psychology, 9*, 266–271. doi:10.1037/h0025911

Gardner, R., & Moriarty, A. (1968). *Personality development at preadolescence.* Seattle: University of Washington Press.

Gaskins, S. (2003). From corn to cash: Change and continuity within Mayan families. *Ethos, 31*, 248–273. doi:10.1525/eth.2003.31.2.248

Gaskins, S., Haight, W., & Lancy, D. (2007). The cultural construction of play. In A. Goncu & S. Gaskins (Eds.), *Play and development* (pp. 179–202). New York, NY: Taylor & Francis.

Getz, I., & Lubart, T. (1999). The emotional resonance model of creativity: Theoretical and practical extensions. In S. Russ (Ed.), *Affect, creative experience, and psychological adjustment* (pp. 41–56). Philadelphia, PA: Brunner/Mazel.

Getzels, S., & Csikszentmihalyi, M. (1976). *The creative vision: A longitudinal study of problem finding in art.* New York, NY: Wiley-Interscience.

Ghiselin, B. (1952). *The creative process.* Berkeley, CA: University of California Press.

Gil, E. (1991). *The healing power of play.* New York, NY: Guilford Press.

Ginsburg, K. R. (2007). The importance of play in promoting healthy child development and maintaining strong parent-child bonds. *Pediatrics, 119*, 182–191. doi:10.1542/peds.2006-2697

Golann, S. E. (1963). Psychological study of creativity. *Psychological Bulletin*, *60*, 548–565. doi:10.1037/h0041573

Goldstein, A. (1999). *Children's fantasy ability and its relationship to understanding literature* (Unpublished master's thesis). Case Western Reserve University, Cleveland, OH.

Goldstein, A., & Russ, S. W. (2001). Understanding children's literature and its relationship to fantasy ability and coping. *Imagination, Cognition and Personality*, *20*, 105–126.

Golinkoff, R., & Hirsh-Pasek, K., Lillard, A., & Russ, S. W. (Eds.). (in press). Special issue. *American Journal of Play*, *6*(1).

Golomb, C., & Galasso, L. (1995). Make believe and reality: Explorations of the imaginary realm. *Developmental Psychology*, *31*, 800–810. doi:10.1037/0012-1649.31.5.800

Goodwin, L. J., & Moran, J. D. (1990). Psychometric characterization of an instrument for measuring creative potential in preschool children. *Psychology in the Schools*, *27*, 204–210.

Gough, H. (1979). A creative personality scale for the Adjective Checklist. *Journal of Personality and Social Psychology*, *37*, 1398–1405. doi:10.1037/0022-3514.37.8.1398

Gough, H. (1988, March). *Gender related descriptions by self and others*. Paper presented at the meeting of the Society for Personality Assessment, New Orleans, LA.

Grandin, T. (2006, June). *The woman who thinks like a cow*. BBC Worldwide documentary.

Groos, K. (1901). *The play of man* (E. L. Baldwin, Trans.). New York, NY: Appleton-Century-Crofts.

Gruber, H. (1981). On the relation between "aha experiences" and the construction of ideas. *History of Science*, *19*, 41–59.

Gruber, H. E. (1989). The evolving systems approach to creativity work. In D. B. Wallace & H. Gruber (Eds.), *Creative people at work* (pp. 3–24). New York, NY: Oxford University Press. doi:10.1080/10400418809534285

Gruber, H. E., & Davis, S. (1988). Inching our way up Mount Olympus: The evolving systems approach to creative thinking. In R. Sternberg (Ed.), *The nature of creativity* (pp. 243–270). Cambridge, England: Cambridge University Press.

Guilford, J. P. (1950). Creativity. *American Psychologist*, *5*, 444–454. doi:10.1037/h0063487

Guilford, J. P. (1967). *The nature of human intelligence*. New York, NY: McGraw-Hill.

Guilford, J. P. (1968). *Intelligence, creativity and their educational implications*. San Diego, CA: Knapp.

Harkness, S., Super, C. M., Axia, V., Eliasz, A., Placios, J., & Welles-Nyström, B. (2001). Cultural pathways to successful parenting. *International Society for the Study of Behavioral Development Newsletter*, *1*(38), 9–13.

Harrington, D. M., Block, J. W., & Block, J. (1987). Testing aspects of Carl Rogers' theory of creative environments: Childrearing antecedents of creative environments in young adolescents. *Journal of Personality and Social Psychology, 52*, 851–856. doi:10.1037/0022-3514.52.4.851

Harris, P. (1989). *Children and emotion: The development of psychological understanding.* Cambridge, MA: Blackwell.

Hartmann, W., & Rollett, B. (1994). Play: Positive intervention in the elementary school curriculum. In J. Hellendoorn, R. van der Kooij, & B. Sutton-Smith (Eds.), *Play and intervention* (pp. 195–202). Albany: State University of New York Press.

Harwood, R. L., Schoelmerich, A., Schulze, P. A., & Gonzalez, Z. (1999). Cultural differences in maternal beliefs and behaviours: A study of middle-class Anglo and Puerto Rican mother–infant pairs in four everyday situations. *Child Development, 70*, 1005–1016. doi:10.1111/1467-8624.00073

Hellendoorn, V. (1994). Imaginative play training for severely retarded children. In J. Hellendoorn, R. van der Kooij, & B. Sutton-Smith (Eds.), *Play and intervention* (pp. 113–122). Albany: State University of New York Press.

Helson, R. (1990). Creativity in women: Outer and inner views over time. In M. Runco & R. Albert (Eds.), *Theories of creativity* (pp. 46–58). Newbury Park, CA: Sage.

Hennessey, B. A., & Amabile, M. (1988). Storytelling: A method for assessing children's creativity. *The Journal of Creative Behavior, 22*, 235–246. doi:10.1002/j.2162-6057.1988.tb00502.x

Herrera, H. (1983). *Frida: A biography of Frida Kahlo.* New York, NY: Perennial.

Hirschberg, S., & Hirschberg, T. (2003). *Past to present: Ideas that changed our world.* Upper Saddle River, NJ: Prentice Hall.

Hirsh-Pasek, K., & Golinkoff, R. (2003). *Einstein never used flash cards: How our children really learn—And why they need to play more and memorize less.* New York, NY: Rodale.

Hirsh-Pasek, K., Golinkoff, R., Berk, L., & Singer, D. (2009). *A mandate for playful learning.* New York, NY: Oxford University Press.

Hoffmann, J. (2012). A pretend play group intervention for elementary school children (Unpublished doctoral dissertation). Case Western Reserve University, Cleveland, OH.

Hoffmann, J., & Russ, S. (2012). Pretend play, creativity, and emotion regulation in children. *Psychology of Aesthetics, Creativity, and the Arts, 6*, 175–184. doi:10.1037/a0026299

Hollingshead, A. A. (1975). *Four-factor index of social status.* Unpublished manuscript, Yale University, New Haven, CT.

Holt, R. (1967). The development of the primary process: A structural view. In R. Holt (Ed.), *Motivation and thought* (pp. 344–384). New York, NY: International Universities Press.

Holt, R. (1977). A method for assessing primary process manifestations and their control in Rorschach responses. In M. Rickers-Ovsiankina (Ed.), *Rorschach psychology* (pp. 375–420). New York, NY: Kreiger.

Holyoak, K. (1990). Problem solving. In D. N. Osherson & E. E. Smith (Eds.), *An invitation in cognitive science: Vol. 3. Thinking* (pp. 116–146). Cambridge, MA: MIT Press.

Hsu, H., & Lavelli, M. (2005). Perceived and observed parenting behavior in American and Italian first-time mothers across the first 3 months. *Infant Behavior and Development, 28*, 503–518. doi:10.1016/j.infbeh.2005.09.001

Hutt, C., & Bhavnani, R. (1972, May 19). Predictions for play. *Nature, 237*, 171–172. doi:10.1038/237171b0

Isaacson, W. (2011). *Steve Jobs*. New York, NY: Simon & Schuster.

Isen, A. M. (1999). On the relationship between affect and creative problem solving. In S. Russ (Ed.), *Affect, creative experience, and psychological adjustment* (pp. 3–17). Philadelphia, PA: Brunner/Mazel.

Isen, A. M., & Daubman, K. (1984). The influence of affect on categorization. Journal of *Personality and Social Psychology, 47*, 1206–1217. doi:10.1037//0022-3514.47.6.1206

Isen, A. M., Daubman, K., & Nowicki, G. (1987). Positive affect facilitates creative problem solving. *Journal of Personality and Social Psychology, 52*, 1122–1131. doi:10.1037/0022-3514.52.6.1122

Isen, A. M., Johnson, M., Mertz, E., & Robinson, G. (1985). The influence of positive affect on the unusualness of word associations. *Journal of Personality and Social Psychology, 48*, 1413–1426. doi:10.1037//0022-3514.48.6.1413

Izard, C. E. (1977). *Human emotions*. New York, NY: Plenum Press.

Jamison, K. R. (1989). Mood disorders and patterns of creativity in British writers and artists. *Psychiatry: Interpersonal and Biological Processes, 52*, 125–134.

Jenkins, H. (1998). Complete freedom of movement: Videogames as gendered playspace. In J. Cassell & H. Jenkins (Eds.), *From Barbie to mortal combat: Gender and computer games* (pp. 262–297). Cambridge, MA: MIT Press.

Johnson, J. (1976). Relations of divergent thinking and intelligence test scores with social and nonsocial make-believe play of preschool children. *Child Development, 47*, 1200–1203. doi:10.2307/1128465

Kagan, J., & Moss, H. A. (1962). *Birth to maturity: A study in psychological development*. New York, NY: Wiley. doi:10.1037/13129-000

Kasari, C., Freeman, S., & Paparella, T. (2006). Joint attention and symbolic play in young children with autism: A randomized controlled intervention study. *Journal of Child Psychology and Psychiatry, 47*, 611–620. doi:10.1111/j.1469-7610.2005.01567.x

Kasari, C., Gulsrud, A., Freeman, S., Paparella, T., & Hellemann, G. (2012). Longitudinal follow-up of children with autism receiving targeted interventions on joint attention and play. *Journal of the American Academy of Child & Adolescent Psychiatry, 51*, 487–495. doi:10.1016/j.jaac.2012.02.019

Kaufman, J. (2009). *Creativity 101*. New York, NY: Springer.

Kaufman, J., & Beghetto, R. (2009). Beyond big and little: The four c model of creativity. *Review of General Psychology, 13*, 1–12. doi:10.1037/a0013688

Kaufman, J., Plucker, J., & Baer, J. (2008). *Essentials of creativity assessment*. New York, NY: Wiley.

Kaufmann, G., & Vosburg, S. (2002). The effects of mood on early and late idea production. *Creativity Research Journal, 14*, 317–330. doi:10.1207/S15326934CRJ1434_3

Kaugars, A. S., & Russ, S. W. (2009). Assessing preschool children's pretend play: Preliminary validation of the Affect in Play Scale–Preschool version. *Early Education and Development, 20*, 733–755. doi:10.1080/10409280802545388

Keller, E. (1983). *A feeling for the organism. The life and work of Barbara McClintock*. New York, NY: Freeman.

Kim, K. H. (2005). Can only intelligent people be creative? A meta-analysis. *Journal of Secondary Gifted Education, 16*, 57–66.

Kim, K. H. (2008). Meta-analysis of the relationship of creative achievement to both IQ and divergent thinking test scores. *The Journal of Creative Behavior, 42*, 106–130. doi:10.1002/j.2162-6057.2008.tb01290.x

Kim, K. H. (2011). The creativity crisis: The decrease in creative thinking scores on the Torrance tests of creative thinking. *Creativity Research Journal, 23*, 285–295. doi:10.1080/10400419.2011.627805

Kim, Y. T., Lombardino, L. J., Rothman, H., & Vinson, B. (1989). Effects of symbolic play intervention with children who have mental retardation. *Mental Retardation, 27*, 159–165.

King, L. A., McKee-Walker, L., & Broyles, S. J. (1996). Creativity and the five-factor model. *Journal of Research in Personality, 30*, 189–203. doi:10.1006/jrpe.1996.0013

King, S. (2000). *On writing*. New York, NY: Scribner.

Klein, G. (1970). *Perception, motives, and personality*. New York, NY: Knopf.

Klein, M. (1955). The psychoanalytic play technique. *American Journal of Orthopsychiatry, 25*, 223–237. doi:10.1111/j.1939-0025.1955.tb00131.x

Kleinman, M. J., & Russ, S. W. (1988). Primary process thinking and anxiety in children. *Journal of Personality Assessment, 52*, 254–262. doi:10.1207/s15327752jpa5202_7

Klinger, E. (1971). *Structure and functions of fantasy*. New York, NY: Wiley-Interscience.

Knell, S. (1993). *Cognitive–behavioral play therapy*. Northvale, NJ: Aronson.

Kogan, N. (1976). *Cognitive styles in infancy and early childhood*. Hillsdale, NJ: Erlbaum.

Kogan, N. (1983). Stylistic variation in childhood and adolescence: Creativity, metaphor, and cognitive styles. In P. Mussen (Ed.), *Handbook of child psychology* (Vol. 3; pp. 631–706). New York, NY: Wiley.

Krasnor, I., & Pepler, D. (1980). The study of children's play: Some suggested future directions. *New Directions for Child Development, 1980*, 85–95. doi:10.1002/cd.23219800908

Kris, E. (1952). *Psychoanalytic explorations in art*. New York, NY: International Universities Press.

Kuhn, T. (1962). *The structure of scientific revolutions*. Chicago, IL: University of Chicago Press.

Kunitz, S. (2005). *The wild braid*. New York, NY: Norton.

Kusche, C. A., Greenberg, M. T., & Beilke, B. (1988). *The Kusche Affective Interview*. Unpublished manuscript, Department of Psychology, University of Washington, Seattle, WA.

L'Abate, L. (2009). *The Praeger handbook of play across the life cycle*. Santa Barbara, CA: Praeger.

Lahr, J. (2007, December 24). Demolition man. *The New Yorker*, pp. 54–69.

Lancy, D. E. (1996). *Playing on the mother ground: Cultural routines for children's development*. New York, NY: Guilford Press.

Lang, R., O'Reilly, M., Rispoli, M., Shogren, K., Machalicek, W., Sigafoos, J., & Regester, A. (2009). Review of interventions to increase functional and symbolic play in children with autism. *Education and Training in Developmental Disabilities, 44*, 481–492.

Langley, P., & Jones, R. (1988). A computational model of scientific insight. In R. Sternberg (Ed.), *The nature of creativity* (pp. 177–201). Cambridge, England: Cambridge University Press.

Lieberman, J. N. (1977). *Playfulness: Its relationship to imagination and creativity*. New York, NY: Academic Press.

Lillard, A. S., Lerner, M. D., Hopkins, E. J., Dore, R. A., Smith, E. D., & Palmquist, C. M. (2013). The impact of pretend play on children's development: A review of empirical evidence. *Psychological Bulletin, 139*, 1–34. doi:10.1037/a0029321

Lorenz, K. (1971). Part and parcel in animal and human societies. In K. Lorenz (Ed.), *Studies in animal and human behavior* (Vol. 2, pp. 115–195). Cambridge, MA: Harvard University Press. (Original work published 1950)

Lubart, T., & Lautrey, J. (1998, July). Family environment and creativity. Paper presented at the meeting of the International Society for the Study of Behavioral Development, Berne, Switzerland.

Lubart, T., Mouchiroud, C., Tordjman, S., & Zenasni, F. (2003). *Psychologie de la creativite* [Psychology of creativity]. Paris, France: Colin.

Luchins, A., & Luchins, E. (1959). *Rigidity of behavior*. Eugene, OR: University of Oregon Press.

Maccoby, E., & Jacklin, C. (1974). *The psychology of sex differences*. Stanford, CA: Stanford University Press.

Mackinnon, D. W. (1962). The nature and nurture of creative talent. *American Psychologist, 17*, 484–495. doi:10.1037/h0046541

Mackinnon, D. W. (1965). Personality and the realization of creative potential. *American Psychologist, 20,* 273–281. doi:10.1037/h0022403

Martindale, C. (1981). *Cognition and consciousness.* Homewood, IL: Dorsey.

Martindale, C. (1989). Personality, situation and creativity. In J. Glover, R. Ronning, & C. R. Reynolds (Eds.), *Handbook of creativity* (pp. 211–232). New York, NY: Plenum Press. doi:10.1007/978-1-4757-5356-1_13

Mazzeschi, C., Salcuni, S., Parolin, L., & Lis, A. (2004). Two measures of affect and emotion in Italian children aged 6–11. *Psychological Reports, 95,* 115–120.

McCrae, R. R. (1987). Creativity, divergent thinking, and openness to experience. *Journal of Personality and Social Psychology, 52,* 1258–1265. doi:10.1037/0022-3514.52.6.1258

McCrae, R. R., & Costa, P. T. (1987). Validation of the five-factor model across instruments and observers. *Journal of Personality and Social Psychology, 52,* 81–90. doi:10.1037/0022-3514.52.1.81

McCune, L., Dipane, D., Fireoved, R., & Fleck, M. (1994). Play: A context for mutual regulation within mother-child interaction. In A. Slade & D. Palmer (Eds.), *Children at play: Clinical and developmental approaches to meaning and representation* (pp. 148–166). New York, NY: Oxford University Press.

Mednick, S. (1962). The associative bases of the creative process. *Psychological Review, 69,* 220–232. doi:10.1037/h0048850

Metcalfe, J. (1986). Feeling of knowing in memory and problem solving. Journal of *Experimental Psychology: Learning, Memory, and Cognition, 12,* 288–294. doi:10.1037/0278-7393.12.2.288

Miller, A. M., & Harwood, R. L. (2002). The cultural organization of parenting: Change and stability of behavior patterns during feeding and social play across the first year of life. *Parenting: Science and Practice, 2,* 241–263. doi:10.1207/S15327922PAR0203_03

Mitchell, R. (2007). Pretense in animals: The continuing relevance of children's pretense. In A. Goncu & S. Gaskins (Eds.), *Play and development: Evolutionary, sociocultural, and functional perspectives* (pp. 51–75). New York, NY: Taylor & Francis.

Monat, A., & Lazarus, R. (1977). Introduction: Stress and coping—Some current issues and controversies. In A. Monat & R. Lazarus (Eds.), *Stress and coping: An anthology* (pp. 1–11). New York, NY: Columbia University Press.

Moore, B., & Isen, A. M. (1990). Affect and social behavior. In B. Moore & A. M. Isen (Eds.), *Affect and social behavior* (pp. 1–21). Cambridge, England: Cambridge University Press.

Moore, M., & Russ, S. (2008). Follow-up of a pretend play intervention: Effects on play, creativity, and emotional processes in children. *Creativity Research Journal, 20,* 427–436. doi:10.1080/10400410802391892

Morrison, D. (1988). The child's first way of knowing. In D. Morrison (Ed.), *Organizing early experience: Imagination and cognition in childhood* (pp. 3–14). Amityville, NY: Baywood.

Morrison, D., & Morrison, S. (2006). *Memories of loss and dreams of perfection*. Amityville, NY: Baywood.

Murray, J., & Russ, S. (1981). Adaptive regression and types of cognitive flexibility. *Journal of Personality Assessment, 45*, 59–65. doi:10.1207/s15327752jpa4501_12

Nagy, E. (2008). Calder's once and future circus: A conservator's perspective. In J. Simon & B. Leal (Eds.), *Alexander Calder: The Paris years, 1926–1933* (pp. 195–211). New Haven, CT: Yale University Press.

Nevile, M., & Bachor, D. (2002). A script-based symbolic play intervention for children with developmental delay. *Developmental Disabilities Bulletin, 30*, 140–172.

New, R. S. (1988). Parental goals and Italian infant care. In R. A. LeVine & P. M. West (Eds.), *Parental behavior in diverse societies* (pp. 51–63). San Francisco, CA: Jossey-Bass.

New, R. S. (1994). Child's play—Una cosa naturale: An Italian perspective. In J. L. Roopnarine, J. E. Johnson, & F. H. Hooper (Eds.), *Children's play in diverse cultures* (pp. 123–147). Albany: State University of New York Press.

New, R. S., & Richman, A. L. (1996). Maternal beliefs and infant care practices in Italy and the United States. In S. Harkness & C. M. Super (Eds.), *Parents' cultural belief systems: The origins, expressions, and consequences* (pp. 385–444). New York, NY: Guilford Press.

Nicolopoulou, A. (2007). The interplay of play and narrative in children's development: Theoretical reflections and concrete examples. In A. Goncu & S. Gaskins (Eds.), *Play and development* (pp. 247–273). New York, NY: Psychology Press.

Niec, L. N., & Russ, S. W. (2002). Children's internal representations, empathy and fantasy play: A validity study of the SCORS-Q. *Psychological Assessment, 14*, 331–338. doi:10.1037/1040-3590.14.3.331

Niederland, W. G. (1973). Psychoanalytic concepts of creativity and aging. *Journal of Geriatric. Psychology, 6*, 160–168.

Niederland, W. G. (1976). Psychoanalytic approaches to artistic creativity. *The Psychoanalytic Quarterly, 45*, 185–212.

Nielsen, M., & Christie, T. (2008). Adult modeling facilitates young children's generation of novel pretend acts. *Infant and Child Development, 17*, 151–162. doi:10.1002/icd.538

Nirvan. (2012, April 9). Caine's Arcade [Video file]. Retrieved from http://www.youtube.com/watch?vfaIFNkdq96U

No Child Left Behind Act of 2001, 20 U.S.C. § 6319 (2008).

Obituary: Erik Erikson, 91, psychoanalyst who reshaped views of human growth, dies. (1994, May 13). *The New York Times*. Retrieved from http://www.nytimes.com/learning/general/onthisday/bday/0615.html

Owens, J. W. M. (2004). Sleep problems in current problems in pediatric and adolescents. *Health Care, 34*, 154–179.

Oyserman, D., Coon, H. M., & Kemmelmeier, M. (2002). Rethinking individualism and collectivism: Evaluation of theoretical assumptions and meta-analyses. *Psychological Bulletin, 128*, 3–72. doi:10.1037/0033-2909.128.1.3

Paley, V. (1990). *The boy who would be a helicopter: The uses of storytelling in the classroom.* Cambridge, England: Cambridge University Press.

Parmar, P., Harkness, S., & Super, C. M. (2004). Asian and Euro-American parents' ethno-theories of play and learning: Effects on preschool children's home routines and school behavior. *International Journal of Behavioral Development, 28*, 97–104. doi:10.1080/01650250344000307

Paumgarten, N. (2010, December 20, 27). Master of play. *The New Yorker*, pp. 86–99.

Pellegrini, A. (1992). Rough and tumble play and social problem solving flexibility. *Creativity Research Journal, 5*, 13–26. doi:10.1080/10400419209534419

Penrose, R. (1989). *The emperor's new mind.* Oxford, England: Oxford University Press.

Pepler, D. J. (1979). *Effects of convergent and divergent play experience on preschoolers problem-solving behavior* (Unpublished doctoral dissertation). University of Waterloo, Waterloo, Canada.

Pepler, D. J., & Ross, H. S. (1981). The effects of play on convergent and divergent problem solving. *Child Development, 52*, 1202–1210. doi:10.2307/1129507

Perry, D., & Russ, S. (1998). *Play, coping, and adjustment in homeless children.* Unpublished manuscript, Department of Psychology, Case Western Reserve University, Cleveland, OH.

Piaget, J. (1932). *The moral judgement of the child.* London, England: Routledge & Kegan Paul.

Piaget, J. (1951). *Principal factors determining intellectual evolution from childhood to adult life.* New York, NY: Columbia University Press. doi:10.1037/10584-006

Piaget, J. (1967). *Play, dreams, and imitation in childhood.* New York, NY: Norton. (Original work published 1945)

Pine, F., & Holt, R. R. (1960). Creativity and primary process: A study of adaptive regression. *The Journal of Abnormal and Social Psychology, 61*, 370–379. doi:10.1037/h0048004

Plucker, J. (1999). Is the proof really in the pudding? Reanalysis of Torrance's longitudinal data. *Creativity Research Journal, 12*, 103–114. doi:10.1207/s15326934crj1202_3

Plucker, J., & Beghetto, R. (2004). Why creativity is domain general, why it looks domain specific, and why the distinction does not matter. In R. Sternberg, E. Grigorenko, & J. Singer (Eds.), *Creativity: From potential to realization* (pp. 153–167). Washington, DC: American Psychological Association. doi:10.1037/10692-009

Poincaré, H. (1952). Mathematical creation. In B. Ghiselin (Ed.), *The creative process: Reflections on the invention in the arts and sciences* (pp. 33–42). Berkeley, CA: University of California Press. (Original work published 1913)

Pollock, G. H. (1962). Childhood parent and sibling loss in adult patients: A comprehensive study. *Archives of General Psychiatry, 7*, 295–305. doi:10.1001/archpsyc.1962.01720040061006

Power, T. G. (2000). *Play and exploration in children and animals*. Mahwah, NJ: Erlbaum.

Powers, R. (2005). *Mark Twain*. New York, NY: Free Press.

Provine, R. R. (2001). *Laughter*. New York, NY: Penguin.

Rapaport, D. (1951). *Organization and pathology of thought*. New York, NY: Columbia University.

Reiter-Palmon, R. (2011). Problem finding. In M. A. Runco & S. R. Pritzker (Eds.), *Encyclopedia of creativity* (2nd ed., pp. 250–253). London, England: Elsevier. doi:10.1016/B978-0-12-375038-9.00180-1

Rholes, W. S., Riskind, J. H., & Lane, J. W. (1987). Emotional states and memory biases: Effects of cognitive priming and mood. *Journal of Personality and Social Psychology, 52*, 91–99. doi:10.1037/0022-3514.52.1.91

Richards, R. (1990). Everyday creativity, eminent creativity, and health: Afterview for CRT issues on creativity and health. *Creativity Research Journal, 3*, 300–326. doi:10.1080/10400419009534363

Richards, R. (2007). *Everyday creativity*. Washington, DC: American Psychological Association.

Richards, R., & Kinney, D. K. (1990). Mood swings and creativity. *Creativity Research Journal, 3*, 202–217. doi:10.1080/10400419009534353

Richards, R., Kinney, D. K., Benet, M., & Merzel, A. P. C. (1988). Assessing everyday creativity: Characteristics of the Lifetime Creativity Scales and validation with three large samples. *Journal of Personality and Social Psychology, 54*, 476–485. doi:10.1037/0022-3514.54.3.476

Richman, A. L., LeVine, R. A., New, R. S., Howrigan, G. A., Welles-Nyström, B., & LeVine, S. E. (1988). Maternal behavior to infants in five cultures. In R. A. LeVine, P. M. Miller, & M. M. West (Eds.), *Parental behavior in diverse societies* (pp. 81–97). San Francisco, CA: Jossey-Bass.

Richman, A. L., Miller, P. M., & Solomon, M. J. (1988). The socialization of infants in suburban Boston. In R. A. LeVine & P. M. West (Eds.), *Parental behavior in diverse societies* (pp. 65–74). San Francisco, CA: Jossey-Bass. doi:10.1002/cd.23219884008

Robert Wood Johnson Foundation. (2010). *The state of play: Gallup survey of principals on school recess*. Retrieved from http://d6test.naesp.org/resources/1/Gallup_Poll/StateOfPlayFeb2010.pdf

Rocke, A. (2010). *Image and reality: Kekulé, Kopp, and the scientific imagination*. Chicago, IL: University of Chicago Press. doi:10.7208/chicago/9780226723358.001.0001

Roe, A. (1953). *The making of a scientist*. New York, NY: Dodd, Mead.

Roe, A. (1972, May 26). Patterns in the productivity of scientists. *Science, 176*(4037), 940–941. doi:10.1126/science.176.4037.940

Rogers, C. (1954). Towards a theory of creativity. *Etc., 11*, 249–260.

Rogolsky, M. M. (1968). Artistic creativity and adaptive aggression in third grade children. *Journal of Projective Techniques & Personality Assessment, 32*, 53–62. doi:10.1080/0091651X.1968.10120447

Root-Bernstein, M., & Root-Bernstein, R. (2006). Imaginary worldplay in childhood and maturity and its impact on adult creativity. *Creativity Research Journal, 18*, 405–425. doi:10.1207/s15326934crj1804_1

Rosen, C. E. (1974). The effects of sociodramatic play on problem-solving behavior among culturally disadvantaged preschool children. *Child Development, 45*, 920–927. doi:10.2307/1128077

Rothstein, M. (2007, July 31). Ingmar Bergman, Master Filmmaker, obituary. *New York Times*, pp. A1, A20.

Rubin, K., Fein, G., & Vandenberg, B. (1983). Play. In P. Mussen (Ed.), *Handbook of child psychology* (Vol. 4, pp. 693–774). New York, NY: Wiley.

Runco, M. (1991). *Divergent thinking*. Norwood, NJ: Ablex.

Runco, M. (1994a). Conclusions concerning problem finding, problem solving and creativity. In M. A. Runco (Ed.), *Problem finding, problem solving and creativity* (pp. 272–290). Norwood, NJ: Ablex.

Runco, M. (1994b). Creative sequelae of tension and disequilibrium. In M. Shaw & M. Runco (Eds.), *Creativity and affect* (pp. 102–123). Norwood, NJ: Ablex.

Runco, M. (1999a). Developmental trends in creative abilities and potentials. In M. Runco & S. Pritzker (Eds.), *Encyclopedia of creativity* (pp. 537–540). San Diego, CA: Academic Press.

Runco, M. (1999b). Tension, adaptability, and creativity. In S. Russ (Ed.), *Affect, creative experience, and psychological adjustment* (pp. 165–194). Philadelphia, PA: Brunner/Mazel.

Runco, M. (2004). Everyone has creative potential. In R. J. Sternberg, E. L. Grigorenko, & J. L. Singer (Eds.), *Creativity: From potential to realization* (pp. 21–30). Washington, DC: American Psychological Association. doi:10.1037/10692-002

Runco, M. (2007). *Creativity*. San Diego, CA: Elsevier.

Runco, M., Millar, G., Acar, S., & Cramond, B. (2011). Torrance tests of creative thinking as predictors of personal and public achievement: A fifty year follow-up. *Creativity Research Journal, 22*, 361–368.

Russ, S., & Cooperberg, M. (2002). *Play as a predictor of creativity, coping and depression in adolescents*. Unpublished manuscript, Department of Psychology, Case Western Reserve University, Cleveland, OH.

Russ, S., & Peterson, N. (1990). *The Affect in Play Scale: Predicting creativity and coping in children*. Unpublished manuscript, Department of Psychology, Case Western Reserve University, Cleveland, OH.

Russ, S. W. (1980). Primary process integration on the Rorschach and achievement in children. *Journal of Personality Assessment, 44*, 338–344.

Russ, S. W. (1981). Primary process on the Rorschach and achievement in children: A follow-up study. *Journal of Personality Assessment, 44*, 338–344. doi:10.1207/s15327752jpa4505_3

Russ, S. W. (1982). Sex differences in primary process thinking and flexibility in problem solving in children. *Journal of Personality Assessment, 46*, 569–577. doi:10.1207/s15327752jpa4606_2

Russ, S. W. (1987). Assessment of cognitive affective interaction in children: Creativity, fantasy, and play research. In J. Butcher & C. Spielberger (Eds.), *Advances in personality assessment* (Vol. 6, pp. 141–155). Hillsdale, NJ: Erlbaum.

Russ, S. W. (1988). Primary process thinking on the Rorschach, divergent thinking, and coping in children. *Journal of Personality Assessment, 52*, 539–548. doi:10.1207/s15327752jpa5203_17

Russ, S. W. (1993). *Affect and creativity: The role of affect and play in the creative process*. Hillsdale, NJ: Erlbaum.

Russ, S. W. (1996). Psychoanalytic theory and creativity: Cognition and affect revisited. In J. Masling & R. Borstein (Eds.), *Psychoanalytic perspectives on developmental psychology* (pp. 69–103). Washington, DC: American Psychological Association. doi:10.1037/10219-003

Russ, S. W. (1998a). The impact of repression on creativity. *Psychological Inquiry, 9*, 221–223. doi:10.1207/s15327965pli0903_7

Russ, S. W. (1998b). Play therapy. In T. Ollendick (Ed.), *Children and adolescents: Clinical formulation and treatment* (pp. 221–243). Oxford: Elsevier Science.

Russ, S. W. (1999a). An evolutionary model of creativity: Does it fit? *Psychological Inquiry, 10*, 359–361.

Russ, S. W. (1999b). Play, affect and creativity: Theory and research. In S. Russ (Ed.), *Affect, creative experience and psychological adjustment* (pp. 57–75). Philadelphia, PA: Brunner/Mazel.

Russ, S. W. (2004). *Play in child development and psychotherapy: Toward empirically supported practice*. Mahwah, NJ: Erlbaum.

Russ, S. W. (2009). Pretend play, emotional processes and developing narratives. In S. Kaufman & J. Kaufman (Eds.), *The psychology of creative writing* (pp. 247–263). New York, NY: Cambridge University Press.

Russ, S. W. (2011). Emotion/affect. In M. Runco & S. Pritzker (Eds.), *Encyclopedia of creativity* (2nd ed., pp. 449–455). London, England: Elsevier. doi:10.1016/B978-0-12-375038-9.00089-3

Russ, S. W., & Dillon, J. (2011a). Associative theory. In M. Runco & S. Pritzker (Eds.), *Encyclopedia of creativity* (2nd ed., pp. 66–71). London, England: Elsevier. doi:10.1016/B978-0-12-375038-9.00014-5

Russ, S. W., & Dillon, J. (2011b). Changes in children's play processes over two decades. *Creativity Research Journal, 23*, 330–338. doi:10.1080/10400419.2011.621824

Russ, S. W., Dillon, J., Fiorelli, J., & Burck, A. (2010). [Pretend play intervention with primary school girls.] Unpublished raw data.

Russ, S. W., & Fehr, K. (2013). The role of pretend play in child psychotherapy. In M. Taylor (Ed.), *Oxford Handbook of Development of Imagination* (pp. 516–528). New York, NY: Oxford University Press.

Russ, S. W., Fehr, K., & Hoffmann, J. (2013). Helping children develop pretend play skills: Implications for gifted and talented programs. In K. Kim, J. Kaufman, J. Baer, & B. Sriraman (Eds.), *Creatively gifted students are not like other students: Research, theory and practice* (pp. 49–67). Rotterdam, the Netherlands: Sense.

Russ, S. W., & Fiorelli, J. (2010). Developmental approaches to creativity. In J. Kaufman & R. Sternberg (Eds.), *The Cambridge handbook of creativity* (pp. 233–249). New York, NY: Cambridge University Press. doi:10.1017/CBO9780511763205.015

Russ, S. W., & Grossman-McKee, A. (1990). Affective expression in children's fantasy play, primary process thinking on the Rorschach and divergent thinking. *Journal of Personality Assessment, 54*, 756–771.

Russ, S. W., & Kaugars, A. (2000–2001). Emotion in children's play and creative problem solving. *Creativity Research Journal, 13*, 211–219. doi:10.1207/S15326934CRJ1302_8

Russ, S. W., Moore, M., & Farber, B. (2004, July). *Effects of play training on play, creativity and emotional processes*. Poster session presented at the meeting of the American Psychological Association, Honolulu, HI.

Russ, S. W., Robins, A., & Christiano, B. (1999). Pretend play: Longitudinal prediction of creativity and affect in fantasy in children. *Creativity Research Journal, 12*, 129–139. doi:10.1207/s15326934crj1202_5

Russ, S. W., & Schafer, E. (2006). Affect in fantasy play, emotion in memories and divergent thinking. *Creativity Research Journal, 18*, 347–354. doi:10.1207/s15326934crj1803_9

Sacks, O. (1995). *An anthropologist on Mars*. New York, NY: Vintage Books.

Sarnoff, C. (1976). *Latency*. New York, NY: Aronson.

Sawyer, P. K. (1997). *Pretend play as improvisation*. Mahwah, NJ: Erlbaum.

Scorsese, M., Lacy, S., Rosen, J., Sinclair, N., & Wall, A. (Producers), & Scorsese, M. (Director). (2005). *Bob Dylan: No direction home* [Motion picture]. United States: Paramount Pictures.

Seja, A. L., & Russ, S. W. (1999). Children's fantasy play and emotional understanding. *Journal of Clinical Child Psychology, 28*, 269–277. doi:10.1207/s15374424jccp2802_13

Shaw, M., & Runco, M. (Eds.). (1994). *Creativity and affect*. Norwood, NJ: Ablex.

Sherrod, L., & Singer, J. (1979). The development of make-believe play. In J. Goldstein (Ed.), *Sports, games, and play* (pp. 1–28). Hillsdale, NJ: Erlbaum.

Shmukler, D. (1982–1983). Early home background features in relation to imagination and creative expression in third grade. *Imagination, Cognition and Personality, 2*, 311–321. doi:10.2190/D0G3-3UM0-J4DQ-2WPV

Shmukler, D., & Naveh, I. (1984–1985). Structured vs. unstructured play training with economically disadvantaged preschoolers. *Imagination, Cognition and Personality, 4,* 293–304. doi:10.2190/WQ65-UNAM-VDV9-PLMR

Silvia, P., Winterstein, B., & Willse, J. (2008). Rejoinder: The madness to our method: Some thoughts on divergent thinking. *Psychology of Aesthetics, Creativity, and the Arts, 2,* 109–114. doi:10.1037/1931-3896.2.2.109

Simon, J. (2008). Alexander Calder: The Paris years. In J. Simon & B. Leal (Eds.), *Alexander Calder: The Paris Years, 1926–1933* (pp. 25–59). New Haven, CT: Yale University Press.

Simón, V. (1998). Emotional participation in decision-making. *Psychology in Spain, 2,* 100–107.

Simonton, D. (1988). *Scientific genius: A psychology of science.* New York, NY: Cambridge University Press.

Simonton, D. (1999). Creativity as blind variation and selective retention: Is the creative process Darwinian? *Psychological Inquiry, 10,* 309–328.

Singer, D. G., & Revenson, T. (1996). *A Piaget primer.* New York, NY: Plume Books.

Singer, D. G., & Singer, J. L. (1990). *The house of make-believe: Children's play and the developing imagination.* Cambridge, MA: Harvard University Press.

Singer, D. G., & Singer, J. (2002). *Make-believe: Games and activities to foster imaginative play in children.* Washington, DC: American Psychological Association.

Singer, D. G., & Singer, J. (2005). *Imagination and play in the electronic age.* Cambridge, MA: Harvard University Press. doi:10.1037/e542072009-030

Singer, D. L., & Rummo, J. (1973). Ideational creativity and behavioral style in kindergarten-age children. *Developmental Psychology, 8,* 154–161. doi:10.1037/h0034155

Singer, J. L. (1973). *The child's world of make-believe.* New York, NY: Academic Press.

Singer, J. L. (1981). *Daydreaming and fantasy.* New York, NY: Oxford University Press.

Singer, J. L., & Singer, D. G. (1981). *Television, imagination and aggression.* Hillsdale, NJ: Erlbaum.

Singer, J. L., & Singer, D. G. (1999). *Learning through play* [Videotape]. New Haven, CT: Media Group of Connecticut and Yale Family TV Center.

Slade, A., & Wolf, D. (1994). *Children at play.* New York, NY: Oxford University Press.

Smilansky, S. (1968). *The effects of sociodramatic play on disadvantaged preschool children.* New York, NY: Wiley.

Smith, P. (2007). Evolutionary foundations and functions of play: An overview. In A. Goncu & S. Gaskins (Eds.), *Play and development* (pp. 21–49). New York, NY: Taylor & Francis.

Smith, P. K. (1988). Children's play and its role in early development: A re-evaluation of the "play ethos." In A. Pellegrini (Ed.), *Psychological bases for early education* (pp. 207–226). Chichester, England: Wiley.

Smith, P. K. (1994). Play training: An overview. In J. Hellendoorn, R. van der Kooij, & B. Sutton-Smith (Eds.), *Play and intervention* (pp. 185–194). Albany: State University of New York Press.

Smith, P. K., & Dutton, S. (1979). Play and training in direct and innovative problem solving. *Child Development, 50*, 830–836. doi:10.2307/1128950

Smith, P. K., & Gosso, Y. (2010). *Children and play*. Malden, MA: Wiley-Blackwell.

Smith, P. K., & Whitney, S. (1987). Play and associative fluency: Experimenter effects may be responsible for positive results. *Developmental Psychology, 23*, 49–53. doi:10.1037/0012-1649.23.1.49

Smolucha, F. (1992). A reconstruction of Vygotsky's theory of creativity. *Creativity Research Journal, 5*, 49–67. doi:10.1080/10400419209534422

Stahmer, A. (1995). Teaching symbolic play skills to children with autism using pivotal response training. *Journal of Autism and Developmental Disorders, 25*, 123–141. doi:10.1007/BF02178500

Sternberg, R. (1988). A three-facet model of creativity. In R. Sternberg (Ed.), *The nature of creativity* (pp. 125–147). Cambridge, England: Cambridge University press.

Sternberg, R. (1998). Cognitive mechanisms in human creativity: Is variation blind or sighted? *The Journal of Creative Behavior, 32*, 159–176. doi:10.1002/j.2162-6057. 1998.tb00813.x

Sternberg, R., & Davidson, J. (1982, June). The mind of the puzzler. *Psychology Today, 16*, 37–44.

Sternberg, R. J., Kaufman, J. C., & Pretz, J. E. (2001). The propulsion model of creative contributions applied to the arts and letters. *The Journal of Creative Behavior, 35*, 75–101. doi:10.1002/j.2162-6057.2001.tb01223.x

Sternberg, R. J., Kaufman, J. C., & Pretz, J. E. (2002). *The creativity conundrum*. New York, NY: Psychology Press.

Suler, J. (1980). Primary process thinking and creativity. *Psychological Bulletin, 88*, 144–165. doi:10.1037/0033-2909.88.1.144

Sutton-Smith, B. (2003). Play as a parody of emotional vulnerability. In D. Lytle (Ed.), *Play and culture studies* (Vol. 5, pp. 3–17). Westport, CT: Praeger.

Sylva, K., Bruner, J., & Genova, P. (1976). The role of play in the problem solving of children 3–5 years old. In J. Bruner, A. Jolly, & K. Sylva (Eds.), *Play—Its role in evolution and development* (pp. 244–257). New York, NY: Penguin Books.

Taylor, M. (1999). *Imaginary companions and the children who create them*. New York, NY: Oxford University Press.

Taylor, M., & Carlson, S. M. (2002). Imaginary companions and elaborate fantasy in childhood: Discontinuity with nonhuman animals. In R. W. Mitchell (Ed.), *Pretense in animals and humans* (pp. 167–180). Cambridge, England: Cambridge University Press. doi:10.1017/CBO9780511542282.014

Tellegen, A. (1989, August). Discussant. In L. A. Clark & D. Watson (Chairs), *The emotional bases of personality*. Symposium conducted at meeting of the American Psychological Association, New Orleans, LA.

Terr, L. (1990). *Too scared to cry: Psychic trauma in childhood*. New York, NY: Harper & Row.

Thomas, N., & Smith, C. (2004). Developing play skills in children with autism spectrum disorders. *Educational Psychology in Practice, 20*, 195–206. doi:10.1080/0266736042000251781

Thorp, D., Stahmer, A., Schreibman, L. (1995). Effects of sociodramatic play training on children with autism. *Journal of Autism and Developmental Disorders, 25*, 265–282. doi:10.1007/BF02179288

Thurstone, L. (1952). Creative talent. In L. Thurstone (Ed.), *Application of psychology* (pp. 18–37). New York, NY: Harper & Row.

Toibin, C. (2012, July 15). What is real is imagined. *The New York Times*, SR 5.

Tomkins, S. (1962). *Affect, imagery, consciousness: Vol. 1. The positive affects*. New York, NY: Springer.

Tomkins, S. (1963). *Affect, imagery, consciousness: Vol. 2. The negative affects*. New York, NY: Springer.

Torrance, E. P. (1966). The Torrance Tests of Creative Thinking—Norms: Technical manual, research edition—Verbal Tests, Forms A and B; Figural Tests, Forms A and B. Princeton, NJ: Personnel Press.

Torrance, E. P. (1988). The nature of creativity as manifest in its testing. In R. Sternberg (Ed.), *The nature of creativity* (pp. 43–75). Cambridge, England: Cambridge University Press.

Torrance, E. P., Ball, E. O., & Safter, H. T. (1992). *Torrance Tests of Creative Thinking: Streamlined score guide Figural A and B*. Bensenville, IL: Scholastic Testing Service.

Trawick-Smith, J. (1998). Why play training works: An integrated model for play intervention. *Journal of Research in Childhood Education, 12*, 117–129. doi:10.1080/02568549809594878

Trevlas, E., Grammatikopoulos, V., Tsigilis, N., & Zachopoulou, E. (2003). Evaluating playfulness: Construct validity of the Children's Playfulness Scale. *Early Childhood Education Journal, 31*, 33–39. doi:10.1023/A:1025132701759

Trowbridge, C. D., Jr. (2009). *Marconi*. Author.

Tudge, J., & Rogoff, B. (1989). Peer influences on cognitive development: Piagetian and Vygotskian perspectives. In M. Bornstein & J. Bruner (Eds.), *Interaction in human development* (pp. 17–40). Hillsdale, NJ: Erlbaum.

Twenge, J. M., Konrath, S., Foster, J. D., Campbell, W. K., & Bushman, B. J. (2008). Egos inflating over time: A cross-temporal meta-analysis of the narcissistic personality inventory. *Journal of Personality, 76*, 875–902. doi:10.1111/j.1467-6494.2008.00507.x

Twenge, J. M., Zhang, L., & Im, C. (2004). It's beyond my control: A cross-temporal meta-analysis of increasing externality in locus of control, 1960–2002. *Personality and Social Psychology Review, 8*, 308–319. doi:10.1207/s15327957pspr0803_5

Udwin, O. (1983). Imaginative play training as an intervention method with institutionalized preschool children. *British Journal of Educational Psychology, 53*, 32–39. doi:10.1111/j.2044-8279.1983.tb02533.x

Updike, J. (2008, November & December). The writer in winter. *AARP*, 38–40.

Vandenberg, B. (1978, August). *The role of play in the development of insightful tool using abilities*. Paper presented at the meeting of American Psychological Association, Toronto, Canada.

Vandenberg, B. (1980). Play, problem-solving, and creativity. *New Directions for Child Development, 1980*, 49–68. doi:10.1002/cd.23219800906

Vernon, P. E. (1989). The nature–nurture problem in creativity. In J. Glover, R. Ronning, & C. R. Reynolds (Eds.), *Handbook of creativity* (pp. 93–110). New York, NY: Plenum Press. doi:10.1007/978-1-4757-5356-1_5

Vinacke, W. E. (1952). *Psychology of thinking*. New York, NY: McGraw-Hill.

Vosburg, S. D., & Kaufmann, G. (1999). Mood and creativity research: The view from a conceptual organizing perspective. In S. Russ (Ed.), *Affect, creative experience, and psychological adjustment* (pp. 19–39). Washington, DC: Taylor & Francis.

Vygotsky, L. S. (1967a). Play and its role in the mental development of the child. *Soviet Psychology, 5*, 6–18.

Vygotsky, L. S. (1967b). *Vaobraszeniye i tvorchestvov deskom voraste* [Imagination and creativity in childhood]. Moscow, Russia: Prosvescheniye. (Original work published 1930)

Waelder, R. (1933). Psychoanalytic theory of play. *The Psychoanalytic Quarterly, 2*, 208–224.

Wallach, M. (1970). Creativity. In P. Mussen (Ed.), *Carmichael's manual of child psychology* (Vol. 1, pp. 1211–1272). New York, NY: Wiley.

Wallach, M., & Kogan, N. (1965). *Modes of thinking in young children: A study of the creativity–intelligence distinction*. New York, NY: Holt, Reinhart & Winston.

Wallas, C. (1926). *The art of thought*. New York, NY: Harcourt, Brace.

Weiner, I. (1977). Approaches to Rorschach validation. In M. Rickers-Ovsiankina (Ed.), *Rorschach psychology* (pp. 77–105). Madison, WI: Kreiger.

Weisberg, D., Hirsh-Pasek, K., & Golinkoff, R. (2013). Embracing complexity: Rethinking the relation between play and learning: Comment on Lillard et al. (2013). *Psychological Bulletin, 139*, 35–39. doi:10.1037/a0030077

Weisberg, R. (1986). *Creativity: Genius and other myths*. New York, NY: Freeman.

Weisberg, R. (1988). Problem solving and creativity. In R. Sternberg (Ed.), *The nature of creativity* (pp. 148–176). Cambridge, England: Cambridge University Press.

Welles-Nyström, B., New, R., & Richman, A. (1994). The "Good Mother." A comparative study of Swedish, Italian and American maternal behaviour. *Scandinavian Journal of Caring Sciences, 8*, 81–86. doi:10.1111/j.1471-6712.1994.tb00233.x

Wolf, A. W., Lozoff, B., Latz, S., & Paludetto, R. (1996). Parental theories in the management of sleep routines in Japan, Italy and the United States. In S. Harkness & C. M. Super (Eds.), *Parents' cultural belief systems* (pp. 364–385). New York, NY: Guilford Press.

Wright, W. (2000). *Maxis: The Sims* [Video game]. Redwood City, CA: Electronic Arts.

Wyver, S. R., & Spence, S. H. (1999). Play and divergent problem solving: Evidence supporting a reciprocal relationship. *Early Education and Development, 10,* 419–444. doi:10.1207/s15566935eed1004_1

Youngblade, L. M., & Dunn, J. (1995). Individual differences in young children's pretend play with mother and siblings: Links to relationships and understanding of other people's feelings and beliefs. *Child Development, 66,* 1472–1492. doi:10.2307/1131658

Zhiyan, T., & Singer, J. L. (1997). Daydreaming styles, emotionality, and the big five personality dimensions. *Imagination, Cognition and Personality, 16,* 399–414. doi:10.2190/ATEH-96EV-EXYX-2ADB

Zimiles, H. (1981). Cognitive–affective interaction: A concept that exceeds the researcher's grasp. In E. Shapiro & E. Weber (Eds.), *Cognitive and affective growth* (pp. 49–63). Hillsdale, NJ: Erlbaum.

# INDEX

225

and memory, 112–113
nonrandom search process of, 100
Associational fluency, 72
Associative fluency, 35
Associative network theory, 69
Associative processes, affect and, 66
Associative theory, 14
Austria, 120
Autism, 102
  play interventions for children
    with, 122
  and Temple Grandin, 101
Autonomy
  creativity and, 148
  cultural differences in, 157
Axia, V., 157

Baas, M., 60, 75
Baer, J., 47
Baez, Joan, 114
Bandalos, D., 47
Barron, F., 11, 103–104
Barton, E., 122
Batey, M., 11, 16
Beghetto, R. A., 9, 10
Behavioral reorganization, 32
Bergman, Ingmar, 108, 111
Bhavnani, R., 53
Bias (in research), 55, 56
Bidirectionality (of processes), 27
Big-C creativity, 9, 10
Big Five personality traits, 11. See also
  individual traits
Bittner, M., 58
Block, J. W., 148
Borges, Jorge Luis, 109–110
Bower, G. H., 69
Boyd, B., 32, 108–109, 112, 115
Brown, D., 58
Broyles, S. J., 11
Bruner, J., 38, 57
Bryant Index of Empathy for Children,
  60
Burck, A., 128–130
Burghardt, G., 30–32, 42
Butcher, H., 103–104

"Caine's Arcade" (YouTube video), 149
Calder, Alexander, 116–117
Cameron, B., 58

Campbell, D. T., 99
Carson, D., 58
Carson, S. H., 11
Case studies. See Arts case studies;
    Science and technology case
    studies
Case Western Reserve University, 6,
    119–120, 123, 165, 174
Cathexis
  defined, 96
  mobility of, 67–68
Cats, pretend play in, 30–31
Cattell, R., 103–104
Cause and effect, 32, 123
Chamorro-Premuzic, T., 12
Chessa, D., 90, 156, 160–163, 171
Child development, 32
  play and, 3
  stage theory of, 36
Child-rearing practices
  and creativity, 148–149
  cultural differences in, 156–158, 161
Christie, J., 57, 77
Christie, T., 122
Clark, P., 53
Cognitive abilities
  development of, 36–37
  increase of, in pilot study, 127
Cognitive–affective framework
  and mood induction, 74–75
  of Singer and Singer, 41–42
Cognitive characteristics, of creative
    scientists, 94
Cognitive deficits, play interventions
    for children with, 122
Cognitive flexibility, 14, 46
  defined, 95
  examples of, in play, 25
  in scientific problem solving/artistic
    production, 105
Cognitive integration and modulation
    of affect, 24, 66
  and dealing with emotion, 27–28
  defined, 18
  in primary-process thinking, 68
Cognitive processes, 3–4, 45–62.
    See also individual processes,
    e.g.: Divergent thinking
  and coping, 58–59
  in creativity, 12–16, 26

# ABOUT THE AUTHOR

**Sandra W. Russ, PhD,** a clinical child psychologist, is the Louis D. Beaumont university professor of psychology at Case Western Reserve University in Cleveland, Ohio. She has served as president of the Society for Personality Assessment; of the Clinical Child Section of Division 12 of the American Psychological Association (APA); and of the Division of Aesthetics, Creativity, and the Arts (Division 10) of the APA. She teaches a psychology of creativity seminar, and her research program has focused on relationships among pretend play, creativity, and adaptive functioning in children. Russ developed the Affect in Play Scale, which assesses pretend play in children, and she and her students are developing a play facilitation intervention. She is the author of *Affect and Creativity: The Role of Affect and Play in the Creative Process* (1993) and *Play in Child Development and Psychotherapy: Toward Empirically Supported Practice* (2004) and coauthor of *Play in Clinical Practice: Evidence-Based Approaches* (Russ & Niec, 2011).